CHILD CARE AND EDUCATION: CANADIAN DIMENSIONS

Isabel M. Doxey
Editor

Nelson Canada

© Nelson Canada
A Division of Thomson Canada Limited

Published in 1990 by
Nelson Canada
A Division of Thomson Canada Limited
1120 Birchmount Road
Scarborough, Ontario
M1K 5G4

Canadian Cataloguing in Publication Data

Main entry under title:

Child care and education

Includes bibliographical references.
ISBN 0-17-603482-X

1. Child development–Canada.   2. Education of children.
3. Education–Canada.   I. Doxey, Isabel M., 1934–

BF721.C45 1989   155.4′0971   C89-095119-5

Printed and bound in Canada

2 3 4 5   BG   98 97 96 95 94

Contents

Introduction, *Isabel M. Doxey*

The easiest way of becoming acquainted with the modes of thinking, rules of conduct and prevailing manners of any people is to examine what sort of education they give their children, how they treat them at home and what they are taught in their public places.

Hector St. John de Crevecoeur
from *Sketches of Eighteenth-Century America, 1769–1775*

Acknowledgements

In the process of developing this book, I often felt like the subject of Socrates' quote describing a teacher as "the midwife at the birth of an idea." The idea for a volume of this type has been gestating in my mind for many years; as an eighth-generation Canadian, I feel committed to defending my Canadian nationality.

The assistance from the contributors at this "birth" has been overwhelming. From my initial invitations throughout the preparation process I always found support and positive responses to all requests. Readers should note that the 25 contributing authors represent more than 17 postsecondary institutions, in addition to public and private schools, governments, and other organizations. As a group they possess more than 500 years of wisdom and experience.

This book also—like the children at its core—reflects the 1990s, for it would not have been possible without access to a computer, modem, fax and copying machine, and mail courier service.

It would also not have been possible without my own enablers and nurturers for my personal care and education: my family—George, Lea, and Michael—and all the young children who have taught and touched me.

Introduction

The glue of the Canadian mosaic is the sense of identity that each citizen has with Canada. Some might claim that there is no specifically "Canadian identity." Others, as this volume suggests, believe that certain qualities and characteristics are indeed uniquely, and indigenously, Canadian. These characteristics can be defined. Furthermore, they have much relevance when considering the why, how, when, and what of programs and services for young Canadian children.

This volume is about Canadian children. It is about their early childhood. It is about their early childhood care and education. It has been designed to help student learners and their teachers appreciate the interdependence and interrelationships among these three dimensions.

To appreciate the range of contributions, some terms and labels need explanations. What, for instance, is *early childhood?* This term now has a far broader meaning that it did even a few years ago. Traditionally, it was used as a synonym for preschool and to refer to programs for children before the formal or compulsory school-entry age—that is, from two or two-and-a-half through five years old or a little older.

During the 1960s, however, early childhood was "abruptly shoved into the economic, political and social spotlight" (Elkind, 1986). Schools and teachers were accused of failing to prepare children for the rapidly changing needs of society that the launching of Sputnik had symbolized. In countering these charges, educators pointed out that the "prime time" for such preparation had already passed by the age of school entry. Thus the early childhood period, from two through six years of age, became an advocacy target for the turbulent social movements of the decade, and a battleground for civil rights activists.

By the 1960s, educators and social scientists had rediscovered cognition; this rediscovery resulted in the resurgence of "academic" education. This trend, however, has been attributed to social, economic, and political forces rather than to any true change in knowledge about how children learn or develop (Elkind, 1986). Children of the 1960s were considered "competent" and able to "cope" (Braun & Edwards, 1972, p. 180). Again, early childhood, particularly the years from three to five, became a fresh target for educators and social scientists.

As we enter the 1990s, the early childhood lifespan continues to be a battleground for theorists, educators, politicians, and researchers from a plethora of disciplines: psychology, sociology, neurophysiology, anthropology, economics, political science. A focus on early childhood has also precipitated a struggle for professional territory among social workers, educators, psychologists, medical personnel, and union organizers. As the focus has changed, so, too, has the scope of the lifespan implied by the term. In this book, the contributions reflect this change: early childhood is defined as the period from birth through eight years of age.

What is *early childhood education*? Here the term is used to identify any program or service for children within the early childhood period: a child-care facility, a nursery school, a kindergarten, or an early primary grade. Such programs and services may be funded and governed through either public or private sources, and may fall within the purview of either the social service or education delivery systems. At one time, programs and services for the *care* of young children not only fell under different auspices or sponsorships from those related to the *education* of young children, but were, in fact, quite different programs. In many ways, the two types of programs still display these differences. Nursery schools (which constituted the traditional early childhood or preschool programs) were usually privately run, outside any formal education or social service system, and focused on providing an enrichment experience, an extension of what was available to children at home. Play was the dominant activity, with the teachers responsible for keeping the children safe, happy, and socially involved. On the other hand, the primary years of school, at least in North America, were part of the formal education system. Children were expected to learn skills for "the three Rs" through teacher-directed lessons. Kindergartens struggled to find some territory between these two approaches (Weber, 1969).

The term "early childhood education" can also imply a philosophy about pedagogy. Inherent in its meaning is an approach to delivering a curriculum that is "developmental" rather than merely custodial. A developmental curriculum is based on knowledge about child development and is geared to the optimal development of the whole child, in contrast to a curriculum that concentrates on intellectual development for academic achievement. These concepts are further explored, explained, and defended by many of the contributing authors.

The number of early childhood programs and services has undergone a phenomenal increase during the past few years in Canada and elsewhere. In the process, the aims and objectives of early childhood education programs and services have become more intertwined. Settings, materials, and methods have also become less sharply differentiated between programs classified as for "care" and those designed primarily for "education." Nursery schools have become more academically oriented. Primary programs are becoming more play-centred.

There have also been organizational changes. More school boards and districts have opened kindergartens and prekindergartens, and even blended kindergarten and primary classes. More child-care programs are being housed in educational facilities. There is greater collaboration and cooperation among people who staff early childhood "education programs" and those who are employed in early childhood "services." Concern for quality is a common goal whether the program is labeled "care" or "education." A phrase used by the Association for Early Childhood Education, Ontario (AECEO) describes the present and offers a vision for the future: "Good care educates, good education cares" (Association for Early Childhood Education, Ontario [AECEO], 1985).

Early childhood education can have positive long-term effects on the attitudes, motivations, and identities of children if it is based on what is known about the best pedagogy and about the developmental processes, combined with respect for each child's circumstances. Our youngest Canadians deserve this kind of care and education. The authors of this volume offer its readers the motivation and the knowledge to ensure that such an approach becomes a Canadian reality.

Part One, "The Canadian Child," helps readers put the child at the centre by becoming aware of the circumstances and conditions of young Canadian children in the 1990s, informed about the roots of our attitudes about children and childhood, and knowledgeable about the nature of play and learning.

Part Two, "The Canadian Context," explains various historical and current influences that have shaped our attitudes and actions, thus alerting the reader to the power of the interactions between children and the milieux in which they develop and function.

In Part Three, "A Canadian Curriculum for Early Childhood Education," the emphasis shifts to the qualities of programs and services for young children, beginning with the challenge of considering what constitutes a "basic Canadian curriculum" for the early years.

In Part Four, "Canadian Programs and Services," the authors offer insights into current initiatives and future trends in theory, practice, and research.

The authors of the chapters in this book challenge the reader to question, apply, interpret, evaluate, and develop the understandings for informed action by which they might enrich the lives of young Canadian children.

REFERENCES

Association for Early Childhood Education, Ontario. (1985). Position paper. Submitted to Early Primary Education Project, Ontario Ministry of Education. Toronto: AECEO.

Braun, S.J., and E.P. Edwards. (1972). *History and Philosophy of Early Childhood Education*. Worthington, Ohio: Charles A. Jones.

Elkind, D. (May 1986). Formal education and early childhood education: An essential difference. *Phi Delta Kappan*, 631–637.

Weber, E. (1969). *The kindergarten: Its encounter with educational thought in America*. New York: Teachers College Press.

PART 1
THE CANADIAN CHILD

Early childhood programs and services exist because, of, and for children. Children and the consideration of their needs and rights should be at the centre of planning, developing, implementing, and evaluating early childhood care and education endeavours. The opening part of this volume starts here—with the Canadian child.

As Isabel Doxey notes in Chapter 1, children are embedded in families, communities, and societies with intertwined histories and heritages. For the reader to appreciate the circumstances and conditions of Canadian children, images of childhood are described and linked to current conditions and implications.

Chapters 2 and 3—by distinguished educators Otto Weininger and Ada Schermann, respectively—present perspectives on two dimensions crucial not only to children's survival, but also to their thriving: play and learning.

Chapters 4 and 5,—the former by Deborah Chant and Isabel Doxey, the latter by Ken Pierce—analyze the experiences of Canadian children in the family and in the curriculum, setting the foundation for the balance of the book.

The Canadian Child

Isabel M. Doxey

What is a Canadian child? Some would see this as a pointless—even rhetorical—question. Are not children just children? Certainly there are some characteristics of children that might be said to be universal. There are, nevertheless, characteristics of children—whether single children or child populations—that are specific to where, when, and how they live. There is a "Canadian child." There is a "Canadian child population."

Although children may be studied as individuals, they do not live in isolation. Their circumstances are affected by their environments: their family, their community, and the overall culture of their society. The social ecological model assumes that this effect is two-way: children are both subjects and objects in their environments (Ishwaran, 1979). Research indicates, for example, that a child's temperament at birth influences the style of socialization adopted by that child's parents (Little & Ryan, 1979). We need to consider these interdependent dynamics to truly understand Canadian children.

Some assumptions need explanation. The first is that although there are values and attitudes that Canadians share with people in other countries, there are nevertheless certain priorities and emphases for these values that are specific to Canada and to Canadians. The discussion of these priorities forms the first part of this chapter.

The second assumption is that the child's early years (from birth to age eight) are critically important for shaping these values and attitudes and for fixing the child's direction on the path of development. This view about the critical early years has been part of societal folk wisdom for centuries, accepted by generations of parents and promoted by the early childhood pioneers Freud and Montessori. Only since the 1950s, however, has the weight of empirical and theoretical research caused scien-

3

tists, policymakers, and educators to accept this assumption about early childhood as a foundation for planning. Children are shaped by a multitude of conditions and circumstances. The second part of this chapter shifts to a sociological perspective to examine some of these current conditions.

A third assumption is that our actions toward children and our decisions on their behalf are determined by what we believe and expect. The concluding section of this chapter illuminates this assumption and explores some of our present and past images of children and childhood.

CANADIAN IDENTITY

It is difficult to establish exactly what a Canadian identity is and what it is not. Many authors, writers, journalists, broadcasters, and philosophers have offered reflections on and even answers to this puzzle. The first place to look for evidence of the identity of any country's citizens is in its constitution. F.R. Scott stated that a constitution reveals the philosophical foundation for the relationships of individuals to social groups and to the state (Karsh, 1978, p. 150). In the Canadian Charter of Rights and Freedoms, Canadians have enshrined a mutual respect for all, regardless of geographic location or of linguistic or ethnic origins. We have enshrined the rights of all individuals to exist without being coerced or transgressed upon. In the words of René Lévesque, a former premier of Quebec, "Canada is a bastion of individual liberties and social justice" (Karsh, 1978, p. 100). Children should be included as citizens with rights.

Our symbol, the beaver, indeed symbolizes many elements of the Canadian character: determination, courage, strength, and persistence. Like the beaver, Canadians need protection from human greed and folly; we find that protection through our laws, regulations, and institutions.

Robertson Davies notes our attachment to civilization (Karsh, 1978, p. 48) and to the ideals of civilized people: dignity, tolerance, and decency. During a recent workshop conducted by this author with other early childhood educators, the participants identified exactly these qualities as illustrative of typical Canadians and as desirable for nurturance in young children.

John Kenneth Galbraith, the internationally recognized economist, describes Canadians as distrusting privilege, authority, and conventional wisdom (Karsh, 1978, p. 60). Sometimes these ideals permeate our behaviour to the extent that we may be described as smug in our considerateness and our reasonableness. As early childhood educators, we must not be smug about our ability to positively affect the lives of children in their early years or to improve our means for so doing.

Canadians are also identified by an opposition to extremism—indeed, even by a certain blandness. Walter Stewart, in his hilarious book

But Not in Canada (Stewart, 1976) also uses the adjective "smug." Author and poet Miriam Waddington considers Canadians to be "full of modest misery / sensitive to double-talk double-take and double-cross / in a country too wide to be single in" (1968, p. 243). In our early childhood approaches we certainly do want to illustrate this "opposition to extremism." Yet, in our relations with children and in their relations with us and each other, we must at all costs avoid the "double-talk, double-cross" of inconsistency and indecision.

How do children develop a sense of identity? One's sense of identity comes from the knowledge of who one is and what one can do. Confidence about one's identity comes from acceptance by others, particularly those who are significant or important to us—for example, parents and teachers. Our sense of identity is also formed by the way our needs are met and the level of need satisfaction we feel. Certainly one need of young children is to be accepted. (Chapter 5 analyzes identity development in more detail.)

We also get a sense of our importance or identity by the way priorities are set and acted on. Priorities are exposed when there are conflicts or incongruences between children's needs and those of adults. Child abuse, for example, generally involves a conflict between the adult's need to be in control and the child's need to be independent: the child then becomes the victim of adult needs and priorities. Children are constantly sent messages by those around them about their worth and about what their society considers valuable.

Traditionally, a sense of identity was instilled in children primarily through the family's authority patterns. Children succeeded or failed in their relationships with their parents and siblings. In the nest of the family, recognition and gratification were given or withheld. This is no longer so in Canada as in other parts of the world. Young children today spend more and more hours involved with children and adults outside the family circle. Young children spend many hours in front of a television set. This quantity of information and exposure usurps the traditionally extensive influence of the family itself. When people outside the family are involved in child-rearing, in shaping the child's identity and self-image, the continuity of our Canadian value tradition is threatened.

How does all this relate to our youngest citizens? If we accept that there are elements in the Canadian character and identity that are unique and idiosyncratic, then we must also accept that there should be elements in the institutions providing care and education to our young children that reflect those characteristics and attitudes that we, as Canadians, have traditionally valued.

The challenge is yet greater. While we must continue to nurture the traditional values that have underpinned our society in the past, we must also recognize that the future will bring new demands and new priorities for our values.

Certainly we would want to deepen our commitment to mutual respect and tolerance for those with diverse beliefs and behaviours, provided that the beliefs and behaviours are not a threat to our Canadian peace and security. We want our young children to understand that being different is permissible, even desirable. Chapter 9 helps us understand this. In our child-care centres and our early childhood education programs we must practise respect and tolerance.

At the same time, we want our young children to maintain respect for the things that we will continue to cherish in common. One of our cherished values is individualism: the celebration of the self and of individual rights. Children should be treated, understood, planned for, and related to as individuals. In the context of early childhood care and education, this means that kindergarten teachers should base their curriculum planning on children's skills, interests, and abilities. It means that child-care teachers should be most tolerant of independent action. It means that teachers in the early primary grades should pay more attention to individual accomplishments than to those of the group. These and other strategies are elaborated in Chapter 11, which discusses what is involved in designing a Canadian early childhood curriculum.

Although our Canadian identity has many admirable and positive characteristics, there are features that could be changed for the better. We might well ask ourselves what identity we would wish for the future, for the next century, and therefore what elements of our identity we wish to nurture in our young.

If we are too bland, too smug, and too reticent, perhaps we could benefit from being more imaginative, from taking more risks. We need to nourish our creative potential, to nourish a forward-looking view, to nourish "anticipatory leadership": a futuristic and optimistic outlook. What we need in Canadian children are possibility thinkers, visionaries, or "wow" thinkers (McPhee, 1988). Perhaps this suggests that early childhood education could benefit from more *glasnost*-style openness in the way we deal with children, in what we expect from them, and in the way we relate to each other as professionals, as well as the way we relate to the public. The challenge is to invite creativity and imagination while not losing those elements of the Canadian identity that are admired and respected, such as our peace-loving outlook and our tolerance.

Young children in Canada need to experience teachers and teaching that liberate them, that release them as explorers of their world and its relationships rather than training them as mechanistic consumers and followers.

Throughout this volume, readers will note other explanations of those elements that contribute to the "Canadianization" of programs and services for our youngest citizens today and tomorrow.

CONDITIONS OF CANADIAN CHILDREN

Although we tend to think of each and every child as being an individual with personal qualities and characteristics, each is part of the population of Canadian children. The child population of the 1990s will be different from that in other generations. They are caught in the midst of one of the greatest social revolutions in the country's history. No children before or who follow will face exactly the same set of societal, familial, or individual circumstances. The culture of Canadian childhood in the 1990s will be radically different. Some trends become visible when we look at certain characteristics of children's lives (*Canadian World Almanac*, 1989; National Council of Welfare, 1979; *Report of the federal task force on child care*, 1986):

1. A Canadian child might be the one of five who lives in economic circumstances below the identified poverty line.
2. The child will probably not have many siblings, and may not have any. As of 1985, women in Canada were having an average of 1.7 children over a lifetime. Their 1960 counterparts bore an average of 3.9 children.
3. The 1990s child could be among the approximately 16 percent of infants who were born to unmarried women in Canada in 1985. This is four times the rate of 25 years ago.
4. If born later than 1985, the Canadian child will have a life expectancy of more than 70 years, the highest in our history.
5. This child has a greater chance of being, at some stage, the child of divorced parents. The divorce rate has increased more than 600 percent in the last 25 years.
6. It is also very likely that this child is a first-generation Canadian with immigrant parents.
7. Our Canadian child of the 1990s might be the one out of every ten children who has French-speaking parents.
8. The child might be the one in three who has both parents working outside the home and who will consequently spend many hours in a variety of child-care arrangements before entering the formal school system.
9. The 1990s child has a higher probability of being part of a single-parent family. The number of such families has increased nearly 20 percent in the last decade and continues to increase at a rate 2.5 times faster than that for two-parent families.

10. The Canadian child of the 1990s also has a greater risk of experiencing some form of abuse—physical, emotional, or sexual (Badgley, 1984).

Combinations of some of these circumstances have contributed to the existence of some special Canadian children in our midst. While it could be argued that all children have special needs, it is commonly accepted that there are specific special needs that demand our consideration and attention as a society.

Some children have special developmental needs. There are those whose life conditions, including their genetic inheritance, have resulted in outstanding and exceptional talents, gifts, skills, and abilities. There are others whose life conditions and genetic inheritance have resulted in physical deformities, emotional disturbances, intellectual retardation, and overall developmental deprivation. (Chapter 19 develops this topic further.) The Canadian child of the 1990s is a child born in the midst of the computer revolution, into an age of information explosion, into a rapidly changing techno-culture. This fact will have extensive impacts. For instance, the difference between the haves and the have-nots, adults as well as children, will be measured more and more in terms of technological literacy. Many Canadian children are already in danger of becoming "techno-peasants." They are without the resources—the economic means, the educational opportunities, and the motivational supports—to even survive in, let alone contribute to, the new techno-culture.

Canadian children are also unique in terms of their psychological needs. Increasingly there is evidence of childhood stress syndrome, which results from the intense organization of their lives, and from unrealistically high expectations imposed by their parents regarding participation, achievement, and success. Even very young children are exhibiting stress-related behaviour and illnesses that previously were the exclusive preserve of adults. Many stresses on children are ecological: war, terrorism, the threat of nuclear disaster. Others are societal: poverty, housing. Some stresses are family-related: separation and divorce, discipline strategies, siblings. Other stresses are individual and personal, resulting from age, sex, intellectual capacity, temperament, peer relationships, and the child's own resilience and coping skills (Honig, 1986). So even children who appear to be "normal" or "typical" may have special needs.

Canadian children of the 1990s will inherit a different legal status and set of rights than children in other parts of the world or in past generations. They will have the right to the social services and programs for which Canada is admired. For example, Canadian parents are entitled to financial assistance through family allowances. Parents also have access to many child-related tax credits and benefits. There are extensive publicly supported education and child-care systems.

IMAGES OF CHILDHOOD

Today's Canadian society holds different images about children and childhood than past generations or other societal systems (Morrison, 1987). But shadows of many previously held images still persist.

In the Middle Ages, children were seen as miniature adults. There was a general absence of interest in children specifically, since little distinction was made between children and adults. Children's clothes, food, rituals, toys, and spaces were miniaturized adult artifacts. Children's experiences were usually shared adult experiences. Children were made to look and act as adults in every way.

In the Canadian society of today, in many ways, similar expectations and experiences for children still do exist. Children have access to the same TV programs as adults. Children's clothing designers provide copies of adult styles. Children are often expected to be adult-like in their behaviours. When angry, for instance, they are often expected to control their feelings. They are also often expected to be able to cope with adult-like activity schedules. They are expected to understand events and relationships with adult-like sophistication, such as "why Daddy doesn't live with us any more." Canadian society, in many ways, still views and treats children as miniature adults.

In Victorian times, under the influence of the widespread belief in original sin, the child was seen to be inherently sinful. Any misbehaviour was a sign of this sinfulness. The adults surrounding the child spent much time and energy (often using practices we would now consider extreme and abusive) attempting to beat out the sin, or the devil, to make the child behave. Controlling, moulding, and shaping were key concepts in describing adult/child relationships of the Victorian period. In Canada today, the number of child-abuse cases being documented suggests that many adults still believe that children are fundamentally evil and need strong, even severe, discipline.

In opposition to this harsh Victorian image was the Romantic image of pure and innocent children. The art of the period—filled with cherubic, angelic children—portrayed these views. Parents and society acted to protect children's innocence inside and outside the home. The birth of psychoanalysis and the psychological theories of Freud sounded the death knell for the idea of childhood innocence, declaring it a myth based on adult wishful thinking (Cleverley & Phillips, 1986). The concept nevertheless persists, providing a framework and foundation for much current legislation and advocacy for the protection of children.

When John Locke advanced the belief that children are born as *tabulae rasa* (blank tablets), the societal system developed different methods and strategies for the care and education of children. It was believed that children's experiences totally determined what they learned and what they became. This view had, and still has, many pleasant and unpleasant implications for Canadian children. If children are viewed as "empty vessels," then their teachers' responsibility is "to fill them": to present knowledge in suitable doses with little regard for the individual child's interests, abilities, or readiness for learning. It is crucial for the child to learn what is taught. Canadian children became, and still become, what adults make of them.

In the past children were also seen as property, commodities, or objects. In the Middle Ages, they could be bought and sold just like any other goods. In Canada, as elsewhere, laws now protect children and control the authority and jurisdiction exercised over them by parents and others. But Canadian children are still, in a real sense, the property of their parents—even before birth, as current court cases reveal. Our legislatures and courts are reluctant to interfere in what is considered a sacrosanct relationship. Parents, teachers, and policy-makers who view children as objects usually put the best interests of adults ahead of the interests or even the needs of children. Current discussions at all policy levels about the provision of child-care services show traces of this image of children as commodities or objects. Even the arguments of many child-care advocates centre more on the needs of single mothers and mothers who work outside the home than on children's needs or rights. Today children are still seen as commodities, and are "serviced" like other objects.

The analogy to a growing plant was an appealing one used to understand children in the past. Friedrich Froebel, often called the father of the kindergarten, adapted and applied this idea. One of the principles of his educational philosophy was the "unfolding" of children. Many believe, as Froebel did, that children need nurturing and stimulation as plants need water and sun. If properly tended, they would fulfil their destiny. It was believed that the innate maturation process was responsible for the rate and the nature of growth and development. The responsibility for parents, educators, and the child's community was to provide the nurturing that would permit this potential to evolve. One could not have much influence in determining it, for it was believed that the child's potential was fixed.

One translation of this image of a child was the use of a child's chronological age to determine educational needs. Children were expected to begin to read at six years and six months, the age at which it was determined they had the mental capabilities to master the process of interpreting print.

Canadian children, like those in the United States and in Europe, are also often seen primarily as consumers. They consume goods: toys, clothes, furniture, equipment. Frequently these are being especially designed with the consuming child as the target. The child is also the consumer of services delivered through the education or the social service system. Unfortunately, children do not have the means, power, or authority to barter or to offer resources or other services in return. They depend on the authority, the power, and the means of adults to either purchase the goods or negotiate the services they might want or need. Consequently, many services (for example, child care) are designed and delivered with parents' needs or the influences of market forces foremost, giving the consuming child only secondary consideration.

Some kindergarten programs illustrate how we have put into practice the perception of the child as consumer. Children in rural areas may need to be bused to the school facility to attend kindergarten. Busing schedules dictate attendance patterns: children may attend for a full day, on alternate days, rather than for a regular daily half-day program. Here the administrative demands rather than the child's best interests drive policy decisions.

Images of children and childhood will continue to evolve and blend. They will vary in strength and degree of influence. They will vary from one region of the country to another and within families. Nevertheless, the images we hold will continue to provide a frame of reference for our personal, political, moral, and legal actions on behalf of children.

CONCLUSION

In this chapter some of the conditions and images of children and childhood have been discussed as they appear in the Canadian context. What will the Canadian child of the twenty-first century be like? Early childhood educators can have a powerful impact in determining the answer to this question. By reflecting on what we believe, understand, expect, and desire for our young children we may contribute to the direction of their lives and, in so doing, ultimately to our own.

REFERENCES

Ariès, P. (1962). *Centuries of childhood*. London: Jonathan Cape.

Badgley, R.F. (1984). *Sexual offences against children* (Vol. 1). Ottawa: Ministry of Supply and Services.

Cleverley, J., & Phillips, D.C. (1986). *Visions of childhood: Influential models from Locke to Spock*. New York: Teachers College Press.

Clift, D. (1989). *The secret kingdom: Interpretations of the Canadian character*. Toronto: McClelland and Stewart.

Cook, K., London, J., Rose-Lizee, R., & Edwards, R. (1986). *Report of the federal task force on child care.* Ottawa: Ministry of Supply and Services.

De Mause, L. (1974). *The history of childhood.* New York: Psychohistory Press.

Honig, A. (1986). Research in review: Stress and coping in children. In J. McCracken (Ed.), *Reducing stress in young children's lives* (pp. 142–168). Washington, DC: National Association for the Education of Young Children.

Ishwaran, K. (Ed.).(1979). *Childhood and adolescence in Canada.* Toronto: McGraw-Hill Ryerson.

Karsh, Y. (1978). Karsh Canadians. Toronto: University of Toronto Press.

Little, B.R., & Ryan, T. (1979). Children in context: The social ecology of human development. In K. Ishwaran (Ed.), *Childhood and adolescence in Canada* (pp. 273–302). Toronto: McGraw-Hill Ryerson.

McPhee, S. (1988, June 9). Keynote address at the regional conference of the Canadian Association for Young Children. Truro, NS.

Morrison, G. (1987). *Early childhood education.* New York: Prentice-Hall.

National Council of Welfare. (1979). *Women and poverty.* Ottawa: National Council of Welfare.

Postman, N. (1982). *The disappearance of childhood.* New York: Delacorte.

Prentice, A.H., & Huston, S. (1975). *Family, school and society in nineteenth-century Canada.* Toronto: Oxford University Press.

Sommerville, J. (1982). *The rise and fall of childhood.* California: Sage.

Stewart, W. (1976). *But not in Canada.* Toronto: Macmillan.

Suransky, V. (1982). *The erosion of childhood.* Chicago: University of Chicago Press.

Sutherland, N. (1976). *Children in English-Canadian society: Framing the twentieth-century consensus.* Toronto: University of Toronto Press.

Waddington, M. (1968). In L. Monk (Ed.), *Call them Canadians* (p. 243). Ottawa: National Film Board.

2

Play: For Survival

Otto Weininger

Two tiny figures, engrossed in piles of sand and small cars without wheels, heads together in the spring sunlight, giggling and laughing. The scene is familiar, from our observation of the world around us and from our memories of childhood. Watching and remembering, we all know why children play—it's fun! During the past two decades, psychologists interested in cognitive development have become increasingly aware of the importance of play as a child's major path to learning. As Sigel and McBane, writing in 1967 on their research with young children, say, "Play allows the child to practise what he has met up with in his world, and gradually, through play, comes to know."

In this chapter we will briefly draw together theories and knowledge from research in ethnology and cognitive psychology, as well as some hypothetical information from traditional psychology, in order to indicate the ramifications of play in a child's development. Play is an important survival skill for the human species: to play is not only to learn, but to learn to survive.

DEFINING PLAY

Developmental psychologists initially looked at play as the basis for learning concepts (Spicker, 1969): play filled the child's need to explore and experiment with the senses. Exploration and experimentation in sensory ways are part of the concrete stage of thought, the stage that, developmentally, precedes the level of abstract reasoning (Piaget, 1962).

Gradually, however, with more detailed observation of play and further in-depth research, it became clear that play was essential to the child's *total* development: emotional, physical, psychological, and cognitive (Weininger, 1979).

Play may be studied from various aspects—physical play, play as a preparation for formal learning, or symbolic play, for example. Generally, play represents "a complex collage of activities," and it has been argued that the wide variety of behaviours that may be included under the rubric of "play" renders the concept itself unscientific (Berlyne, 1969). In our view, however, play's very complexity invites further investigation. We need to relate the findings of disparate studies to specific elements of play in order to come to a full understanding of play's true nature and function.

Play may be defined as any of a wide variety of behaviours through which human beings attempt to discover what sort of people they are, what they are able to do, and how they can learn about their environment (Weininger, 1979). "On balance, it appears that the phenomenon of play has been defined in a reasonably consistent manner using fairly standard criteria. Across studies, the same categories and psychological features have been used to study play, and within studies, these categories have been recognized with a high degree of reliability. Investigators seem to mean somewhat the same things when they use the term play" (Eckler & Weininger, 1988).

PURPOSES OF PLAY

Play is the earliest opportunity provided by the species for the child to acquire some of the enormous amount of information necessary for his or her effective functioning as an adult in society.

Zoological observation shows that the more prolonged the growing-up process is and the longer a baby animal is allowed to play, the greater is the amount of information and the number of skills that must be acquired before the young animal can successfully separate from its mother. The behaviours of the larger primates come close to the human experience. For example, observation of the play of chimpanzees shows that they too are attempting to find out how they influence their environment. Jane Goodall's (1972) work shows that play is an important part of the chimp's activity, particularly in relationship to the mother, and that play is a very serious activity that enables the animal to understand more of the world around it. For example, when the chimp's mother dangles her baby by one foot, she not only displays a kind of close attachment behaviour, but also provides her baby with the opportunity to experience what it would feel like to dangle from the limb of a tree.

Play helps infants to understand the potentialities of their own body, of their body in space, of the ways various stimuli will impinge on it, and of how it must organize and/or adjust itself in relationship to those stimuli. The serious preoccupation that most babies—whether they be human, primate, lion, or dog—bring to scratching at a small hole in the ground, making variations of a sound, watching a speck of light dust, or gazing at a fly reflects the effort to acquire information, to acquaint themselves with their world, and, in so doing, to ensure their own survival. Play is at the service of survival. The higher the species is on the evolutionary scale, the more information needs to be learned in order to survive. Therefore it is not at all surprising to find the human baby and child involved in a great deal of play activity.

Play has to do with exploration, curiosity, sensory-motor activity, social activity, verbal imitation, and divergent thinking. There are many activities we would all categorize as play—a child moving and piling up blocks; a parent crawling on all fours pretending to be a cat chasing a giggling and laughing child; a child fascinated by a bit of string or a tree branch; a baby exploring fingers and toes, sounds and tastes. The child colouring and painting, thinking and gazing into space, or digging a hole in the sand and making a wall; the adolescent bouncing a ball or trying to score a basket; the adult walking through the woods or playing golf or swimming—these are all activities that are subsumed under the term "play." In every case the actions are intrinsically motivated, and there may be considerable pleasure, emotionally and/or physically, in *performing* the acts regardless of the goal or outcome of the activity.

Thus, although the basic "function" of much play is quite clear, we must also keep in mind play's apparently "functionless" quality. From another point of view, play does not seem to be so much a "goal-directed" activity as an intrinsically motivated expression of inner needs (Neuman, 1971), closely associated with intense emotions of pleasure and attachment. It seems to be exactly this complex interrelationship between fact and feeling, between learning and expression, between self and other, that accounts for the crucial importance of play in the development of the child.

Something of this pattern can be seen in the relationship between play and cognitive development. Physical activity and playing with objects allow the child to investigate the "hard realities" of the world. As Piaget's pioneering research showed, play represents children's first attempts to explore and understand their environment as they move from what is at first a series of discrete stimuli or events toward more coherently integrated cognitive schemata. Play helps develop the child's earliest conception of the permanence of objects. Beginning with manipulative play using hands and gaze, the infant gradually develops a sense of the function of objects and more complex conceptions of his or her possible relations to them. A child playing with a ball, for instance, may discover that it bounces when dropped or thrown; that it bounces higher on a hard surface, such as a sidewalk, than on soft earth; that if thrown up it always comes back down; that if thrown "just right" against the side of a building it can be made to return directly to the child or to bounce in another direction. The child learns the skills involved in doing all these things with the ball, and learns that different things can be done with balls of different sizes—the child's hands learn the skills of catching and throwing a ball, a process that gives the child a feeling of accomplishment and knowledge about how balls "work."

As Piaget (1962) suggested, through play children are striving to find an equilibrium between themselves and their world. Children examine new stimuli in their experience: they not only look at a new toy, for example, but touch it, taste it, try to manipulate it as they did an older toy and/or as sounds and sights gained from their first sensory exploration of the new object might indicate. Through the first tentative explorations the "new" seem to be accommodated to the "known"; as it is assimilated and made use of, the child develops further mental "schemata" with which to account for the new experience. The free exploration and accommodation provided by play seem to allow the child to arrange what might otherwise be a bewildering variety of incoming information.

Clearly, very young children must do a great deal of "new" investigation. Thus, four-year-olds have been found by one study to be more interested in examining toys—"specific exploration"—while adults who recognize the toys' function immediately "do" things with the toys—"diversive exploration" (Hutt, 1970; Vlietstra, 1978). Children may also be daunted or repelled by a stimulus of too great complexity: playing, in the young child, appears to occur with less complex stimuli. Generally, as children become more acquainted with a toy, both their specific exploration and their investigative exploration decrease, and play behaviour increases.

But even very young children do not spend all their time in quasi-scientific "investigative explorations"! They "pretend," they play symbolically with objects, and there is some very striking evidence of a relationship between this sort of free "symbolic" play and one of the more basic cognitive skills, the ability to "conserve" quantity—that is, to recognize that equal amounts of a substance remain equal when their shapes are changed. Golombe and Cornelius (1977) compared two groups of four- to four-and-a-half-year-olds. The first group was given six symbolic play situations in three daily sessions lasting approximately fifteen minutes each. They pretended, for example, that they were preparing some food to take on a picnic, or that they were in a truck driving through mountains. The other group was presented with three "constructive" play tasks, one a day in sessions of about fifteen minutes each. They were asked to assemble two animal puzzles and to construct designs using a mosaic set, then given a drawing task. Results indicated that symbolic play facilitates conservation. The authors suggest that "symbolic play is an important antecedent of operational reversibility." Symbolic play, rather than being something that we expect the child to outgrow, should perhaps be fostered as a technique to help the child develop reversible representational thought structures.

Weininger's (1985) work, focusing on a sequence of thematic play, had observable effects on children who were physically handicapped as well as on children who were suffering from serious emotional disturbances. Children in one study were involved in listening to and playing at the theme of a story that was read to them; in a second and third study children aged four to five years were involved in "pretend" play four days a week starting in the third month of the school year. These children came into a small room and sat around a table with their teacher. Their play became increasingly complex as they demonstrated the capacity to engage in more detailed play. Gradually the teacher introduced the ideas of story-telling, story-writing, and story-reading. The group continued to meet for seven months, with the time of their play increasing from five minutes a day to sixty minutes a day. A control group was also observed during this same period of time.

The play of the experimental group was certainly different from the control group. Observations indicated that as the experimental play group began to "write" and "read" their stories, they showed considerable improvement in linguistic processes, were no longer withdrawn and angry, showed sustained activity, and were able to pay attention, to concentrate, and to remember. Their interpersonal relationships improved greatly. They talked to each other, played games with each other, and interacted in other than angry ways. When they left the small room and went into their large classroom, they still played cooperatively and used words appropriately; although they still had fights, these fights were less intense and were over faster. Surprisingly, the spatial capacity, fine motor movements, and memory of these children improved. They behaved in purposeful ways; they planned and could even monitor their own progress. They apparently gained a great deal from this play—in contrast to the control group, which did not show these gains. The control-group children still played in fragmentary and isolated ways, were generally angry and screaming at each other or the teacher, had poor control over their feelings, and could not sit still or concentrate. The children of the control group were very much like the children in the experimental group at the start of this research. Play, when provided in a consistent manner and at the "level" required, is "a powerful tool for children's learning" (Weininger, 1985).

PLAYING AND KNOWING

Through play, children seem able to assimilate sections of new experience that can be dealt with in more or less familiar terms, while at the same time extending their knowledge through progressive integration of new material. Cognitively, play seems to allow the child to make a rough selection or organization of incoming information so that he or she can make use of it. At first, only a small amount of information will be processed; later on, this "chunking" of information will be increased, so that an older child is able to grasp larger sections of information—in this way, becoming almost automatically able to be involved in various kinds of learning processes. When the learning is novel, the child will have to return to "chunking" and take in manageable bits at a time. This response is very similar to the way in which novel stimuli will affect any behaviour. For example, if the stimulus is too novel—for example, when chimps are presented with models of chimps that lack heads or arms—the stimulus is too disturbing to approach; only when the chimps have been able to do some preliminary exploration do they approach the stimulus (Goodall, 1972). So too with the human child. If the stimulus is too novel, the child seems to avoid looking or perhaps is unable to view the stimulus effectively. It is almost as if the stimulus does not "register" cognitively and emotionally—there is no prior organization to admit this unusual stimulus. If the stimulus is stale or completely known, the child may ignore it as well—unless, because of fear or anxiety, the child needs to go back to known information, so as to regroup his or her internal processes. Consequently, for children and perhaps for other young animals it is very important that the novelty of stimuli not be so great as to prevent the organism from looking at it and in that way acquiring information. The rough-and-ready selection and reorganization processes involved in play seem to provide for the progressive integration of a perhaps initially confusing abundance of new experiences—at a pace suited to the individual child's needs and stage of development.

Spatial competencies may be significantly underestimated if young children are not given enough experiences through play to examine their environment (Herman & Siegel, 1978); cognitive maps of their environment are correctly made only after children are provided with sufficient experience with that environment. If children are given an adequate amount of experience in any of their learning environments, their degree of accuracy about their environment and perhaps the subsequent usefulness of the experience to integrative learning is significantly enhanced, provided that the cognitive mapping does not require, at first anyway, "translation of scale or stimuli" (Siegel et al., 1979, p. 584).

Cognitive mapping seems to take place in a "strip" manner at first: the child plays with some of the toys in a special way and only in some of the space of the room. The child seems to move about the room developing strip maps (Tolman, 1948); later, the child integrates these content-filled strip maps into a comprehensive map of the toys' function and full-room/full-building space. The comprehensive map allows children to know where they are going, what they are going to do, and how they are going to do it. It allows them to function in an "automatic" way, for learning through play has now become part of their cognitive unconscious (Weininger, 1979)—an ensemble of structures and functions unknown to children except in their results.

Through play, children internalize a process that enables them to use and integrate the processing styles of both cerebral hemispheres in a complementary manner. This internalization process is most vividly reflected in the transfer of learning that has been observed to take place outside the sociodramatic play situation. This process, according to our model, involves an ability to routinize certain aspects of a task by gradually transferring the information gained through play experience (and initially processed by the right hemisphere) to the left hemisphere. The ability to internalize the structure of a story through sociodramatic play is paralleled by the emergence of the ability to begin to work with symbol systems such as reading and printing. These symbol systems require the internalization of certain rules of grammatical structure (Weininger & Fitzgerald, 1988, p. 34).

Through play, children find out more about the world around them and their own capacities to deal with and affect the world. Play helps a person to discover "what *I* can do to an object to make it change its function, what *I* can do in relation to my world that helps me learn about it." Whether it is learning about water, air, sand, or fire, play provides for environmental learning. It involves sociocultural role-playing, as well as safety knowledge, and is of survival value. Through play, the child also learns to generate ideas for alternative means of performing acts—whether they be real or fantasy. To explore an object is almost to say "What can the object do?" The child may begin by exploring the object in a sensory-motor style. In exploration, the stimulus of the object may seem to be most important. However, its importance can only be as great as the capacity of the child (or adult) to think, "What can I do to explore the *function* of the object?" Play permits the child to stay with an object, to explore it, to find out how it functions—first, in relation to patterns that the child already knows; then, in relation to alternative patterns. Play subsumes exploration and teaches the child the consequences of his or her acts. Play provides for the opportunity for people to explore how *they* function as well as how the object they are using functions. Play is the acquisition of information related to the potentials around and within the self.

PLAYING FOR UNDERSTANDING

For this reason it is important to examine the relationship of play to the shaping of the self, through the basic processes of attachment and separation. Winnicott's conception of the development of the "observing ego" may illuminate the complex relationship between cognitive and emotional growth from the perspective of traditional psychiatry. For Winnicott, as for Piaget, play helps to develop the sense of equilibrium between the self and the world. Winnicott believes that play helps children to understand what is happening around them, inside them, and outside themselves. It helps them to begin to distinguish the "not me" and allows them to begin to recognize, sometimes with difficulty and with pain, what is outside their omnipotent and narcissistic control. "To control what is outside one has to do things, not simply to think or to wish, and doing things takes time, playing is doing" (Winnicott, 1968).

Winnicott talks about the "potential space between the baby and his mother," which is a position that varies according to the experiences of the baby in relationship to the mother. In this space, the baby is free to play and to experiment with his relation to his mother by examining, testing, finding out, observing what is under his control and what is not. Essentially, the baby is using this potential space between mother and infant as a way of examining his own relationship to his environment. At this point, in the normal, healthy child, this is a child communicating with some part of himself—what Winnicott calls the "observing ego."

This observing ego allows the child to reflect upon and receive information from the environment and to modulate the incoming information in a way that is acceptable and capable of integration within the full ego. In this way, the ego and its perception of reality may become broadened, strengthened, and stabilized. In order for the child to further his perceptions of reality, it is important to have this original experience of play in the safe yet new "potential space" between himself and mother. Without this play in the potential space, we suspect that the child will not be able to make use of the crucial transitional concept of the observing ego—that is, the child would have to try to develop his ego prematurely by forced identification with the mother, which prevents the child from becoming a separate person.

Play, in the normal child, helps the observing ego, and acts as a kind of self-healing mechanism. The child is able to play out and observe some of his own poorly organized, if not inadequate, responses to his environment—in particular, to his mother. The play then becomes exceptionally exciting, for in a sense it takes place on the edge of a precipice where the child explores unconscious aspects, at times not under conscious control. It is as if a kind of magic relationship evolves that the child uses to explore his own unconsciousness. It is, however, the potential space and the state of confidence that is present between the mother and the baby that permit the baby to play. As Winnicott says, "In playing, the child manipulates external phenomena in the service of the dream and invests external phenomena with dream meaning and feeling." If play seems to be purposeless, then, it may only be that we have not understood the goal. In some instances, the goal is not the conscious one of learning specific information, but rather the unconscious one of attaining greater emotional maturity.

Children at play may seem to be totally independent, particularly when they are in the narcissistic, omnipotent phase of their development, but they quickly run into the frustrating wall of not being able to accomplish all that they set out to do, and quickly move back to the attached relationship. If this relationship permits the child to explore his or her world, the attachment fosters the individuation process, and the child becomes a separate person. The child has learned control over behaviour and can satisfy his or her own needs; the child has learned some of the cultural mores and is able to move within these systems. With an increasing feeling of being able to do things effectively, we would expect increased exploration and risk-taking. But only when children have a secure foundation of *knowing* that they can perform will they take risks in situations where they might fail. And only when they realize that failure is also part of learning are they on the way to becoming an independent person, more ready to leave their parents.

Certainly, observations of infants at play show that the child's simultaneous sense of attachment to and freedom from the mother provides the natural context for the gradual "socialization" of play. As Eckerman, Whatley, and Kutz (1975, p. 48) note, it really seems to be the mother who provides "the setting for the infant's exploration of his inanimate world. At 10 to 12 months, play with the mother and direct play with the peer is infrequent; by 16 to 18 months, play with mother and play with peer is more frequent, but play with mother exceeds that of the peer. By 22 to 24 months, play with the mother declines, while direct play with the peer increases markedly."

Another study of two- to three-year-olds emphasizes the support provided by the presence of the mother, or the beloved "transitional object" that symbolizes her presence, in a novel situation. Like other studies, this experiment demonstrated that the frequency and duration of a child's play are greatest in an environment where maternal support is available: "Without exception, having the mother in the setting prevented distress and promoted play more than either a familiar non-social agent such as a favourite toy, or no familiar agent." But the study also pointed out that children who have an attachment to a blanket can play and explore without showing distress, at least as long as children exposed to their mothers, and always longer than non-attached children. The presence of the transitional object seems to facilitate exploration and play in novel settings (Passman & Wiseberg, 1975).

Perhaps it is because the baby is too immature to be separate from her parents that nature has given her the time to play. The time gives the infant a chance to learn how to make use of objects and herself, and, as well, enables her to develop the kind of attachment to her mother that lets her go on and make use of social interactions. It has been argued that in the earliest stages the stronger the "understanding attachment" between mother and baby, the more effective the learning (Klaus & Kendell, 1976). When the child is ready, the mother prepares her to become more and more independent, and so she negotiates on her own in her playing world. Playing now provides the opportunity for the child to interact with and develop affection for peers; once the ability to develop such affection has been acquired, "new affectional ties can develop without playing" (Harlow & Harlow, 1976).

PLAY VARIATIONS

In the social arena, children play with each other and learn how to interact. Their activities evolve: solitary play gives way to spectator play, then to parallel play, associative play, and group play. Children learn to respond to one another's experiences, but at their level of emotional growth. They are stimulated by the interactive experiences. Children imitate in play; cooperative behaviour emerges in play and children begin to accept instruction. Children begin to evaluate their activities honestly and not entirely egocentrically. They are learning how their behaviour and that of others affect themselves and the others. Children learn to wait, to postpone gratification, to recognize that they do not know everything. But, although the gradual "socialization" of play is clearly a crucial step toward maturity, we must recognize the continuing importance of solitary play. As one study reminds us, "To be playing on his own does not necessarily mean that a child is lacking in social ability; it may mean that he has the confidence to play so" (Roper & Hinde, 1978, p. 577). Of course, it would be absurd simply to state that solitary play represents "poor social adjustment," when such play may, in fact, be energetically "goal-directed" activity (involving arts and crafts, for example); it may involve large-muscle play and educational play. Solitary play may be independent and task-oriented behaviour, and may be functional; an indication not of immaturity, but rather of maturity. There may even be a continuum of solitary play, along which children move from passively watching others or their environment, to more active and expressive activities, to becoming independent and accepting challenges from their environment and objects in their environment (Moore, Evertson, & Brophy, 1974).

Moreover, the concept of the observing ego reminds us of the important developments that may be taking place through play, which need not be active or goal-directed in the usual sense. For the toddler, the infant, and the baby, play involves a kind of symbolic activity. While Piaget suggests that sophisticated symbolic activities start to occur in an interiorization of movement at about 18 months of age, other studies suggest that this kind of activity occurs much earlier (Bower & Patterson, 1973; Corrigan, 1975; Demany, McKenzie, & Vurpillot, 1977; Mehrabian & Williams, 1971; Monoud & Bauer, 1974–1975). Bower and Patterson's work suggests that babies are capable of a kind of reversibility and even a kind of calculation; and perhaps Piaget's whole idea of egocentricity is called into question, when, in fact, it is simply one state in which children are involved in an attempt to gain further information from their world. Perhaps egocentricity must be viewed as simply one developmental act among many others such acts, not as the overriding one.

Through imitation and role-playing in the strictly "presocial" world of "pretend," solitary play seems to allow children the chance to re-explore, to clarify, to some extent to master, and perhaps even to generate further hypotheses about, the world and their own potential creativity. This is most obvious in dramatic play, perhaps beginning by using small replicas of the adult world and later being able to behave "as if it were here" and participate in social drama. Children can pretend that they are going on a visit to a mountaintop, or that they are in the middle of a hurricane. They then present the play using the information that they have acquired in other activities. In this way children make use of language and gradually broaden their skills to acquire greater comprehension and meaning for the words. The drama almost asks for more words, and so more words are required by the child. The drama allows for imitation and identification and helps the child sort out the very difficult question of "who I am and what I do." Dramatic play gives information about "where I stand in relationship to other people, how I feel about what my parents are doing, and what I think makes things happen."

In pretend play the child explores the worlds of imagination. Imagination is the thinking function of play and the "what if" function: imagining "What if I were a cook?" sets the stage for the actual play itself—the "now I am a chef cooking foods." In thinking about the pretend activity itself, one child remarked, "You imagine it in your head and that tells you how to play." As the child continues to play, imagining continues and becomes the planning process for further play activity; the "what if" precedes the "as if" (Weininger, 1988).

Obviously, pretend play with the simplest objects allows the child not only to experiment with tool-using but also to abstract from and relate disparate experiences—so, a spoon is a spoon, is a sailboat, is a shovel, is a thermometer, is a baby. A fascinating experiment by Dansky and Silverman (1973) with children aged three to five years indicated that free play with one set of 16 objects—as opposed to imitation of a tutor/experimenter, or the achievement of an intellectual task involving the 16 objects—facilitated the generation of alternative associations regarding a *second* set of objects presented afterwards. The development of language in association with play also reflects and may reinforce children's growing awareness of both the nature of the world and their own creative capacities with regard to it. In play, words are repeated, made up, rhymed. Props that are used to represent objects in the child's environment are given names. With these names, the child is exploring their functions. For example, if the child sets the table and says it is now dinnertime, the child is perhaps suggesting "I am trying to free myself from the concreteness of the object in order to be able to use language in its symbolic pure form." The child is progressively freeing herself, through play, to be able to say "Let's have dinner"—that is, to use language in its purely abstract form. Language seems to become increasingly independent of the conditions of its use (De Laguna, 1970).

⁂ In another example, following a brief period of play, small groups of children from three to five years of age were given two sets of materials. Set A consisted of paper clips, blank 3″ by 5″ cards, empty matchboxes, small corks, empty spoons, pipe cleaners, clothespins, and a pair of pliers. Set B consisted of a paper towel, a plastic cup, a screwdriver, and a coat hanger. The experiment consisted of two phases. In the first phase, groups of two children seen together were given one of the following tasks, using the objects in Set A. Some groups were instructed to play with the objects however they wished. Other groups were instructed to watch and "then imitate the experimenter, who performed a series of actions with the objects. The intellectual task subjects were shown the objects and told to arrive at a joint decision about which object the experimenter was thinking of on the basis of the various verbal clues that they would be given" (Dansky & Silverman, 1975, p. 104). In the second phase, following immediately, each subject was seen individually by one of the experimenters and the subject was asked to generate all the uses he or she could for all the objects in Set B. The subjects in the play condition produced significantly more standard and non-standard uses than did the subjects in either the imitation or intellectual-task conditions. Play seems to create an attitude conducive to generating alternative associations, whether or not the objects in question are encountered during the play activity. Playful activity perhaps provides children with a greater opportunity to integrate and organize their experiences, and perhaps stimulates them to think more about what they are doing and about what objects mean (Dansky & Silverman, 1975).

Play also enables children, in a manner that allows for abstraction without loss of intensity, to deal with an activity that may in fact be serious, perhaps even disturbing. By pretending, children can distance them-selves from the activity and thus see aspects of their own and others' behaviour more clearly. The intensity, the seriousness, often means that the child is not able to gauge the effects of the activity; play apparently allows for a kind of "intentional" activity, with the intent to understand and if necessary to circumvent or to coordinate relationships in order to understand what is going on in the world. As Piaget (1962) suggested, play involves an ability on the part of children to disengage from immedi-ate consequences, keep the goal in mind, and perform the kind of actions that may allow them to understand more about what is going on. In social play behaviour, both animals and human children must keep in mind that the activity is in fact playful—that play "fighting" is not the "real" thing, for example. If the play changes from pretence to reality, the child has not been able to distance himself and the involvement has not allowed the child really to understand what is going on in the "act." Distancing means that the child must form a kind of representation—to understand signs and signals as the representation of the actual act. The child signifies that *this* act means *this* particular thing, so that when a child sets up a stick, he states that this stick is the goal post or this stick is the house. The stick signifies the playful activity; the task is then to decide what to do with the goal post, or what to do with the house. The child has the capacity to make intention and representation through play activity and to learn the various kinds of alternatives (which he has made part of the rules of the game) that he may in fact employ in reaching the desired end. The rules have in fact been developed as a result of the social interaction between the child and other children—at first, though, as we have suggested, between the child and his mother. The child is able to use the signified pole to represent an object and to deal with it in a symbolic style. Thus, the cognitive capacities of intentional activity and representational goal-directed activity appear to be built up through the play in which the child has been involved to date.

PLAY AS PREPARATION

The way in which children organize their play is an indication of their ability to deal effectively with the world. Research findings on class differences in cognitive development have emphasized the importance of play in the foundation for early learning and expression. Working-class children appear to be less able to function on representational levels than their middle-class peers. Sigel & McBane (1967) suggest that working-class children's cognitive structures are not sufficiently developed so that new experiences may be assimilated. In other words, it appears that the working-class child has not had sufficient opportunity for play. Borowitz et al. (1970), in a study of preschool ghetto boys, shows that the organization and amount of creative play and quality of speaking are related to cognitive competence. Of course, play is not merely a "preparation" for "higher" forms of learning. Even if children do develop the more complex mental schemata necessary for dealing with specific correlative tests, this does not ensure that they will use those schemata (Premack, 1977). The importance of play involves more than developing basic problem-solving skills. Play also provides a core for the child's social, emotional, aesthetic, and intellectual development, organizing different aspects of experience into wholes, opening up new insights, and extending learning in the most natural way possible. As Bruner (1973) has said, "Play during early childhood permits the child to explore combinations of things and acts that would never be explored if he kept just to reasonable problem solving. It is for this reason that we can properly speak of play as the serious business of childhood."

Given the crucial importance of play in the child's development, it hardly seems necessary to argue here at length—as I have frequently done elsewhere—the value of a play-based curriculum for early schooling (Weininger, 1979). The importance of play as an element of or a model for early curricula has been widely recognized (Karnes et al., 1972; Spicker, 1969; Weikart, 1971). Comparative studies of classroom structures have indicated that the least-structured format that allows for imaginative play fosters the child's ability to persist in pursuing an independent task (Faggott, 1973; Huston-Stein, Freidrich-Cofer, & Susman, 1977; Singer, 1973). Moreover, a sensitively handled play-based program that respects the needs of individual children for both freedom and direction in learning can compensate for the distinctive distortions of a cognitive style, which seems, as I have argued elsewhere (Weininger, 1979), to be the product of the failure to achieve what Winnicott calls the proper "potential space" between mother and child in the earliest stages of development: such distortions include, for example, the passive, perfectionistic, frequently language-delayed "over-protected" child and the aggressive, hostile, "rejected" child. For children whose early experiences have deprived them of this foundation or distorted it, the opportunity the classroom offers for play will be crucial in helping them to reconstruct and reorganize their experiences and to develop the schemata for acquiring knowledge. At the same time, play itself also provides an important opportunity for the teacher to recognize, evaluate, and make adjustments for the particular problems, abilities, and learning styles of individual children.

CONCLUSION

To sum up, through play children begin to form their first conceptions of themselves and the world and to develop their emerging cognitive capacities. From the infant's earliest play with mother and explorations of objects, through the more elaborate and creative play behaviour of the older child, play allows children both to adapt themselves to their environment and to gain a measure of control over it and thus confidence about their own place in it. Vandenberg (1973) has spoken in more general terms of the cultural functions of play: "Play serves important adaptive functions and . . . through cultural transmissions, these adaptive (and some not so adaptive) activities can change group life. It is a two-way street; through play animals learn the important adaptive behaviours for group life, and group life can itself be altered by the adaptive consequences of new behaviours discovered in play. To benefit in such a way from play means that that species must be flexible enough to invent new behaviours, generalize them to a new situation and culturally transmit them."

Since in the child's cognitive, emotional, and social development play peculiarly serves this simultaneously adaptive and creative function, it does not seem too much to argue that play is necessary for survival. In one sense, play may seem to be a secondary activity—that is, it is often changed, and when there is sufficient novelty or stress, play behaviour stops. On the other hand, it may be correct for children to stop playing under stress in order to mobilize whatever skills, competency, and schemata it would be wise for them to have. And in the broader view, it is perhaps the alternatives, the diversity, the schemata that are developed by children during play that enable them to survive stress and adapt to their environment. Play seems to be, in effect, a way of trying to control the environment.

And, of course, play does not end with childhood. It continues for the rest of one's life—golf, tennis, squash, sailing, skiing, chess, dancing, and art are all recognized as useful adult play. Although we talk of work when we are adults, we find that a large group of people approach their work in terms that can be seen as playful. That is, when the adult's job offers the opportunity to "play with" his or her work, to bring in novelty, to create an environment so as to produce ingenious solutions, or to vary the order of tasks, or the routine of the day, then it is perceived as more interesting and fulfilling. At the extreme is a scientist who discovers some great chemical in a serendipitous fashion by mentally playing with his or her work while on the golf course! It is unfortunate that our society has, for the past hundred years or more, created the kinds of occupations that can be truly called *only* "work"—occupations where the person simply stands at a machine and watches as it routinely performs the same activity over and over. We may need to offer people who stand at machines the opportunity to re-create the machine's task so that its operator no longer feels like a mere extension of it, and thus feels less human, but is once again able to bring playful attributes to the job.

At the other extreme, who but a species needing the mental diversions of play would turn games *into* jobs, and very lucrative jobs at that, such as professional hockey, tennis, golf, racing, football, and so forth? It is a sad commentary on our society that in so doing we routinize and intensify these "games" so that the fun of playing them becomes "work," with a desperate intensity. And the money involved turns these workers into interchangeable commodities just as surely as it does those on the assembly line.

So we play our whole lives long, in one way or another. What begins as a learning need—part of the cognitive and psychological development of infants, children, and adolescents—becomes not only a habit but an emotional and intellectual need. I suspect that the enormous upsurge in organized recreation and leisure activities in this country directly parallels an increase in the number of adult jobs characterized by routine and boredom in an increasingly technological society. It also provides a release from the tensions of our highly competitive and very organized, but often not physically active, lives. Whenever children play, they absorb ideas, build skills, further concepts, become more individual; whenever adults play, we return, somewhere in our mind, to those hazily remembered, slower, wonder-filled days of childhood, if only for the time it takes to bicycle through the park. And as surely as children play, albeit unknowingly, to learn enough to survive, so adults continue to play, knowing that play is a part of surviving they don't *want* to live without.

REFERENCES

Berlyne, D.E. (1969). Laughter, humor and play. In G. Lindzey & E. Aronson (Eds.), *The handbook of social psychology* (Vol. 3, Reading, MA: Addison-Wesley.

Borowitz, G.H., et al. (1970). Play behavior and competence in ghetto four-year-olds. *Journal of Special Education, 4,* (Spring/Summer), 215–220.

Bower, T.G.R., & Patterson, J.G. (1973). The separation of place, movement and object in the world of the infant. *Journal of Experimental Child Psychology, 15,* 161–168.

Bruner, J. (1973). Organization of early skilled action. *Child Development, 44,* 1–11.

Corrigan, R. (1975, April). *Relationship between object permanence and language development: How much and how strong?* Paper presented at the Eighth Annual Stanford Child Language Forum, Stanford, CA.

Dansky, J.L., & Silverman, I.W. (1973). Effects of associative fluency in preschool-age children. *Developmental Psychology, 9,* 38–43.

Dansky, J.L., & Silverman, I.W. (1975). Play: A general facilitator of associative fluency. *Developmental Psychology, 11*(1), 104.

De Laguna, G. (1970). *Speech: Its function and development.* College Park, MD: McGrath.

Demany, L., McKenzie, B., & Vurpillot, E. (1977). Rhythm perception in early infancy. *Nature, 266,* 718–719.

Eckerman, C.O., Whatley, J.L., & Kutz, S.L. (1975). Play with peers during the second year of life. *Developmental Psychology, 11*(1), 42–49.

Eckler, J., & Weininger, O. (1988). Play and cognitive development in pre-schoolers: A critical review. *Alberta Journal of Educational Research, 34*(2), 179–193.

Faggott, B.I. (1973). Influence of teacher behaviour in pre-school. *Developmental Psychology, 9,* 198–206.

Golombe, P., & Cornelius, C.B. (1977). Symbolic play and its cognitive significance. *Developmental Psychology, 13*(1), 246–252.

Goodall, J. (1972). *In the shadow of man.* New York: Dell.

Harlow, H.F., & Harlow, N.K. (1976). Learning to love. *American Scientist, 54,* 244–272.

Herman, J.F., & Siegel, A.W. (1978). The development of cognitive mapping of the large-scale environment. *Journal of Experimental Child Psychology, 26,* 389–406.

Huston-Stein, A., Freidrich-Cofer, L., & Susman, E.J. (1977). The relation of classroom structure to social behaviour, imaginative play and self-regulation of economically disadvantaged children. *Child Development, 48,* 908–916.

Hutt, C. (1970). Specific and diversive exploration. In H.W. Reese and L.P. Lipsitt (Eds.), *Advances in child development and behaviour.* New York: Academic.

Karnes, M.B., et al. (1972). A five-year longitudinal comparison of a traditional versus a structured pre-school program on cognitive, social and affective variables. Bureau of Research, Illinois University, Urbana. Washington, DC: Office of Education, (ERIC Document Reproduction Service No. ED 062007)

Klaus, M.H., & Kendell, J.A. (1976). *Maternal-infant bonding.* St. Louis: C.V. Mosby.

Mehrabian, A., & Williams, M. (1971). Piagetian measures of cognitive development up to age two. *Journal of Psycholinguistic Research, 1,* 113–126.

Mounoud, P., & Bauer, P. (1974–1975). Conservation of weight in infants. *Cognitive Psychology, 3,* 29–40.

Moore, N.V., Evertson, C.M., & Brophy, J.E. (1974). Solitary play: Some functional reconsiderations. *Developmental Psychology, 10*(6), 830–834.

Neuman, E.A. (1971). *The elements of play.* New York: MMS Information Corporation.

Passman, R.H., & Wiseberg, H. (1975). Mothers and blankets as agents for promoting play and exploration by young children in a novel environment: The effects of social and non-social attachment objects. *Developmental Psychology, 11*(2), 170–177.

Piaget, J. (1962). *Play, dreams and imitation in childhood.* New York: Norton.

Premack, D. (1977). The human ape. *The Sciences, 17*(1), 20–23.

Roper, R., & Hinde, H.R. (1978). Social behaviour in a play group: Consistency and complexity. *Child Development, 49*, 570–579.

Siegel, A.W., Herman, J.F., Allen, G.L., & Kerasic, K.C. (1979). The development of cognitive maps of large- and small-scale spaces. *Child Development, 50*, 582–585.

Sigel, I., & McBane, B. (1967). Cognitive competence and level of symbolization among five-year-old children. In J. Helmuth (Ed.), *Disadvantaged child* (Vol., 1). Seattle: Special Child Publications.

Singer, J. (1973). *The child's world of make-believe: Experimental studies in imaginative play.* New York: Academic.

Spicker, H.H. (1969). The influence of selected variables on the effectiveness of pre-school programs for disadvantaged children. Washington, DC: Office of Child Development. (ERIC Document Reproduction Service No. ED 049835)

Tolman, E.C. (1948). Cognitive maps in rats and man. *Psychological Review, 55*, 189.

Vandenberg, B. (1973). Play and development from an ecological perspective. *American Psychologist, 8*(78), 724–738.

Vlietstra, A.G. (1978). Exploration and play in pre-school children and young adults. *Child Development, 49*, 235–238.

Weikart, D.P. (1971, February). Relationship of curriculum teaching and learning in pre-school education. Ypsilante, MI: High/Scope Educational Research Foundation. (ERIC Document Reproduction Service No. ED 049837)

Weininger, O. (1979). *Play and education: The basic tool for early childhood learning.* Springfield, IL: Charles C. Thomas.

Weininger, O. (1985). Just pretend: Explorations in the use of pretend play and teaching handicapped and emotionally disturbed children. In J. Kase-Polisini (Ed.), *Creative drama in a developmental context.* Lanham, MD: University Press of America.

Weininger, O. (1988a). "What if" and "as if": Imagination and pretend play in early childhood. In D. Nadaner (Ed.), *Imagination and education.* New York: Teachers College Press.

Weininger, O., & Fitzgerald D. (1988b). Symbolic play and inter-hemispheric integration: Some thoughts on a neuropsychological model of play. *Journal of Research and Development in Education, 21*(4), 23–40.

Winnicott, D.W. (1968). Play: Its theoretical status in the clinical situation. *International Journal of Psychoanalysis, 49*(4), 591–599.

3

The Learning Child

Ada Schermann

The Concept of Environmental Readiness
Program Implications
Barriers to the Teaching/Learning Process
Conclusion
References

This chapter presents the reader with the challenge of understanding how young children learn, and the conditions that best promote learning. Learning is assumed to have occurred when behaviour changes as a result of experience. In some instances it is easy to see that learning has taken place, as children use the new knowledge and skills that they have acquired; on other occasions, the learning represents an increase in the likelihood that certain responses will occur.

Young children are natural learners, endowed with immense curiosity and a talent for finding out about the world. By the time children enter nursery school or kindergarten, they know a great deal about the physical world, have many social skills, and are able to use language to communicate effectively. All this learning has been achieved without either formal instruction or the assistance of specially trained teachers. There have, however, been many people who have created the conditions and climate that enable learning to take place and who must therefore be regarded as the child's teachers. A teacher, then, may be defined quite simply as someone who helps another person to learn. In order to teach effectively, the teacher should never plan a program without reference to the learner's developmental level, interests, and abilities. The teacher should also remember that the incidental learning that is happening while children are playing and casually interacting with people and things is preferable to teacher-dominated instruction.

A challenging environment for learning is one that affords opportunities for many different behaviours. These include looking, listening, questioning (both verbally and by manipulating materials), handling objects, experimenting, constructing, playing with ideas and things, and moving around in space to gain different views. In the course of the child's interactions with the environment, it is assumed that positive reinforcement has been present in one form or another, providing both an incentive to learn and the acknowledgement that the response is acceptable. When children fail to learn, it has been customary to look for what is wrong with the learner and to ascribe the problem to a lack of readiness and/or an absence of motivation. Readiness in the learner implies that responses may be learned in a relatively short time, with some (but not excessive) effort. The view that children had to be "ready" for programs often caused teachers to make little effort to help some children learn, because the teachers were not prepared to modify their programs to suit individual children. These adults were refusing to accept that it is far easier to restructure the environment than to quickly change the behaviour of the child. All children are capable of learning, and it is the teacher's responsibility to find out what individual children know and can do so that the teacher may plan a learning environment that will enable all children to further their learning. The concept of *environmental readiness* should become an important part of the teacher's thinking, for it is essential that the environment be responsive to all children irrespective of their developmental level; the program must be adjusted to the child rather than being an obstacle to progress or an excuse for a lack of progress.

THE CONCEPT OF ENVIRONMENTAL READINESS

Environmental readiness implies the creation of an environment in which the central feature is a respect for the learner together with a willingness to arrange the environment to accommodate the needs of individual learners. There are five key factors for the teacher to keep in mind.

In a responsive environment, *individual differences are seen as natural to human beings, and the uniqueness of each person is taken into account when designing the environment.* Teachers find it easy to accept differences in physical characteristics, and no educator would attempt to make all children of the same age equal in height and weight. Yet these same educators often expect children to develop intellectually at the same rate as their peers. Chronological age is a measure of time, not of development. It cannot be assumed that because children are close in age, their learning has followed the same path. Accordingly, children should be allowed to take different routes to common goals—or, better yet, individual goals should be set for each child. Teachers must understand that each child has a personal timetable for learning and must therefore be reluctant to base their expectations on age. In addition to having physical and intellectual differences, individual children perceive the world according to their own needs, interests, and sensitivities.

In a responsive environment, *each child's learning is measured in terms of movement from that child's personal starting point.* The purpose of evaluation is to find ways of promoting learning rather than to assign labels and levels or to compare children with their peers.

In a responsive environment, *reinforcement or encouragement is very much in evidence.* Behaviour that brings rewards is more easily learned. The rewarding of behaviour, known as *reinforcement,* serves to strengthen the chances that the behaviour will be repeated. Each child has a personal reinforcement history; what is reinforcing for one child will not necessarily be encouraging for another. The art of providing reinforcement lies in finding responses to reinforce, in identifying appropriate rewards for each child, and in noting the effect of the reinforcement on the learner. It is a mistake to wait for a perfect response to occur before offering encouragement, since the learner may not be able to achieve perfection in the initial stages of learning. Some adults believe that to reinforce a poor attempt amounts to a lowering of standards, but it cannot be emphasized too strongly that the worth of the child's response must be seen in relation to the child's starting point rather than in terms of what the teacher expects the child to achieve. While behaviourists have advocated the use of tangible rewards, it is better for the child if the rewards are natural outcomes of the task—for example, pleasure and a feeling of competence. Children find activity rewarding and should not learn to expect concrete rewards.

In a responsive environment, *there is time and opportunity for practice.* It is recognized that much of the child's learning will result from the child's own activity, whether it be observation, discussion together with demonstration, or fine or gross motor movement. In this environment, the teacher learns to wait patiently while the child is learning. Young children seem to have a natural understanding of the value of repetition; they can often be seen performing similar actions and requesting the same stories to be told or read to them.

Finally, in a responsive environment, *the content to be learned and the skills to be acquired are relevant to the young child's own world.* This does not mean that the environment deals only with reality; it also provides the stimuli for imaginative thinking. It is a world in which the child is allowed the luxury of being a child; it is not a world in which the child is seen as a miniature adult and is being hurried out of childhood.

In summary, an environment that is ready for individual children is child-centred. It is one that adjusts to the child rather than forcing the child to conform to adult standards. It is a place where the child's interests and strengths are the starting points for learning—and where learning, in turn, is measured in relation to these factors. A respect for the child's talents, needs, interests, and preferred ways of learning forms the basis for the teacher's decisions, thereby creating an environment that develops the child's natural talent for learning and lays the foundation for a lasting commitment to learning.

PROGRAM IMPLICATIONS

Play is the ideal medium for learning, since all the conditions necessary for learning are present. While the teacher influences the play by providing the setting and the materials, it is the spontaneous activity of the child that is the most significant factor. Children choose play activities and materials for which they are ready. These activities also present challenges in which they are likely to meet with success. Teachers must provide a choice of open-ended activities so that each child may find materials that are interesting and offer realistic challenges in terms of each child's readiness. Observing children's choices and how the materials are used will give the teacher much information as to what the children are ready to learn.

Reinforcement occurs as a natural consequence of play when children are successful in what they are doing and when they derive much pleasure from the play. The teacher's role is to provide play materials that will extend the child's skills, ensure success, and enable the child to delight in learning.

Children do not have to be persuaded to practise what they are learning in their play. The repetition of responses is almost always a part of play, with children building variations into their activities to keep them interesting.

The space provided for play will affect what is learned. For example, when a very small floor area is provided for building with blocks, structures will become much taller, requiring better fine motor coordination than when a large floor space is available. Children will learn more about the stability of a structure when building a tall tower. The arrangement of materials for painting will either encourage or limit experimenting and learning. When painting is confined to an easel with a narrow ledge for the jars of paint and where each colour has its own paintbrush, there will be little or no possibility for varying the shade of the paint. There should be only one brush, adequate space for a water container in which to wash the brush, and spare containers in which to mix paint. Children will then be able to learn how to lighten or darken colours and to experiment with textures. If the easel prevents this arrangement of the materials, painting should take place on the floor or at a table with the paper pinned onto a board and the paint in muffin tins. If children are to learn about the possibilities of paint, opportunities should also be created for painting on different surfaces such as fabric, cardboard, wood, textured paper, or clay.

Rules are necessary for the smooth functioning of any society, and children have to learn that there are occasions when they will have to conform to rules. However, many environments are unnecessarily restrictive. Teachers should question all rules, other than those relating to safety, asking whether the rule exists to promote learning and development or purely for administrative convenience. If the latter is the case, the rule should be revised or abandoned.

While many texts on child development describe the young child as having a short attention span, anyone who is familiar with young children must seriously question this generalization and its implications for learning. Accepting it at face value would lead the teacher to allow very short time periods for tasks to be undertaken by the child or by the group. Observing young children at play, one is struck by the length of time that a child can spend blowing bubbles and learning about their characteristics, dressing up in adult or superhero clothes and trying on various roles, exercising creative talent while making a collage of found materials, figuring out how to build a snow creature, or listening attentively to a story. Apparently, when a child has a choice of activity, materials, and companions, and to some extent of space and time, long periods of concentration are the rule rather than the exception. The young child's attention span is a protective device that shields the child from adults who would force learning; lack of attention is a way of indicating little interest, insufficient prerequisite knowledge, or inadequate skills for a task. In most instances adults misinterpret the message that the child is sending and limit learning by offering the learner too little time.

The best device for providing enough time for learning new responses as well as consolidating responses already learned is to allow children to leave materials in place and to return to them the next day. This will require a careful examination of the use of space, particularly in the case of blocks. Children should not have to tear down their block structures because it is time to tidy the room; when buildings are left in place, the child may proceed to more complex arrangements, thereby furthering learning. What may be learned will also depend on the quantity of the material that is available. When a long story is chosen by the group or by the teacher, the reading may be spread over a number of days, beginning each time with the recall of what was read the day before. Reviewing what one knows is part of learning, so conditions should be created in which this is a logical step in the activity.

Messing around with tools and materials is an important part of gaining knowledge and skills. Children should not be hurried or forced into producing something that is acceptable by adult standards. Much learning can occur when there is play with something and no lasting end product. Watching and listening to children's talk while they are playing will aid the teacher in seeing the learning that is occurring. For example, a group of three-year-olds were playing with clay. They discovered that they could squeeze it, flatten it, roll it, stretch it, pinch it, poke holes in it, tunnel through it, and make tracks in it. At the end of the play time, the clay was recycled for future use. In addition to learning about the potential of the clay, the children learned new words to describe their actions.

Learning is often hidden in a product; unless the teacher has observed the development of the product, the teacher will be unaware of what has been learned. A young child, new to a nursery-school class, was painting for the first time. Her completed picture was a brown and green affair with large areas of the paper covered with paint except in one place, where she had made neat imprints to reveal the shape of the paintbrush. The child began her painting with yellow paint and then began to use the blue. She was clearly astonished and delighted when she saw the yellow turning green as she applied the blue paint; she then proceeded to work very carefully with the blue paint to make sure that all the yellow parts turned green. As she was doing this, she became aware of the fact that the brush strokes could be broad and sweeping or single imprints. The teacher's observation of the child's actions enabled her to chat meaning-fully with the child and to celebrate the event. Too often adults insist on titles for children's pictures or require children to tell stories about their pictures, believing that these steps are important for language develop-ment. Language, however, has many uses; reflecting on what has been accomplished will not only provide language practice but will also lay the foundations for the language of planning. Children should not be forced to talk about their play or their products; in a friendly environment, most children will do so voluntarily.

Learning is more easily achieved when the information to be acquired or the skill to be developed is relevant to the child's daily life. Children's play should give them time to rehearse what they have learned in the outside world and should also alert them to new possibilities in terms of observations to be made and actions to be taken outside the school. This rehearsal and heightened perception of the real world was seen in a nursery school where a group of four-year-olds were making a house out of a very large cardboard carton. Each time they wished to enter their house, they had to lift the box and crawl underneath it. After a while the novelty of this approach wore off and they consulted the teacher as to what to do. The teacher asked them how they had entered the playroom and what they did at their own homes. This discussion led them to cut a door in one side of the box. But each time they tried to open the door, they scraped their fingers; this new challenge prompted them to make a door handle from loops of brightly patterned ribbon. Their next problem was how to light the inside of their house; they asked the teacher if she could find them a lamp. Because the house was small, however, it was agreed that a hot light bulb might prove to be a hazard. The teacher urged them to find another solution to their problem by looking around their playroom. She pointed out that there was plenty of light, although the overhead lights were not switched on. The children soon realized that the answer to their problem was to construct windows. They painted their house, deciding that to save themselves some time they would not paint the roof but would instead paste their paintings, which they had been saving to take home, onto it. The house was a masterpiece; it was colourful, functional, and represented hours of creative thinking and problem-solving. Moreover, it changed the way the children looked at buildings on their next walk around the neighbourhood. They began to comment on stained-glass windows, the shapes of roofs, the design of doors and door handles, and the variety of external finishes. Their play had opened a new window on the world and the learning that accrued was both significant and substantial.

It has already been stated that the purpose of evaluation is to further the children's learning; it should do justice to the children, representing what they know and can do. Observing play is crucial to the evaluation of learning, since it provides the teacher with a wealth of information regarding readiness, preferred strategies, levels of performance, and the transfer of learned actions and ideas to a variety of situations. On the basis of these observations, the teacher will choose an appropriate range of equipment and activities that will allow for the children's interests, be relevant to their lives, and provide realistic challenges. The extent to which the children's behaviour changes to meet these reasonable challenges may then be described. Achievement will be seen as the distance travelled rather than only as the point that a child has reached.

BARRIERS TO THE TEACHING/LEARNING PROCESS

Children differ from adults in a number of ways. Unless teachers are mindful of these differences, they may constitute barriers to learning.

First, each child comes to school with a different experiential background. The children who are well prepared to enter the school are those who have been encouraged and helped to be independent but who are able to request and accept adult help when it is needed. They have been allowed the luxury of being children and have been given every opportunity to develop their powers of observation, language, and motor skills through play and interaction with caring adults or older siblings. Unfortunately, many children have not had such a favourable start to their lives. Their language may be limited, they may lack interpersonal skills, and they may have been given to understand that children are supposed to be passive observers of the passing scene. Home visits by teachers prior to children entering nursery schools or junior kindergartens would provide a wealth of information regarding the type of program and the supports that should await the child at school.

Second, young children have a different view of the physical world. For example, a low bookshelf or cupboard can create a visual barrier for the child. Children who are secure will not be deterred by physical obstacles. They will quickly review the scene and then will search for something that interests them. Insecure children will be reluctant to explore and will wait for the teacher's instructions. Teachers must therefore provide different information and support for each of the learners, depending on their previous experience and feelings of security. Secure children are constantly taking steps to further their own learning, while less secure children must be supported by the teacher until they are comfortable. Teachers would do well to view their classrooms or playrooms from the child's-eye level.

Third, instructions given by teachers are often misinterpreted by children, because children's concepts, understanding of language, and manner of thinking is different from that of adults. Children make very broad distinctions and learn later to fill in the details. For example, when a group of four-year-olds was about to make cookies, the teacher assigned each child a place at the table and then told the children that they would take turns to mix the cookie dough. She said, "Angelina, you will be first; Theo, you will be second; Carrie, you will be third; and Dylan, you will be fourth." Theo burst into tears. Between sobs, he managed to gasp, "I'm last! I don't want to be last." The teacher could not understand Theo's comment until he explained that since he was not to be first, he must be last. He was able to distinguish between extremes on a scale but could not yet fill in the details. The teacher tried to reason logically with Theo, but he was inconsolable and continued to weep loudly. Finally, the teacher put the bowl in front of Angelina and said, "Stir the ingredients, Angelina; then it is Theo's turn, then Carrie's, and then Dylan's." At last she had used language that all could understand, and the cookie-making proceeded happily. The next day, the teacher told a story about a family who set out to do four things. She described what they did first, second, third, and fourth. The last thing that they did that day was to go to the ice-cream parlour. Each week the family in the story went on a different outing, doing more things each time; the children gradually learned that last is a position that depends on the length of the series.

Fourth, the child's reasoning is characterized by an inability to cope with a number of dimensions at the same time. The child will focus on one aspect of a situation and will base an explanation of the phenomenon solely on that single feature. To the adult, this will seem to be an incorrect answer. But it should be remembered that it is the best that the child can do at the time. On one occasion when I was photographing nursery-school children, a child who was nearing her fourth birthday was wondering what she might do. Her teacher gave her a sheet of coloured paper and a pair of scissors and showed her how to fold the paper and cut out pieces to make a pattern. The child quickly grasped the idea and in a short while made an interesting pattern, which she brought to my attention. She asked me to take a picture of her pattern. She placed the paper in front of her face and waited for me to take a picture. Her delight in what she had learned was evident and I told her that I would like to have her smile in the photograph as well as the pattern. She considered the situation for a moment and then said, "I know why you can't see my smile. Your face is there and mine is here." She fetched two low chairs and placed them opposite each other, telling me to sit on one while she sat on the other. Having sat down, she again held the patterned paper directly in front of her face and announced that she was ready to have her smile photographed. Clearly, the dimension that occupied her thoughts was the difference in our heights, not the fact that she had covered her face with a piece of paper. I thanked her and took the picture.

Finally, barriers are created when parents and teachers disagree regarding approaches to learning. Many parents prefer a formal style of education and are unable to see that young children learn through play. When they pass this view on to their children, the children soon learn that the path to parental approval is to describe school as boring; they often become reluctant to learn. If children are to learn in school, they must have the support of their parents. Teachers can break down the barrier to learning that is created by conflicting priorities by observing learning and by helping parents to see what their children have learned. Instead of trying to persuade parents that play is beneficial, teachers must show how children's behaviour has changed as a result of their play and describe activities in terms of what has been learned rather than as work or play. It is well to remember that work may be the mindless repetition of responses in which no learning is taking place.

CONCLUSION

Attitudes toward young children's learning are changing. It is now recognized that care and education must be closely linked and that both these aspects of children's lives must be catered to both in child-care settings and in elementary schools. There is no justification for a division between care and education, since the child's style of learning is the same. Teachers in the nursery-school world and in the elementary school have much to offer each other in terms of understanding and programming for the young child. Fortunately, there is now increasing dialogue among child-care workers, nursery-school teachers, and elementary school teachers.

A second change of perspective involves the recognition that the function of learning in the early years is not merely to ready children for programs that will follow, but rather to allow children to develop to their fullest potential.

A third change of perspective can be seen in the relationship between parents and teachers. Parents are more often being viewed as partners in nurturing their children's learning; their participation in programs is being encouraged. When parents volunteer to act as program assistants, teachers should vary their requirements in terms of each parent's readiness and talents. Teachers should clearly understand that while their role is to set standards for the playroom or classroom, they need to appreciate the parents' viewpoints. To that end, there must be an ongoing dialogue between parents and teachers. The presence of other adults is invaluable; it enables the teacher to avoid large-group instruction. Because groups consist of individual learners, the size of a group should always be small enough to give each of the learners the opportunity to participate actively.

Perhaps the most important element in the broadening of our perspectives entails differentiating between education and schooling. Doing so affects what we want children to learn. A school has been defined as a place in which children receive instruction, usually in adult-determined curricula relating to particular skills. Education has much wider implications; it involves the development of intellectual, social, physical, and moral capacities. This development begins at birth and should continue throughout life. The teacher as educator will be keenly aware of the learner's potential and will demonstrate flexibility in arranging the environment to accommodate individual children. The implications of the concept of environmental readiness, together with the importance of reassurance and relevance, will guide teachers. They will appreciate that there is neither a season nor a special place for learning. Children will learn wherever and whenever new knowledge is available or there is the opportunity to acquire or to practise a new skill. If children are to become educated and their learning is to continue throughout their lives, all those who have the privilege of helping them learn should remember that today's experiences are tomorrow's memories. It is characteristic of human beings that they return to activities and situations in which they have been offered reasonable challenges, have achieved a fair measure of success, and have derived satisfaction from their effort.

REFERENCES

Day, B. (1975) *Open learning in early childhood.* New York: Macmillan.
Federation of Women Teachers' Associations of Ontario. (1978). *Early Childhood Education.*

Federation of Women Teachers' Associations of Ontario. (1986). *Active Learning in the Early School Years.*

Hymes, J. (1981). *Teaching the child under six.* (3rd ed.) Columbus, OH: Charles E. Merrill.

Seefeldt, C. (1987). *The early childhood curriculum: A review of current research.* New York: Teachers College Press.

Yardley, A. (1970). *Discovering the physical world.* London: Evans Brothers.

Yardley, A. (1970). *Reaching out.* London: Evans Brothers.

Yardley, A. (1971). *The teacher of young children.* London: Evans Brothers.

Yardley, A. (1973). *Young children thinking.* London: Evans Brothers.

4

The Child In The Family

Deborah Chant and Isabel M. Doxey

A family is a system that a child must accept, but it is also a system that defines him or her. The family has been and will continue to be accepted as the cornerstone of our society. It has been described as "the bastion and support of personal life and individuality" (Hayford, 1988, p. 6). Yet family structures and family life are changing dramatically. Concomitantly, the lives of young children within Canadian families have great diversity.

As early childhood educators interact with children and their parents on a daily basis, they come face to face with the unique and complex interrelationships that occur in families. An awareness of the conceptual approaches to understanding families with young children is an important component in a teacher's responsibility for the education and care of children. This chapter begins with a discussion of some assumptions and images we use to define and understand the family phenomenon. In the next part, four models of the family/society link are presented. Following that, the issue of child abuse is considered, with a discussion of conditions within healthy and vulnerable families. The final section offers readers the opportunity to improve their understanding of the child in the family with a discussion of some specific circumstances arising from current family lifestyles.

DEFINING THE CHILD'S FAMILY

In our present Canadian society, the family is accepted as the base of security for the child. It is the parents who have the primary responsibility for the physical and psychological well-being of their children. Parents are also the first educators. It is within the family that roles are defined for parents and children. It is primarily within the family context that children develop their sense of themselves and their relationships to adults and others. It is through children's dependency on the adults in their family that they develop their sense of trust in people generally. It is through the living arrangements of the family that children learn the roles, the rules, and the behaviours that our Canadian society values.

The family has come to be seen as an adaptive social group form. The group that we label family is undergoing some redefinition, but the changes we are witnessing are signs of the family's adaptability and strength, not of its breakdown. It has responded to the challenge of acting as the cradle of individual confirmation by giving the child authenticity amid the perils of our postindustrial bureaucratic conditions. From the child's viewpoint, the family needs to have supports that will guarantee health and vitality.

Historically, the family has been seen as a self-contained, self-sufficient unit that provides for the economic, educational, recreational, physical, and emotional needs of its members. Many of these functions are now served by other societal institutions. Schools, for instance, have supplemented, extended, and replaced or compensated for the family. Social programs such as old age pensions and unemployment insurance have replaced elements of the family's economic and security functions. Most recently, advances in biological technology have begun to alter even the family's procreative function.

Families were once viewed as sacred institutions, functioning to socialize, educate, and care for their members according to cultural practices and patterns. Examining these experiences was viewed as intrusive. Only in recent years have we been able to acquire a greater knowledge of family relationships and interactions and the phenomenon of family life. Social scientists and demographers, for instance, have revealed specific characteristics of the circumstances of children within contemporary Canadian families: more are born into families in which the parents are older at the commencement of parenthood; more have only one sibling; and more experience some form of family breakup—either separation or divorce—during childhood or adolescence.

Even the interpretations of the word family have changed over the years. Although historically the word, from the Latin root *familia*, meant a household or large group of kin, today it evokes many different images. Attempting to define the term becomes a very complex task when we try to incorporate the various configurations different individuals call "my family." These may be same-sex unions, commuting couples, lone-parent families, or remarried families. Eichler (1988) addresses this ambiguity by suggesting the following definition of the family:

A family is a social group which may or may not include adults of both sexes, (e.g. lone parent families), may or may not include one or more children, (e.g. childless couples), who may or may not have been born in their wedlock (e.g. adopted children or children by one adult partner of a previous union). The relationship of the adults may or may not have its origin in marriage (e.g., common-law couples) they may or may not share a common residence (e.g. commuting couples). The adults may or may not co-habit sexually and the relationship may or may not involve such socially patterned feelings as love, attraction, piety, and awe) (p. 4)

This definition captures the rapid changes that have been taking place in family values and organization, and highlights the potential variety in family conditions for young Canadian children today.

MODELS OF THE FAMILY

Various models of the family have been developed for purposes of locating the family within the broader society. Models from social, legal, demographic, and economic domains will be discussed in this chapter.

One model of the Canadian family involves an idealized image (Eichler, 1988) and is often called a *monolithic* or *normative* model. It presumes common structures, functions, and organization. The nuclear family, for example, has been presented as "normal," along with various assumptions about what lifestyles and behaviour patterns ought to occur. Eichler (1988) suggests the need for a more realistic approach, a "multi-dimensional model" that views families as having diverse patterns of lifestyle, structure, and function. For children whose families do not conform to the "norm," the monolithic model may result in a preoccupation with their own shortcomings and an undue indictment of their family as inadequate. One result is that we create "sick" children or "victim" children. We then attempt to diagnose and treat these children through our network of social policies and services. In Canada, the stigmatization of subsidized child care is one example of the application of this model of the family.

A second model of the family is found in the legal domain—particularly in legislation that governs behaviour and relations between and among family members in situations involving divorce, property division, and child-custody decisions. With conflicting definitions in the regulation, it is difficult to interpret the rights and obligations of family members, particularly children. Nevertheless, the use of this model in family law has an extensive impact on the status of many young children.

A third model of the family/society relationship is a demographic model used primarily for census purposes. Here, family patterns are defined by household arrangements, sex and age organization, or relations to the labour market. These variables are often projected as "natural" or "average" family forms—as with, for example, the "head of the household" concept.

A fourth model describing the family/society link is the producer/consumer model, which assumes that the primary link between the family and society is an economic one and that the family is the cornerstone of economic viability. This concept has underpinned our notions of work. We do not separate work in its social and economic sense from the family. Work is our labour, whether it gets a wage or not. Children "work" when they go to a child-care facility or to school. This model identifies a crucial connection between the family and society whether or not a given family's structure is compatible with current morals or statistics. Recognition of the family and of family members as consumers gives rise to a different set of rights for parents and children: for example, the right of parents to negotiate for such services as child care.

SOME FAMILY CONDITIONS

The condition of the family has been seen as a marker of the general health of a society, because the family is the vehicle that supports the mental and physical health of its members. When the degree of family conflict increases, and more and more families are identified as being "at risk," this too is seen as a mirror of the larger society. Many have traditionally believed that the link between healthy families and healthy children is as strong as the prenatal umbilical cord. Experience and research suggest that this is not necessarily the case. Many children survive family disruptions, family stress, and unpleasant and unhealthy conditions and continue to thrive. (Chapter 6 presents some of the research related to this issue.) Some children may even become stronger mentally through experiencing adversity.

Healthy families nevertheless provide a moral and spiritual foundation for children. Parents model what they believe to be right and wrong, and reinforce codes for acceptable behaviour. In characterizing a healthy family, it is not the type of spiritual or moral code that is critical, but the fact that such a code exists. Healthy families also offer children stability, with clear rules for conduct that are consistently applied. Children feel secure and thrive within this atmosphere.

Unfortunately, many young Canadian children must survive in "unhealthy" families, experiencing family violence. Violence has been described as a natural part of the repertoire of human behaviour. Societies have undertaken and undergone war and punishment in a myriad of forms for centuries. Many forms of violence are considered legitimate;

some even receive rewards and approval) Straus (1983) states that "violence between family members is a normal part of family life."

Indeed, the history of childhood (De Mause, 1974) reveals patterns of abuse, neglect, and cruelty beyond any that might be documented today: "The history of childhood is a nightmare from which we have only recently begun to awaken. The further back in history one goes, the more likely children are to be killed, abandoned, beaten, terrorized and sexually abused" (p. 1). De Mause leads us to conclude that such treatment of children was once the norm rather than the exception, with brutality reinforced by the nature of life and by daily routines as much as by the behaviour of parents and other family members.

(Until recently, family violence has been a private, family matter.) Patterns of family violence were not known, not studied, and not even considered to be the concern of society or anyone other than family members. It was not that violence did not occur; it was just not discussed. The privacy of violence, particularly any violence within the family that involved children, was sanctioned by the legal system and by religious institutions as well as by general social norms. (Only within the last two decades have family violence in general, and child abuse in particular, become public issues and targets for policies, laws, and research.)

Canadian law no longer permits either child or wife abuse. In spite of this, estimates reveal that at least 50 to 60 percent of Canadian families experience some form of family violence (Eichler, 1985, p. 55). For many young children, violence is apparently as typical an experience of family relationships as are affection and nurturance.

As is the case with physical abuse, sexual abuse of children has a higher incidence than was previously believed. In a 1984 national survey conducted in Canada, one in every two females (53.5 percent) reported having experienced unwanted sexual acts as a child (Badgley, 1984). A greater proportion of females than males are likely to have been abused as children. Such abuse is most often inflicted within the family by family members rather than by strangers; most victims live under the same roof as those who abuse them.

The incidence of physical abuse of children is also widespread. Children are expected to be obedient. They are expected to conform without question to parental wishes, desires, and direction. They are rewarded for being respectful to older family members. Consequently, violent punishment may be considered justifiable if children display what a parent deems to be deviant behaviour. Young children are generally powerless to prevent or stop the abuse. Very young (that is, preverbal) children are unable even to report it, while children who do attempt to report abuse may not be believed by the adults to whom they turn.

Child abuse often involves an abuse of power by parents. Child abuse can occur in any family; it does not occur only within families that are "at risk," dysfunctional, or "unhealthy." It has been documented that over 90 percent of parents punish their children physically and feel that spanking and slapping are good and normal, even necessary, forms of discipline and punishment. In the family training ground, children learn that violence is appropriate with those we love. It is also well documented that violence breeds violence; children who are abused will be more likely to perpetuate this pattern of control and discipline with their own children.

Three factors appear to be common to all experiences of domestic violence, including child abuse: violence is learned by children; it is built into the hierarchical structure of power within the family; and it is the tool for resolving conflicts and maintaining family viability. As noted earlier, the family's condition as a private institution makes it more prone to violence and less accessible to intervention. When the social attitude that parents "own" their children is combined with isolation of the family, conditions are created that enhance the potential for abuse and violence within the family and toward the children.

The challenge for the early childhood educator is to become knowledgeable about the legal requirements for recognizing and reporting child abuse while providing compassionate and sensitive care and education for the child.

UNDERSTANDING THE YOUNG CHILD IN THE FAMILY

To adequately understand the young child in the family, early childhood educators should be alert to some of the issues and challenges that face the contemporary Canadian family throughout its existence as a unit of society.

An understanding of the life cycle of a family is one step. This view borrows from the lifespan approach of studying individual development: the family is a unit moving through time experiencing a series of events and tasks (Carter & McGoldrick, 1980). Evelyn Duvall (1957) was the first to outline this theory, depicting eight stages: beginning families; childbearing families; families with preschool children; families with school-age children; families with teenagers; families as launching centres; families in the middle years; and aging families.

Since this theory was first introduced, a number of variations on the original model have been proposed. Suggested modifications have included changing the sequence of categories, names of stages, and time frames (McGoldrick & Carter, 1980). Early childhood educators benefit from an understanding of the family life cycle stage. To apply this theory realistically we must recognize the family as diverse in its forms, practices, and sociocultural contexts. "The timing, the tasks, the rituals for transition, the themes, coping mechanisms and meaning attached to the different stages of the family life cycle vary from culture to culture" (Falicov & Karrier, 1980, p. 383.)

A number of challenges exist for families as they make the transition to parenthood and proceed through the stage of a family with young children. Many of these events can be found in all families. However, certain aspects may differ as a result of family structure and of culture.

Most individuals about to become parents, whether single, married, or cohabiting, report the anticipation of parenthood to be a time of excitement and joy coupled with anxiety as they reflect on their ability to be "good parents" and to be able to provide for the needs of the child. Early childhood educators may encounter this anxiety as parents question them regarding their child's behaviour, comment about their child's development compared with other children, and deal with entrusting their children to other caregivers.

Another issue facing family units is being able to make a shift to the parenting role while maintaining other responsibilities. This may be a particular issue for the dual-career couple, as both partners come to terms with balancing their career and family commitments. There is no doubt that role strain is likely to accompany this lifestyle, with particular impacts on young children. The division of labour the family chooses can affect the early childhood educator's role. A teacher may, for instance, have more contact with one parent than with the other, have daily contact with both parents, or communicate primarily with grandparents. The teacher may also observe role strain on the part of parents attempting to meet all their commitments.

Another challenge for families is adapting to the expanding social network of the child (Bradt, 1980). When children begin to expand their social network to relatives, babysitters, teachers, and peers, parents feel the impact. Not only is the family now coming under scrutiny from others, but these associations are also having socializing influences on the child. Sometimes these influences are enriching. In other cases, they may be in conflict with family preferences and approaches.

Families vary in the degree to which they favour and nurture such outside contacts. For some it is important that child-care responsibilities be maintained within the family network—with grandparents, cousins, and so on—to ensure that certain family values and practices are maintained. Child-care centres and schools may be viewed as places that threaten the family's status quo. It is extremely important that teachers do not confuse certain parents' need to maintain a certain degree of insulation around their family with lack of interest in their child's development and education.

For some families, the social network traditionally provided by the extended family may not be present (McGoldrick & Carter, 1982). Resources that previously furnished support for learning and practising the many skills involved in parenting have been removed, often without being replaced. As parents come under closer examination, and doubt their skills, they may tend either to seek assistance from teachers or to distance themselves from those viewed to be more powerful. In either case, the early childhood educator may offer support.

How are child-rearing tasks maintained in non-nuclear family forms, such as post-divorce and remarried families? There are significant challenges for both mother-led and father-led families. Assuming responsibility for all major household tasks and parenting, as well as outside employment, may be a significant source of strain. For fathers, it may mean undertaking more child-rearing tasks, while for mothers, it may involve finding employment outside the home and/or added home responsibilities. The degree to which parents successfully make this transition depends on how these roles were organized prior to divorce (Hetherington, Cox, & Cox, 1978). If there is a non-custodial parent with access or custody rights, some parenting may be shared. Nevertheless, teachers need to recognize that lone-parent families are under some stress in accomplishing child-rearing tasks.

Due to emotional upheaval in the family at the time of separation and divorce, parenting capacity may diminish (Wallerstein & Kelly, 1980). The resulting disequilibrium in the family is usually short-lived (Goldsmith, 1982) but can have both advantages and disadvantages for family members. For example, a child may fill the place of an absent father, which makes it difficult for the child to separate. On the other hand, a child may be stimulated to develop more independence and responsibility. Because it is also likely that children will manifest some behavioural changes over the course of a year following separation, parents have the difficult task of coping with their children's feelings as well as with their own (Wallerstein & Kelly, 1980).

In the case of the non-custodial parent, maintaining a presence in the child's life can be difficult. Temporal, geographical, psychological, or legal factors may act as barriers. Current legislation in Ontario, however, permits parents who have access rights to get information about the education, health, and welfare of their child.

The situation of the remarried family (also referred to as a "blended," "reconstituted," or "step-family") is even more complex. Just as divorce is now considered to be a phase in the family life cycle, so is remarriage (Beal, 1980; McGoldrick & Carter, 1980). The experiences of remarried families differ from those of biological families, however, in that the former tend to bypass the lifespan stage of "family with young children" because of certain structural variations (Visher & Visher, 1982). One distinction is that children are often members of two households. Psychologists and educators have expressed concern about the ability of young children in particular to deal with this lack of continuity. On the other hand, as Visher and Visher (1982) point out, the diversity may be a benefit for the children; they are exposed to different lifestyles and learn to adapt to parenting by a number of adults. Some children may experience difficulty in adjusting to a step-parent as a full participant in carrying out discipline (Visher & Visher, 1982).

In cases involving divorce and remarriage, educators are just as important a resource for parents as in first unions. Because of their daily contact with the children, educators may be the first to observe changes in the children, stress in parent/child relationships, or other conditions in which assistance is needed. Specific strategies should include discussions and modelling acceptance of various family lifestyles, being sensitive to the needs of children and parents without focusing on adjustment problems, maintaining a stable environment for children, and assisting parents in finding support services if needed (Leahy, 1984).

CONCLUSION

The Canadian family unit will continue to adapt and change as it experiences the pushes and pulls from membership within and from the society without. As the family manages these changes, it manifests its own unique set of characteristics. In planning and providing for young children, early childhood educators must keep children centred within the context of their family values and lifestyles.

REFERENCES

Badgley, R.F. (1984). *Sexual offences against children* (Vol. 1). Ottawa: Ministry of Supply and Services.

Beal, E. (1980). Separation, divorce and single parent families. In E. Carter, & M. McGoldrick (Eds.), *The family life cycle: A framework for family therapy*. New York: Gardner.

Bradt, J. (1980). The family with young children. In E. Carter & M. McGoldrick (Eds.)., *The family life cycle: A framework for family therapy*. New York: Gardner.

Carter, E. & McGoldrick, M. (1980). *The family life cycle: A framework for family therapy*. New York: Gardner.

De Mause, L. (1974). *History of childhood*. New York: Psychohistory Press.

Doxey, I. (1983). Focus: The family of the future. In *Geneva Park Papers* (pp. 74–86.) Lake Couchiching, ON: Ontario Liberal Party.

Duvall, E. (1957). *Family development*. Philadelphia: J.B. Lippincott.

Eichler, M. (1985). *Families in Canada today: Recent changes and their policy consequences*. Toronto: Gage.

Eichler, M. (1988). *Families in Canada today* (2nd ed.) Toronto: Gage.

Falicov, C. & Karrier, M.A. (1980). Cultural variations in the family life cycle: The Mexican American family. In E. Carter & M. McGoldrick (Eds.), *The family life cycle: A framework for family therapy*. New York: Gardner.

Goldsmith, J. (1982). The post-divorce family. In F. Walsh (Ed.), *Normal family processes*. New York: Guildford.

Hayford, A. (1988). Outlines of the family. In K. Anderson (Ed.), *Family matters: Sociology and contemporary Canadian families*. Toronto: Nelson.

Hetherington, E.M., Cox, M., & Cox, R. (1978). The after-math of divorce in mother-child, father-child relations. In Stevens, J.H., Jr. (Ed.), *Mother-child, Father-child Relations*. Washington: NAEYC

Leahy, M. (1984). Findings from research on divorce: Implications for professionals' skill development. *American Journal of Orthopsychiatry, 54* (2).

McGoldrick, M., & Carter, E. (1980). Forming a remarried family. In E. Carter & M. McGoldrick (Eds.), *The family life cycle: A framework for family therapy*. New York: Gardner.

McGoldrick, M. & Carter, E. (1982). The family life cycle. In F. Walsh (Ed.). *Normal family processes*. New York: Guildford.

Nett, E. M. (1981). Canadian families in social-historical perspective. *Canadian Journal of Sociology 6* (3).

Schlesinger, B. (1983). *Families in Canada today*. Toronto: Gage.

Statistics Canada. (1985). *Vital Statistics*. (Vol. 1). Ottawa: Supply and Services.

Straus, M. A. (1983). Ordinary violence, child abuse and wife beating: What do they have in common? In D. Finkelhor et al. (Eds.), *The dark side of families*. Beverly Hills: Sage.

Wallerstein, J., & Kelly, J. (1980). *Surviving the break-up*. New York: Basic Books.

Visher, J., & Visher, E. (1982). Step-families and step-parenting. In Walsh, F. (Ed.), *Normal Family Processes*. New York: Guildford.

5

The Child in the Curriculum

Ken Pierce

Self-Concept
Self-Esteem
The Early Childhood Educator's Role
Self-Concept Development
Conclusion
References

Early childhood educators are having a profound influence on the next generation of Canadians. It is commonly assumed that this occurs through the high-quality curricula provided to the children. This chapter will explore this assumption by examining the relationship between the curriculum, the child's emerging self-concept, and the early childhood professional. It will culminate by offering ways for early childhood educators to recognize their special role in influencing Canada's future decision-makers.

Through the early childhood curriculum, we are really preparing children directly for their future and indirectly for our future. Today's Canadian children are tomorrow's Canadian decision-makers. So the early childhood curriculum must provide children with experiences that will enable them to learn to be good decision-makers.

What can we provide to assist them in making effective decisions? Anything tangible or material we might offer—such as wealth, knowledge, or power—is fleeting and temporary. What is left transcends time and circumstance and guides each of our interactions with the world. What is left are the attitudes and beliefs we have about ourselves and each other.

SELF-CONCEPT

The self-concept in children is a collection of attitudes that they have about themselves and their effectiveness. If children are to be contented and competent people, capable of contributing to Canadian society, they will need to learn three attitudes from us. First, they will need to learn respect—for themselves and for others. Second, they will need to learn honesty with themselves and others. Third, they will need to learn trust—first, in themselves and their own abilities; then, in those around them.

What our children most need now, what they will need even more in the future, and what we have the opportunity and the responsibility to help them develop is a positive concept of themselves. Children need to acquire the belief that they are loved, capable people who can meet whatever the future holds. Our own future and Canada's will depend, to a great extent, on our children's ability to assess situations and make appropriate decisions. To do so, each child will require the self-confidence to try and the ability to be honest and trusting. Such attitudes reflect a positive self-concept, an individual with high self-esteem.

Karen Owens (1987) postulates that "every action we take or decision we make is predicated on some implicit assumption of what we are like" (p. 268) and that children's biased evaluations of themselves become the core element in structuring their behaviour. Berne (1985) points out that "the more positively children feel about their ability to succeed, the more likely they are to exert effort and feel a sense of accomplishment when they finish a task" (p. 411). Feeney, Christensen, and Moravcik (1985) contend that the "self-concept influences children's ability to develop meaningful relationships with people, ideas and the physical world" and that "one of the goals of Early Childhood Education is to help children develop strong, positive and realistic self-concepts" (p. 411).

Others offer even stronger recommendations regarding the importance of the self-concept. Coopersmith and Silverman (1964) refer to it as the most important key to children's behaviour and a better predictor of success in school than intelligence. Kiester (1973) holds that it is the foundation on which personality is built and the primary determinant of behaviour. Finally, Briggs (1975) argues that "self-esteem is the mainspring that slates every child for success or failure as a human being" (p. 3).

A positive self-concept involves feelings of being loved, of personal worth, of competence and control. A negative self-concept entails feeling helpless, incapable, and not valued by those important to us.

SELF-ESTEEM

Why is a feeling of self-esteem so important? A child's level of self-esteem is the basis for what is often called motivation and is critical to the child's survival. Perhaps what is most important about self-esteem is that it is *learned.*

From our earliest moments we begin collecting information about ourselves and our world. As infants, we soon learn what causes discomfort, eases pain, satisfies hunger, and gets us attention. If a child cries with the intent of receiving attention, and is picked up, the child achieves a *success*, a feeling of control over his or her environment. As this same process occurs repeatedly in various circumstances, children retain these successes and failures as the foundation of their self-concept, their feelings of being worthwhile and effective.

If children do not achieve successes at these early stages, they will eventually, through repeated failures, stop trying. They have learned that their actions do not help satisfy their needs. They lose the motivation to try. They learn not to try. In extreme cases, the child can wither and die. The research on infant development contains many examples of this phenomenon.

Usually, children experience a combination of successes and failures that together help generate a prevailing attitude about their effectiveness and worth. This attitude becomes a filter through which they process all their experiences and impressions of life. For example, one of our first experiences with failure in life occurs when we are weaned. Breast-fed babies usually reject spoon feeding initially, since the spoon and the food are the wrong taste, temperature, texture, shape, and consistency. They scream for the object they know is right. If we do not restore the desired object, they soon realize that they cannot always control their environment. They learn that in certain situations they are more successful than others.

If children experience a lot of failures, they come to believe that they have little control over their world. Since others really control it, there seems little reason to try. On the other hand, if they have had significant successes, they learn that they can and usually do control their environment. This is the basis for self-motivation and self-confidence.

In this way, we all develop a self-concept. This process never ends. We, as human beings, like the world around us, are constantly changing and evolving. Our self-concept, too, is constantly being developed. According to Adler and Towne (1975), "the self-concept is extremely subjective, being almost totally a product of our interactions with others" (p. 34). Thus, significant others like parents and early childhood professionals have an important role to play in children's emerging self-concept.

THE EARLY CHILDHOOD EDUCATOR'S ROLE

Parents and early childhood educators have a significant impact on the child's self-concept because the child spends so much time with and is so dependent on them in these crucial years. Subsequently, the peer group and other people with whom children interact frequently or during important situations also affect their self-concept. In describing children with positive self-concepts, Swayze (1980) states that "children with positive self-concepts feel capable, likable, and valued and can meet successfully the demands of the world. They have dignity and are happy human beings" (p. 40).

By the time children are six years old, their self-concept is already well established. Their reactions to challenges in their world will be determined directly by the beliefs and attitudes they hold about themselves. So, as Heathington (1980) has noted, "no other time is as critical as childhood for establishing positive self-concepts" (p. 63).

The experience of growing up in the 1990s will have a profound influence on a child's self-concept. Children today have a lot more information than did their counterparts in the past. They have a lot more issues to understand, a lot more decisions to make, and a lot less time in which to make them. Increasingly, they must also make many decisions at a younger age.

As early childhood professionals, as adults and as parents, our role in preparing children for Canada's future is threefold. Our first role is that of *protector*. We have a responsibility to protect children by ensuring that their needs are adequately met. Our second role is that of *advocate*. We have a duty to continually advocate more and better services for children and families. Our third role is that of *facilitator*, and this is where our curriculum becomes so important. We have a responsibility to nurture self-confident, honest, trusting children by creating, in our learning environments, relationships that are characterized by attitudes of caring, respect, openness, and trust.

SELF-CONCEPT DEVELOPMENT

To fulfil these three roles, we must look to the child for the content and direction of our programming. The needs of each child in a program should be the focus of that program's curriculum. Only if we meet children's needs as *they* define them will we give them the chance to develop the attitudes so crucial to achieving a positive self-concept. The best curriculum has little to do with factual knowledge or sophisticated equipment and much to do with attitudes and relationships.

We do not need to spend a lot of time debating the merits of young children being able to recite the alphabet, count to 100, or identify the colours of the rainbow. In this age of computers, our alphabet has expanded, our number system has changed, and the colours of the rainbow have developed so many new hues we now need a computer just to list them. All this information is of limited value to children who have not been respected or loved, and who do not believe they are competent, capable people.

It becomes essential, then, that we design our curriculum to consider children's needs and how to meet them. "If, as parents or professional persons, we have a basic understanding of how a healthy self develops and the conditions and interpersonal relationships that nurture it, we are then in a position to move actively in the direction of creating these conditions" (Owens, 1987, p. 295). This is the challenge that faces early childhood educators.

One approach to understanding children's needs is with a control-theory model, as outlined in the writings of Glasser (1984) and Good (1989). The control-theory model views an individual as having two types of needs—physical and psychological.

The physical needs involve conditions or substances required by our body to survive:

1. safety;
2. air;
3. nutrition;
4. rest;
5. reproduction; and
6. movement.

The psychological needs represent four equally important areas that become the focus of most of a person's attention: once the physical needs are satisfied psychological needs are:

1. *belonging* (that is, a sense of being loved, of sharing, and of cooperating with significant others);
2. *power* (that is, a sense of importance, recognition, or influence);
3. *fun* (that is, a sense of pleasure); and
4. *freedom* (that is, a sense of having and making real choices).

Children, like adults, are in a constant struggle to have these needs met. With less experience from which to learn, children often choose dramatic ways to achieve satisfaction. As a result, they often infringe on others who are engaged in the same process.

If we, as early childhood professionals, understand this process, we can do much in our learning environments to help children learn positive ways to get their needs met. And people who are effective in getting their needs met invariably possess a positive self-concept.

It therefore behooves us to remember that children will show little interest in our carefully prepared learning activity if they are focusing their attention on their unsatisfied physical need for nutrition, because they missed breakfast.

We may convince ourselves that a child who has withdrawn into himself because his belonging need has been jeopardized by a family argument will set it aside without our help and will participate in a excursion to a local bakery. But it is unlikely that a child who has focused on his unmet need to feel loved will make much time to watch bread rise.

The very specificity of children's needs suggests some qualities that a curriculum must have in order to be effective (see also Chapter 11). For example, the curriculum must have a high degree of flexibility, so that it can be adjusted for the changing situations. Children tend to shift their focus constantly as they struggle to understand, and to cope with meeting, their needs. An observer might inappropriately conclude that children are unpredictable or have a short attention span. The curriculum must also be practical, to allow professionals to use the resources at their disposal in creative and novel ways. Finally, the curriculum must be sensitive to each child in a way that challenges that child to grow in relation to his or her individual needs.

Many people still believe that an early childhood program's curriculum consists of a planned list of activities in which the children will engage over a specified period of time. They may also believe that such a curriculum will require special, and sometimes sophisticated, equipment and experiences. Both notions are incorrect.

The curriculum is not the schedule, or the equipment, or facts, or skills—it is you, as the early childhood educator.

You are the one who significantly influences children in their development of a positive self-concept by your relationship with them, and by your attitudes. As an early childhood educator,

> you are a significant person who has the power to influence self-concept and self-esteem. What you teach may not be nearly so important as how you teach and what kind of person you are as you teach. Young children need teachers who accept them as they are and who encourage them to value and positively evaluate themselves. (Feeney, Christensen, & Moravcik, 1987, p. 181)

It is your ability to show respect, honesty, and trust that has such a powerful impact on children.

It has been estimated that the typical early childhood professional will work personally and directly with a minimum of 1200 children over the course of his or her career, spending approximately 2000 hours a year with each child. Multiply these figures by the number of early childhood professionals in Canada, and we can appreciate the impact that they are having on the next generation of Canadians.

You are an important model for each child with whom you interact. Your opportunity to influence a child is probably exceeded only by that of the child's family. Observe how often you are discreetly watched by children, how often they imitate your words, actions, and attitudes.

The activities and experiences in your program provide a framework for this important learning to occur. Having long since forgotten falling off the balance beam, children will still remember your caring, sensitivity, and support. What was said that hurt them will soon be lost, but they will recall your arm around their shoulder, and how good it felt.

The best possible curriculum in any type of program involves sensitive, caring adults—who, through their relationships with children, enable all the children to develop a positive attitude about themselves and others.

A quality curriculum requires a group of people committed to assisting young children in their attempts to learn to meet their needs in positive ways. Lero and Kyle (1985) define quality care as "care provided by knowledgeable, committed and sensitive caregivers in a milieu that supports their efforts to provide an optimal environment designed to foster children's well being, development and competence" (p. 88).

Too often we approach our curriculum by identifying our goal, but forgetting the crucial process needed to achieve it. Picture an early childhood student diligently "helping" a special-needs child by making an Easter basket exactly like those of the other children. Meanwhile, the child sits silently, bored and frustrated.

Remember one of your favourite teachers. What comes back to you? Is it the facts you learned and the skills you developed? Or was it this teacher's attitude? Perhaps his or her smile, sense of humour, respect for you, acceptance of you, or confidence in you?

There is a Chinese proverb that reads, "A child is like a piece of white paper; everyone who passes it leaves a mark." As early childhood professionals, as adults, and as parents, we leave a lot of marks on children. It is our responsibility to make those marks positive by nurturing the child's self-image.

There is one catch. One is not given the opportunity to influence thousands of young minds without some cost. If you really want to help children develop a belief in themselves, something is required of you. You must display the attitudes you want them to learn. This will require you to take the risks you will be expecting children to take. You will have to believe in yourself and believe in the children. Otherwise, the children can never learn these things from you.

Increasing attention is given to the concept of choice in our society, since it is considered to form the basis of our uniqueness from other animals. Each of us is responsible for our own choices. Each of us can choose to be happy or sad, competent or incompetent. But we do not "choose" to be a model for children. If we are in their world, then we are automatically a model for them. So "to be able to bolster the self-concept of children, you must yourself possess an adequate self-concept" (Lero & Kyle, 1986, p. 88). Marshall McLuhan's famous saying "the medium is the message" certainly holds true in early childhood education.

CONCLUSION

One final image may be valuable. Take a moment to remember your own childhood. Go back to those important times in your own past. Think about the hard times and the good times of your childhood.

Think about a special person from those times—someone who was special to you because she or he accepted you as a person, with no conditions. This person was there for you when you needed it. This person was there in the way you needed. This person accepted both your strengths and weaknesses. This person provided unconditional support and made the time to accept you for what you were. Think about the impact that person had on you, then and now, about how that person affected, probably forever, how you grew as an individual.

As Bos (1984) states so succinctly, "The most important thing an adult can do to give a child a positive self-concept is to give time." As an early childhood educator, you have the time and the opportunity to be like your special person for the children in your care.

If you can be that special person to children by providing them with time to learn positive attitudes toward themselves and others, then you will go a long way in assisting them to develop a positive self-concept.

If you believe in yourself, if you are committed to developing your own self-confidence with honesty and trust, this will have a significant impact on all children with whom you interact, giving them a better chance, through your modeling, to develop a belief in themselves. In this way young Canadian children can be nurtured to develop self-confidence and self-esteem. The child is the core of the early childhood curriculum.

REFERENCES

Adler, R.B., and Towne, N. (1987). *Looking out looking in.* (5th ed.). Toronto: Holt, Rinehart and Winston.

Berne, R.M. (1985). *Child, family, community.* Toronto: Holt, Rinehart and Winston.

Briggs, D.C. (1975). *Your child's self-esteem.* New York: Doubleday.

Bos, B. (1984). *Before the basics: Creating conversations with children.* Roseville, CA: Turn the Pages Press.

Coopersmith, S., & Silverman, J. (1964). How to enhance pupil self-esteem. *Today's Education, 58,* 28–34.

Feeney, S., Christensen, D., & Moravcik, E. (1987). *Who am I in the lives of children?* (3rd ed.). Toronto: Merrill.

Glasser, W. (1984). *Control theory: A new explanation of how we control our lives.* Toronto: Fitzhenry and Whiteside.

Good, E.P. (1989). *In pursuit of happiness: Knowing what you want, getting what you need.* Chapel Hill, NC: Newview.

Heathington, B.S. (1980). Needed: Positive reading self-concepts. In T.D. Yawkey (Ed.), *The self-concept of the young child* (pp. 63–71). Provo, UT: Brigham Young University Press.

Kiester, D.J. (1973). *Who am I?: The development of self-concept.* Durham, NC: Learning Institute of North Carolina.

Lero, D.S., and Kyle, I. (1985). Day care quality: Its definition and implementation. In *Report of the task force on child care* (Series 3: Child Care Standards and Quality, pp. 85-149). Ottawa: Ministry of Supply and Services.

Owens, K. (1987). *The world of the child.* Toronto: Holt, Rinehart and Winston.

Swayze, M.C. (1980). Self-concept development in young children. In T.D. Yawkey (Ed.), *The self-concept of the young child* (pp. 33–48). Provo, UT: Brigham Young University Press.

PART 2
THE CANADIAN CONTEXT

In Part Two, the reader is alerted to some dynamics of the Canadian context, beginning with an introduction to some influential precedents "on the premise that we must understand where we have been to know where we are going."

Chapter 6, by Mary Taylor, gives us a frame of reference by presenting the major influences from research and theory over the past 500 years that provide the foundation and the context for our current programs and practices. In Chapter 7, Alan Pence focuses on the true roots of the Canadian child-care profession. Barbara Corbett's study of Friederich Froebel, in Chapter 8, provides a closer look at this important influence on early childhood education in Canada.

Chapters 9 and 10 offer a more modern look at specific challenges presented by the Canadian context. In Chapter 9, Karen Mock discusses multiculturalism, a particularly Canadian concept, and locates related issues for early childhood care and education within the broader scope of race relations. Finally, in Chapter 10, in this part, Anne Lindsay applies some of these principles in her work on the sociocultural backgrounds and the discourse of Native Indian children.

Foundations of Early Childhood Education

Mary Taylor

This chapter offers the reader an overview of research in child development spanning 500 years. The intent is to reveal how our awareness of childhood has grown through observing children, studying their growth and development, and formulating theories about how to reform or enhance this development through schooling.

As Western cultures developed greater social, psychological, and scientific understanding of the human being, the various theories of child development gradually fragmented child psychologists into various camps: the environmentalists, the geneticists, the developmentalists, the clinicians, and the behaviourists. As Doxey has observed in Chapter 1, with the age of relativity came a greater consciousness of the whole child and the interrelatedness of physical, mental, emotional, and social development. Longitudinal studies revealed the many variables and influences that affect the process of development and learning, making clear the complexity of childhood and the need to re-examine educational practices. Long-term research in language and communication is gradually having an impact on some primary-school programs. But the challenge that still daunts many is accepting play as the essence of childhood.

EARLY VIEWS OF CHILDHOOD

In his book *Centuries of Childhood*, Philippe Ariès (1962) reveals that the concept of childhood as a distinct phase of life is a comparatively recent development in Western civilization. For many centuries, except for the recognition of the infant Jesus and of angels, childhood was considered a transitional period and largely forgotten. Artwork from the twelfth century depicts children as little people with adult faces and body structure.

Among intellectuals during the Middle Ages, a major pursuit involved pondering the "ages of life." Childhood became that period of time that lasted seven years from birth.

> Thus the child six summers old is not worth much when all is told. But one must take every care to see that he is fed good fare, For he who does not start life well will finish badly one can tell. (Ariès, 1962, p. 22)

By the end of the fifteenth century, because work was of short duration and not too important to society, games, amusements, and festivities where children and adults were equal participants had become the main preoccupation. This helped society form collective bonds and a sense of community. Toys were miniatures of prized possessions, and were manufactured for adults rather than for children.

The sixteenth century brought the recognition of childhood as a separate life stage. Distinctive costumes were created for aristocratic boys, and parents were advised to "coddle" (that is, pamper, treat gently) their children.

At the same time, the clergy and moralists became instrumental in removing the child from adult society. Condemning adult immorality—especially adult games—and eager to ensure that society developed manners and discipline, they viewed children as helpless, fragile creatures needing to be cared for and also reformed. The responsibility for doing so, they believed, rested on both the family and the school. By the seventeenth century, they succeeded in shifting the ideas held by many: children's morality was to be safeguarded by forbidding them to play. Coddling, no longer considered conducive to building a moral structure, was not to be condoned.

The seventeenth century, marked by an earnest effort to understand children as well as to reform them, produced writers with varying viewpoints. Balthazar Gratien wrote,

> Every man must be conscious of that insipidity of childhood which disgusts the sane mind; that coarseness of youth which finds pleasure in scarcely anything but material objects and which is only a very crude sketch of the man of thought. . . . Only time can cure a person of childhood and youth, which are truly ages of imperfection in every respect. (Ariés, 1962, p. 132)

The insipid child of Gratien's time who found pleasure in material objects and the "child in perpetual motion" of another author of the period became a thinking, feeling, and perceiving child in the eighteenth-century writings of Jean Jacques Rousseau. Although Rousseau identified distinctively functioning stages of development that were regulated by constant laws, his theories were intuitive rather than scientific. He made society cognizant of the child's intellect as different from the adult's, but failed to recognize the influence of the social environment on the child's development.

Heinrich Pestalozzi (1746–1827), a disciple of Rousseau, recognized the importance of both social and moral influences within the sphere of intellectual development. With only an intuitive sense of child development, Pestalozzi determined in 1781 to "psychologize education." The school must do what the home failed to do; the teacher must relate to the pupil (a child from eight to fourteen years old) as a good mother relates to her child; the pupil must learn through direct contact with the everyday world; learning must begin with sense-perception of objects; words and arithmetical symbols must be introduced only in relation to familiar content. In these ways, Pestalozzi believed that the school could reform society.

Pestalozzi became revered by his contemporaries for his teaching methods, particularly the "object lessons." In retrospect, "Pestalozzi was tainted with a certain systematic formalism which made itself evident in his timetables, in his classification of the subjects to be taught, in his mental gymnastic exercises, and in his passion for demonstration lessons. His excesses in this direction demonstrate just how little account he took, in detail, of the true development of the mind" (Phillips, 1957, p. 413). Nearly a century later, in 1871, Egerton Ryerson, chief superintendent of schools in Ontario, disturbed by "neglect of elementary education, word-mongery and superficial teaching, and the frequent use of the rod," introduced Pestalozzi's object lessons as a formal part of the prescribed course of studies in all schools (Phillips, 1957, p. 413).

Friedrich Froebel (1782–1852), a disciple of Pestalozzi, was likewise eager to devise a new type of education that would bring joy and self-confidence to young children. Froebel's methods were accepted in Canada for kindergarten only, because the Church of England took exception to his most important book, *The Education of Man*. In 1883 Toronto established its first Froebelian kindergarten. Today many Ontario kindergartens reflect Froebel's didactics (Phillips, 1957, p. 422), as Chapter 8 outlines.

THE CHILD STUDY MOVEMENT

The political and economic circumstances that evolved from the Industrial Revolution created the myth, particularly in England, that, because the white middle-class adult male was most likely to succeed in manufacturing or business, such people must somehow be intellectually superior. In close harmony with this view was Darwin's theory of the survival of the fittest, which emphasized "the competitive selection of able individuals by a harsh environment" (Henderson & Bergan, 1976, p. 35). An extension of Darwin's theory of the evolution of species was the idea of cultural evolution. In 1859, Darwin pointed out that, in any population, environmental factors probably influenced the selection of genetic traits. During the next decade Gregor Mendel and Sir Francis Galton each made significant discoveries in genetics and heredity, while Charles Dickens, through his literary art, explicitly described the environment and society in which children of the time were forced to survive and compete. Photographs of children gained favour over portraits. All these factors increased the social, industrial, and genetic consciousness of Western societies and brought about the child study movement.

G. Stanley Hall (1844–1924), considered the founder of child psychology, thought that development was determined mainly by genetic influences. Already strongly influenced by Darwin, Hall incorporated Freud's psychoanalytic principles into the child study movement—which, in the 1890s, was strong enough to bring about educational reform, influencing the progressive views of John Dewey (1859–1952), an authority on curriculum and education rather than on child development. Hall believed that education should revolve around the natural stages of the child's growth. He believed that these stages recapitulated human history.

Also in the vanguard of the child study movement was Maria Montessori (1870–1952), a medical doctor. She was greatly influenced by Joseph Sergi, an Italian anthropologist who was attempting to revolutionize educational practices through child study. It was apparent to Montessori that the afflictions suffered by many "abnormal" or "backward" children were psychological rather than medical in nature. At first committed to understanding the intellectual development of abnormal infants, after 1906 she devoted herself to studying the education of the young child. Through skilful observation, Montessori realized that young children's learning develops through acting on the environment, leading to knowledge that surpasses that offered by the best books or by language itself. She identified by ages critical periods of growth, describing development as a series of rebirths.

She was the first to construct a framework of child development on scientific principles, linking children's physical, emotional, social, linguistic, manipulative, and intellectual growth to the unfolding of their spiritual embryo.

For the baby and toddler, Montessori's principles had practical meaning. Probably because of her lack of training in education, the formalization of her principles into teaching methods distorted them as thoroughly as object lessons had distorted Pestalozzi's theories. Child-development theories cannot be realized without an understanding and preparation of the environment in which the child responds spontaneously. Pestalozzi, Froebel, Hall, and Montessori all helped to select some of the components for the foundation of early childhood care and education.

In the late 1800s, failure in school was not linked to heredity or environment.|Socialization practices such as schooling were strongly influenced by the concept of original sin. Children were considered immoral when they did not meet adult expectations. In France at the close of the nineteenth century, Alfred Binet (1857–1911) began the construction of the first practical test of intelligence, hoping to correct the harsh treatment given to those having difficulty in school.

H.H. Goddard translated Binet's intelligence test into English in 1905. Although it was ultimately discovered that the test was limited because many of the test items measured similar abilities, numerous tests have nevertheless been patterned on Binet's and children are still tested, parceled into groups, and "blessed" accordingly.

Around the same time, there was a general increase in knowledge about human mental evolution—in particular, the integrative action of the nervous system. On a broader spectrum, the United States launched an investigation into child labour in 1910. Subsequently, greater credence was given to the theories of Montessori and Hall, who stressed that growth preceded learning. By 1924, child psychology, though still in its infancy, had already fragmented into several insular subfields: genetic, physical, intellectual, and emotional. With the birth of behaviourism in 1913, social scientists began the construction of a new monument.

The roots of behaviourism are embedded in the influence of science on Western cultures following the Industrial Revolution. In less than a century, people had learned how to gain control over nature and the environment by designing and producing technical devices and machines. Believing that human beings could be similarly controlled, John B. Watson (1878–1958) called in 1913 for a scientific study of human behaviour. This new science, behaviourism, would be committed to observing, describing, measuring, predicting, and controlling behaviour. Mental processes previously identified as perception, thought, and reflection were rejected as being introspective. Science was considered objective. Behaviourists viewed all individual variations in observable behaviour as stemming entirely from experience. Watson wrote confidently,

> Give me a dozen healthy well-formed infants and my own specific world to bring them up in and I'll guarantee you to take any one at random and train him to become any type of specialist I might select—doctor, lawyer, artist, merchant-chief, and yes, even beggar man and thief, regardless of his talents, penchants, tendencies, abilities, vocations, and [the] race of his ancestors. (1930, p. 104).

The 1920s saw the beginning of research organizations for the study of child development and educational experiments. In Ontario, the influence of the American research led to the creation of the Institute of Child Studies at the University of Toronto. Behaviourism was well entrenched, for this new science brought new hope to a country on the brink of the Great Depression.

Within the same period as Watson's early research (1912 to 1920), Montessori visited the United States; H.H. Goddard observed an increase in intelligence in the earthworm. E.L. Thorndike established a new discipline—educational psychology; Freud produced his biological theory of behaviour; Stoddard found that the IQ could be changed by changing the environment; and in 1919, the first Rudolf Steiner school was established in the Waldorf–Astoria factory in Stuttgart, Germany, for the workers' children.

Rudolf Steiner (1924) was concerned that, although many theories abounded, there was no true knowledge about human beings. He believed that the art of education should be based on anthroposophy ("study to find knowledge of man"). It should be concerned with the whole person—body, soul, and spirit—and should be in the hands of autonomous teachers who, through their observations of the child, would align teaching methods and curriculum content with the child's stage in biological development.

So the polarities in child-development theories were well entrenched by the end of the first quarter of the twentieth century.

In 1921, Jean Piaget (1896–1980) began a study of intellectual development that would eventually span six decades. During the first decade, Susan Isaacs—who was trained in psychology, logic, and psychoanalysis, and was principal of the Malting House School in Cambridge, England—was influenced by Piaget and in turn influenced him in modifying his research techniques. Through careful observations of children playing together spontaneously, she gained evidence of children's thinking of a different calibre than that witnessed by Piaget when he interviewed his subjects. Isaacs was successful in putting into practice her theories about children's thinking. "Play is indeed the child's work, and the means whereby he grows and develops. Active play can be looked upon as a sign of mental health; and its absence, either a sign of some inborn defect or [a sign] of mental illness" (1968, p. 152).

In 1929, Arnold Gesell published *The Mental Growth of the Preschool Child*. He introduced innovative techniques as head of the Yale Clinic for Child Development. From studies of twins and of the effects of training on stair-climbing, it was concluded that motor-skill development was predetermined by genetic factors. Gesell is regarded as the pioneer in longitudinal investigation methods, but because he used age as the basis for defining developmental stages, his research does not reflect the range of individual differences within the developmental patterns.

Other studies conducted during the 1930s revealed that favourable changes in the economic and cultural character of an area brought about marked changes in the IQs of schoolchildren and that the IQs of preschoolers could be raised through environmental alterations. The behaviourists and the genetic developmentalists moved toward common ground.

Five years after Einstein published his theory of relativity, researchers began relating the various areas of child development. Nancy Bayley, after looking at the relationship between mental and physical development in babies, began the first long-term observation of individuals from birth to age 18 years. Later, in 1932, she began a 32-year study of 76 babies. Best known for Bayley's Scales of Infant Development, she views intelligence as a complex of separately timed developing functions, with the more advanced functions in the hierarchy depending on the maturation of earlier, simpler functions. In 1968, after completing a long-range study of the correlation between behaviour and mental growth from birth to age 36, Bayley called for "scientific inquiries" into sex-linked processes of interaction between the genes and various environments in the growth of intelligence.

During the 1920s and 1930s, the study of child development was regarded as secondary to more traditional disciplines. Argument about whether it belonged to the field of psychology, mental health, or house-hold science restricted its pursuit, leaving the Watsonian influence to dominate the teacher-training institutions.

"American family life in large cities is admittedly on the wane," wrote J.B. Watson in *Behaviorism*. He went on to suggest that, because of more divorces, fewer marriages, fewer children among the well-to-do, and greater promiscuity among both husbands and wives, the home was "inadequate, unqualified, and unwilling to care for children" (1930, p. 55).

Several authorities maintain that Watson had a devastating effect on child development, leading parents to subject their children to rigid controls (for example, no rocking or otherwise stimulating babies). But such child-rearing practices fell into disrepute with the advent of Arnold Gesell's growth norms in the 1930s and Benjamin Spock's child-care advice, first popularized during the 1940s. Nursery schools were established privately or with the support of government offices concerned with health and welfare, but education departments were little influenced by the child-development movement, particularly in Canada, until the middle 1930s.

In 1930, a White House conference named the twentieth century "the Century of the Child," stressing the need to study "the whole child" and the interrelatedness of his or her physical, mental, emotional, and social development. The enormous increase in child-guidance clinics for testing children was not accompanied by the provision of psychiatrists trained to treat children. Likewise, child-development centres had difficulty finding psychologists who had any experience in studying children. Little was known as yet about treatment or therapy for the young child.

Sigmund Freud's research represented a major thrust toward seeking causal relationships in behaviour. Scientifically, Freud himself never moved from observing the attributes of behaviour to seeking the causes of behaviour. His theory of development reflected a distortion of normal development, because his data were derived from clinical observations. In 1938 he formulated the first comprehensive theory of socialization based on the interactive viewpoint. Freud's psychodynamic theory pictures the human being as a dynamic system, subject to the laws of nature. The child passes through a series of psychosexual stages, each related to erogenous zones. Freud influenced two key figures in child development: Erik Erikson, who became the first psychoanalyst in the Boston Clinic in 1934; and Arthur Jersild of the Child Development Institute at Columbia Teachers' College, who pursued the significance of the self-concept and personality development in the young child, the teacher's self-concept and personality, and the interrelatedness of teacher and pupil.

Carl Rogers, who wrote one of the first books on child psychotherapy in 1940, believed that children's perception of their own adequacy or inadequacy is the major determinant of their behaviour. A.H. Maslow (1943) proposed the theory that people have a hierarchy of needs set up in an invariable order. Once a given need has been satisfied, the need at the next level of the hierarchy then becomes the motivating force that elicits an individual's behaviour.

By 1946, Gesell and Ilg had completed a major lifetime study of children, *The Child from Five to Ten*. The major areas they examined included motor characteristics, personal hygiene, emotional expression, fears and dreams, interpersonal relations, play and patterning, school life, ethical sense, and philosophical outlook. These were studies of observable behaviours detailed by ages in separate, unrelated categories.

Gesell believed that each child has a unique pattern of physical and mental growth that constitutes the core of his or her individuality. According to him, one task of the life sciences should be to make that individuality more intelligible. He was concerned that many areas of child development remained unexplored. Much of the existing research and knowledge was disjointed. He called upon those involved in medicine, sociology, embryology, neurophysiology, biochemistry, genetics, and anthropology to carry on fruitful observations of the young child in order to understand the interplay of organisms and personal environments.

There appear to be no outstanding leaders who heard Gesell's plea. Within 35 years he had compiled the most descriptive record of children's development ever to be constructed; his work is still widely read. The major weakness of his work involves his concept of time. Age since birth cannot be a measure of development. The science of the child must become part of a broader science of humanity.

While Watson's theories on child development faded away, his contributions to scientific research on behaviourism remained in full force. Since 1931 his disciple, B.F. Skinner, has been recognized as the greatest contributor to behaviourism, particularly with regard to controlling animal behaviour. According to Skinner, development occurs as a result of learning—a viewpoint in direct opposition to that of Montessori, Piaget, and others who believed that new learning occurs as a result of further development. By 1954 Skinner had applied his principles of behaviourism to the socialization of young children. When it was found that positive reinforcement could control an enormously wide range of behaviours, behaviourism became a primary thrust both in child-guidance clinics and in schools. In 1955, behaviour modification programs were born. Skinner used the results of pigeon-training experiments as examples to support his argument that a child could learn better through the careful sequencing of instructional content coupled with immediate positive reinforcement for adequate responses. He convinced many educators that programmed learning would solve all school problems.

When children are trained to be controlled by science or technology, when they are denied opportunities to perceive, think, reflect, and make decisions, they never learn to control their environment wisely, for their environment has controlled them.

UNDERSTANDING LEARNING

Born in Neuchâtel, Switzerland, in 1896, Jean Piaget became the most renowned and the most controversial researcher studying young children and their learning. With a doctoral degree in biology and a background of readings in sociology, religion, psychology and philosophy, he became interested in the relationship between biology and and learning. While working on a postgraduate degree in developmental psychology in Paris, he received valuable training from Alfred Binet. While preparing and administering test items for the Binet intelligence tests, Piaget perceived a consistency in the "similarity" of wrong answers and began to question not only the validity of formal testing but also the source of human knowledge. What is intelligence and how does it develop? What is knowledge and how does it develop?

During the 1920s, Piaget made highly specific observations of his own three children, noting their behaviour in close detail. From this "scientific" approach, he developed his theory of intelligence in the infant and the young child, followed by a theory about the actual process of thinking and the development of logical thought from birth to maturity. His theory that the growth of human intelligence is highly affected by children's interactions with the people, places, and things in their environment spawned innumerable studies in the field of psychology but had little effect on society generally until October 4, 1957, when the Sputnik launch sent thousands of American educators scrambling for ideas on how to make children brighter, more quickly, so that the U.S. would be able to catch up to and surpass the Soviet Union in the "space race."

Many educators, psychologists, and sociologists have replicated isolated aspects of Piaget's research. His is the most frequently cited name of the century in books on child development. His major contribution to society may be that he influenced, inspired, prodded, or angered a vast number of people throughout the world to argue about, inquire into, study, and reflect on how children develop and learn. His theories are revolutionary in the field of education, revealing that intellectual development depends on four interdependent influences beyond heredity: experience, maturation, social transmission, and equilibration.

The research of Piaget and others reveals that a stimulating physical environment in an atmosphere that allows the young child, out of curiosity, to act freely on this environment must be provided. As they act on the environment and view the environment reacting, children form new intellectual structures (schemata) that relate the world around them to their inner world of images and thoughts. This kind of action, always self-directed, is biologically determined.

Piaget's theories represented a blending of the research, folk wisdom, philosophy, and scientific knowledge of his day. His work is yet to be totally understood by the majority of psychologists and educators, particularly in North America, for they have been steeped in measurement, testing, and teaching approaches grounded in behaviourism.

These approaches accommodate Piaget's information by testing children on the Piagetian concepts of intellectual development. They discovered cognitive psychology without ever discovering the developing child. However, a small band of educators and psychologists, under

Piaget's influence or otherwise, did spearhead further inquiry into the related structures of the child's development.

Several important studies were reported in the late 1950s and early 1960s. Sears, Maccoby, and Levin (1957) found that hostility and aggression in young children could relate to patterns in child-rearing practices. Olson (1959) observed that, for the individual child, growth patterns over short time periods tend to be quite uneven, characterized by sharp spurts and declines. He castigated the schools for putting children into stair-step programs according to grade level, and provided research to prove that since individual differences in development span several years, failing children because of academic progress is of little value.

Kagan and Moss (1962) produced a longitudinal study that followed children from birth to maturity. Personality in childhood and adulthood was related to the mother's protective or over-protective behaviour during the child's first three years of life. Children who developed independence, explored freely, ventured forth curiously, and whose mothers took considerable interest in their achievements and encouraged them to master the environment showed rising IQs during the years from six to ten.

White (1959) found that motivation has biological significance and that action on the environment through play is the child's expression of the desire for competence. Hunt (1961) reported changes of from 20 to 60 points on intelligence test scores arising from environmental influences. Intellectual development, although not stable over a period of time, could be maximized by matching environmental circumstances to the child's intellectual level, as reflected in Piaget's developmental theory.

By 1970 there were many more specific bits of research that, put together in a coordinated structure, began to form the foundation of child-development theory as we now understand it. In Ontario, the 1966 revision of the primary and junior curriculum incorporated much of the foregoing research. Yet many children in the 1990s are still in graded lockstep programs that are unrelated to their natural development process.

Extending the understandings provided by Piagetian theory is the work of Erik Erikson (1963). A friend of Freud and a psychiatrist at the Gesell Clinic, Erikson believed that humans develop through a number of invariant stages, each stage presenting its own unique problems for the individual to solve. While Freud saw developmental problems as psychosexual, Erikson saw them primarily as psychosocial, arising out of the ever-widening range of social encounters with which the individual must cope. Of the eight stages Erikson defined for the lifetime of human development, the first four are significant to the child's first decade: Basic Trust versus Mistrust; Autonomy versus Shame and Doubt; Initiative versus Guilt; and Industry versus Inferiority. In formulating his stages,

Erikson recognized that interaction between individuals and their culture contributes to personal growth. He believed that the development of trust lays the groundwork for a feeling of security throughout life.

As a result of direct observation of and interaction with children, followed by deep reflective thinking, Erikson, like Piaget, painted broad, realistic pictures of children as he perceived them in time and space. He saw development as a lifelong process, each stage uniquely significant. Time to develop in an environment of mutual trust is the essence of childhood. If the child cannot respond, the environment should be changed.

When Dr. Spock faced the challenge of dealing with parents who sought his help in rearing children, parent/child relationships became a major field of research. Among the experiences essential to establishing a sense of trust in the child, a warm relationship with a mother figure was thought to be of greatest importance. John Bowlby, who pioneered the study of attachment in infants, discovered that infants are ready to make their first attachment between the ages of three and six months. A first attachment can be formed after six months, but with greater difficulty. If by the age of two there is no attachment, many difficulties arise in the child's further development. The first attachment is vulnerable for several years after the first birthday (Bowlby, 1969). Bowlby, along with many others, proposed that the roots of attachment are biological in nature. Viewed in the context of evolutionary theory, infant/mother attachment is seen as a biological function that promotes species survival, and exploratory behaviour is seen as a biological function that promotes interest, exploration, and learning. Because attachment is so significant to intellectual and social development, it is an important consideration of the child's education (see also Chapter 15).

THE URGE TO EDUCATE VERSUS THE DESIRE TO LEARN

In *The Process of Education*, Jerome Bruner (1960) shook psychologists and education theorists with his declaration that any school subject can be taught effectively in some intellectually honest form to any child at any stage of development. Benjamin Bloom (1964) in a long-term look at earlier and later intelligence, reported that he could predict, at age four, 50 percent of children's potential IQ (the IQ they would reached by age seventeen); at age eight, he claimed, 80 percent of that potential IQ could be predicted. This information was assimilated in many ways, but few asked "Why not delay schooling until age eight, when 80 percent of a child's IQ will have developed and the child will be better able to profit from school experience?" Because school enrolment in the early grades was beginning to decline as the baby-boom bulge passed through,

Bloom's research was used as an argument for having children come to school earlier. Since 1966, there has been a steady increase in school programs for four- and five-year-old children, across Canada and elsewhere.

Child-development studies as an honest pursuit rapidly succumbed to a marked increase in research in "early childhood education" and "preschool instruction," the major aim of which involved increasing the child's IQ. The efforts of the learning theorists were spurred on by three separate government reports on children: Coleman (1966) in the United States, Ryan (1972) in Canada, and Davie (1972) in England. That "equality of input does not produce equality of output" was already known by anyone who had taught young children. The public, however, was baffled. What did schools do? Poverty was identified as a major cause of school failure. Few gave heed to Davie's findings that the parent/child interaction was the biggest influence in the child's learning and that by age seven the advantaged child was at least four years ahead of the disadvantaged child in academic achievement.

At a time when educators had no theoretical basis for understanding intelligence, knowledge, and the difference between memory and learning, they imposed an increasing amount of instruction on younger children, paying little attention to researchers who were evaluating the disquieting results of such instruction. Cole and Bruner (1971), for example, pointed out that using middle-class behaviour as the measure of success had changed children with differences into children with deficiencies. "Not only is there no clear-cut longitudinal data to support the claims of lastingness of preschool instruction, there is evidence in the opposite direction," wrote David Elkind (1974), who pointed out that environmental variations during the school-age period (from age six to twelve) are more significant for intellectual attainment.

Work by other researchers and theorists from the 1950s explored correlations between the learning processes, maturation, personality, behaviour, and intellectual attainment. This work resulted in the constant creation of new learning theories.

Bandura (1971) developed a social learning theory within behaviouristic psychology. He viewed imitation as the basic mechanism of learning and saw children as playing an active part in shaping the conditions around them, even though they themselves are controlled by adults. This phenomenological theory was based on the belief that people are conscious agents who experience, decide, and act as an integrated whole with an inner need to fully develop their potential. This theory challenged many social scientists, who were accused of treating humans as inanimate objects susceptible to measurement and manipulation.

The question is why tests that measured intelligence in terms of verbal skills that relate mainly to school success continued to hold supremacy over child-development and learning theory. A child's learning can be manipulated, but as yet it cannot be accurately measured. Testing then becomes a moral issue, not a question of testing theory or techniques.

Although learning is a necessary part of development, it cannot be understood until development is understood. Many of the theories up to this time did not take this fundamental fact into account.

LANGUAGE ACQUISITION

Except for Piaget, who was one of the first to examine in children up to the age of seven the development of language as a function, little research in language development was done until the 1950s. References to language prior to that time were normative–descriptive, lacking a linguistic theory and therefore a foundation for learning language. In 1957 B.F. Skinner published *Verbal Behavior*, which set forth his theoretical views on language acquisition based on a form of rule-learning. He called the language-learning the process of "operant conditioning."

A number of behaviourists supported Skinner's views on this subject but found failures in imitative language learning. Also found were novel responses in the child's language not influenced by imitation. Skinner's ideas remain highly influential in the language-teaching field, although they were severely attacked and discredited as a plausible explanation of language acquisition.

Chomsky's Language Acquisition Device (LAD) describes innate knowledge of linguistic patterns and distinctive features of speech found in human beings (1968). With his research came the awareness that language is not acquired merely through learning lists of words and sentences, but instead must be viewed in a much deeper context of human development.

Halliday (1973) researched the functions of speech, concluding that imitation cannot explain all of the child's language learning. For children, all language is doing something: in other words, it has meaning in a very broad sense. If children are to continue their learning in school, it is essential that adults extend their meaning of language to include all the functions that language has—especially the personal, heuristic, and imaginative functions. Halliday identifies seven models of language functions with which the normal child is endowed by the age of five.

Bernstein (1972) wrote that educational failure is often language failure, involving a fundamental mismatch between children's linguistic capabilities and the demands that are made on them. He contributed an elaborate theory that characterized social-class differences in language development. He described lower-class speech as "restricted: concrete rather than abstract, unconcerned with motives and intentions and emphasizing roles" (for example, boys don't cry). Middle-class speech was "elaborated: descriptive, explanatory, reflective, full of reasons and personal concerns."

Lenneberg (1969) linked language development with a biological predisposition of the human brain. His evidence rested on the existence of language universals: every human culture develops language; moreover, its onset is age-correlated, with the same acquisition strategies used by every learner. He found that language development was much more correlated with motor development than with chronological age and that language capacity follows its own natural history. If the environment provides a minimum of stimulation and opportunity, children can avail themselves of this language-development capacity.

Reflecting on the past, researchers recognized that the formal testing settings had helped classify children as verbally deprived. Outside the testing situation, verbal or language deprivations were hard to find. The notion that there are class and ethnic-group differences in developmental rates, and that these differences lead to verbal deprivation requiring compensatory linguistic training, seems utterly unfounded. (For further evidence of this point, see Chapter 10's discussion of the verbal discourse patterns of Native Indian children.)

There is, however, the paradox that children learn to speak well without either parent or child focusing on language structure. It is not the structure, but the limited range of language function, that distinguishes less-favoured children. Children are encouraged to say what a particular adult values, and this can be a limiting influence. Children learn what they practise, not what they are taught. By encouraging the child to talk, the adult is providing the necessary aid.

If we know that both the structure and the function of language develop best when there is powerful communicative intent, and if we want to stimulate language development, we must learn how to make early childhood environments less didactic. We must maximize talking time for children with children and for children with adults.

The significance of the optimum environment for language development in the young child has also been extensively researched. An effective language environment requires a low adult/child ratio with ample opportunity for face-to-face dialogue combined with staff stability and staff autonomy. Studies have shown that the staff with the most autonomy spoke in longer and more complex sentences, made more' informative comments, gave more explanations, fewer negative commands, answered children more frequently, and were more often answered by the children.

Bruner (1960) explored how communicative functions are actually realized in the very young and how the quality of mother/child interaction gives language acquisition its distinctive function. Language acquisition depends not only on the nature of this interaction but also on the child's prior mastery of concepts about the world to which language will refer. With all further advances in communication dependent on the quality of the interaction between the baby and the primary caretaker, communication is undoubtedly rooted in attachment. Both mother and child have been described as innately endowed with the skill to communicate. What children undergo within themselves in the process of developing this skill remains a mystery.

THE ROOTS OF COMPETENCE

Michael Rutter (Institute of Psychiatry, University of London) has called attention to the "distressing lack of curiosity about the early sources of security and competence" (1978). Not all children from stable, loving homes do well; and children with unfortunate home experiences often do well. What makes the difference? Rutter urges inquiry into the conditions that enable children to do well in spite of stresses and disadvantages. Currently it appears that while attachment is essential for toddlers, bonding is essential for the older child.

> Bonding is best differentiated from attachment by the presence of selectivity in relationships which persists over time and place.... Circumstantial evidence suggests that these early selective bonds provide the basis for later social development. However, if development is to proceed optimally, it seems that the bonds must not only be strong but also [be enduring]. The nature and quality of these early relationships is probably crucial. (Rutter, 1978, p. 39)

Once children have developed bonds, they can transfer those bonds to other people. But the ability to form bonds in the first place can be lost. The extent of disadvantage suffered by the child and the quality of the child's environment at ages three, four, and beyond will determine the possibility of bonding if it has not occurred by the critical age of two.

Rutter and his colleagues have done important research, concluding that if circumstances improve later in childhood, the child is not likely to be harmed by stressful early experiences. Good experiences outside the family, particularly in school, can mitigate stresses experienced in the home. In summary, recurrent or multiple acute stresses are most likely to be harmful to the child. Emotional security and social competence can be maintained by a child who experiences stress and disadvantage if a first bonding has been established. Many studies suggest that cognitive and emotional skills depend on what has been called a "hidden curriculum" in the home.

The school scene can be one of despair for the young child. The great press to construct an educational technology that produces middle-class values and skills has in reality produced only evidence that we simply do not understand what conditions are most conducive to learning. Bruner, reflecting on the 1960s, remarks that learning outcomes are not achieved through teaching subroutines that can then be recombined to fulfil the requirements of specific tasks. "We in modern technological settings took for granted that children learn this way. We know better now. Research over the last several years has taught us much" (Connolly & Bruner 1974). If children feel inadequate in dealing with the challenges and tasks imposed on them, they become passive and unwilling to risk themselves. If they lack confidence in their ability to cope, they, will take rewards in the short run for their efforts but will no longer risk the bigger rewards of the distant future, those of success through persistent and high-risk endeavours. Over the generations, society has evolved conditions, both at home and at school, whereby the young child becomes a victim of despair.

PLAY

More and more educators, parents, and researchers are becoming consciously aware that children's play is their true art, the activity that allows them to practise the skills of living. (See also Chapter 2). Through play, children can risk exploring the novel and the difficult. Their learning is enriched not only by what they discover by acting on the environment, but also through the growing awareness that they can recognize and come to value their ideas, feelings, and strivings as their own. Through play, their sense of self and of others is enhanced and becomes more firmly rooted. Children who cannot play do not learn. This is a scientific fact.

Scientific studies of the brain and the integrative action of the nervous system have been carried on for more than a century. Only now are we learning something about brain development in the young, particularly beyond infancy. Intelligence remains a cultural invention. To continue to base instruction on a theory that seeks to increase intelligence is to place the child at high risk.

The freedom to move in a stimulating environment is necessary for the brain to grow. Moreover, the quality of that growth depends on maintaining coordination among the different parts of the brain. It is the child's own actions that work out this synchronization; to force such things as eye–hand coordination or fine visual discrimination is to limit the brain's own regulatory system.

Over the years, scientists have amassed a basic picture of how the human brain works. Most revealing is how much still needs to be learned. However, much exciting research is currently taking place that will undoubtedly have many implications for the education and development of young children in the next decade.

In the meantime, Piaget's work remains the most valid research available for relating the child's observable cognitive behaviour to the maturation of the brain cortex. Brierley (1975) has concluded that "play gives the child power to generate learning," if we define play as "the total of all the spontaneous creative activities in which children freely choose to engage" (Sister Valerie, 1972).

Bronowski (1978) expressed concern for the importance of childhood and of playing in his intensive and skilful analysis of human development.

> For most of history, children have been asked simply to conform to the image of the adult.... The ascent of the young, the ascent of the talented, the ascent of the imaginative became very halting many times.... By one test [civilizations fail]: they limit the freedom of the imagination of the young.... In a sense all science, all human thought is a form of play. (pp. 426 & 432)

A childhood of play allows the plasticity of the mind and the spirit of the self to unfold freely.

IMPLICATIONS

From child-development research by more than 1000 authors during the past 500 years, there is sufficient data to revolutionize education, yet we do not know enough about the child to formulate a theory of learning. This is the mighty paradox.

Learning takes a long time. Time allows for the movement of these elements, things, symbols, ideas. To move ideas in time and space is not only to reflect but also to anticipate. Reflection and anticipation are reciprocal functions of thinking. Understanding what we are learning depends on physical, spatial/temporal relationships within the mind.

For the child the process of play—relating to things spontaneously as one moves freely in time and space—is like the process of thinking for the adult. Both children and adults gain understanding and insight as new structures and new ideas emerge from what was already part of their thinking. Children require a long time to play if they are to become adults who can think reflectively. It is as natural for people to anticipate as it is for them to breathe, yet there is little information in child-development research or developmental psychology about the natural laws of human functions related to thinking.

That is to say, there is no scientific basis for the child's traditional school curriculum. We continue to feed children thousands of bits of information, mostly abstracted into words, while, at the same time, we know this is not an efficient way to learn. We still have much to learn about learning by observing the child at play (see also Chapter 3).

Children are always more than what they know and what they can do. Being in time and space allows them to do more, to know more, to become more. This is their potential and it is directed toward the future. The movement is toward infinity and children's encounters are infinite, for they may be physical encounters of the external world or imaginative encounters of their inner being. Language is infinite. Learning is infinite.

CONCLUSION

Human beings invented the alphabet, the computer, the satellite, and atomic energy as a means of fulfilling basic needs. In turn, these inventions are shaping humanity.

Little information was presented in any of the literature reviewed that indicated an awareness of the child's natural development in the expressive arts—dramatic play, building and constructing, music, movement, modeling, painting and drawing. Each expression has its own form and structure that the child creates. Each one makes its unique contribution to the process of reading. Until children are consciously aware of these expressions, they have not established within themselves the basic foundation for further learning and for reading.

We can see that as a society we have a haphazard, fragmented, limited awareness of the child rather than a comprehensive view of childhood. Our urge to teach, our urge to test and measure, our urge to judge—all conflict with the child's potential to learn and the adult's potential to think. We are the children of the past, living now with our mutated potential.

A quick review of a day in the life of a child will reveal how many of his or her waking hours are programmed by adults. How much time is left for spontaneous play in a trusting, stimulating environment? To pattern children's thinking, to program their activities, is to slow down their natural development of movement and awareness.

If the child and society are to survive, we must cease to fragment the child. We must open our eyes to see how little we know. The cooperative efforts of all researchers in disciplines related to childhood and society are essential. There currently appears to be very little discussion among those who teach child psychology, child development, early childhood education, elementary education, physical education and health, the arts, medicine, neurology, sociology, communication disorders, linguistics, and family life. Each subfield operates in isolation.

Cooperative research is on the horizon. Psychobiologists have begun to discover ways in which biological and behavioural development may be related. Neuropsychologists, psycholinguists, sociobiologists are all attempting to transcend outmoded patterns of thought, but will the new synthetized disciplines enhance our awareness of the child? Who is the authority on children?

If academics are caught up with their disciplines and politicians are caught up with standards, finances, and enrolments; if the administrators are caught up with organization, politics, curriculum, and testing and the teachers are caught up with instruction, programming, accountability, and society, who has time for the child? Early childhood programs must offer an atmosphere that accepts young children and their culture and provides them with time and space to grow and learn.

Over the past 50 years, the schools have increasingly been pressed into raising the IQ of the young child. What is the meaning of intelligence? Do the test-makers confuse intelligence in the young with precocity, the ability to conform, the ability to verbalize, and the ability to excel in the school curriculum?

Do we know the effects of malnutrition, diseases, sedation, drugs, radiation, abnormal chromosomes, birth trauma, and premature birth on brain development, behaviour, and growth beyond infancy? Do we know the effects on parents, children, and teachers of young children being labeled because they are who they are? Have we identified those things that are now being taught at an early age but that can in fact be learned more rapidly, more effectively, and with greater understanding at a later age? Do we know which developmental skills are being delayed because of early intervention?

Before the process of education is understood, the early childhood educator must distinguish among genetics, heredity, environment, development, maturation, growth, intelligence, teaching, learning, knowledge, skills, concepts, impression, and expression, then find out how all these things combine within each child. Before the process of thinking can be understood, the early childhood educator must know the differences among imitation, imagination, intuition, insight, and integrity, then find out how they form a unity.

In neuro-cortical, physical, and biological development, the child is his or her own authority. No one else can tell the time of the child's biological clock. No one can measure the beat of his or her inner rhythm. The adult needs to be an authority on the child's physical needs—for food, shelter, warmth, sleep, activity, health, and safety. It is within the authority of the adult to nurture the child. It is within the authority of the adult to cherish the child; to establish an atmosphere of trust, attachment, bonding, and love; to provide time and space for the child to play. It is also within the authority of the adult to share with the child his or her own culture, heritage, thoughts, dreams, humanity, and celebration of life.

REFERENCES

Anderson, J. (1956). Child development: An historical perspective. *Child Development, 27,* 181–196.

Ariès, P. (1962). *Centuries of childhood* (R. Baldick, Trans.). New York: Random House.

Bandura, A. (1969). *Principles of behavior modification.* New York: Holt, Rinehart and Winston.

Bandura, A. (1971). *Social learning theory.* New York: General Learning.

Bernstein, B. (1972). A sociolinguistic approach to socialization with some references to educability. In J.J. Gumperz & D. Hymes (Eds.), *Directions in sociolinguistics.* New York: Holt, Rinehart and Winston.

Binet, A. (1973). *The development of intelligence in children.* New York: Arno.

Bloom, B.S. (1964). *Stability and change in human characteristics.* New York: John Wiley and Sons.

Bowlby, J. (1969). *Attachment and loss: Vol 1. Attachment.* London: Hogarth.

Brierley, J. (1975). *The growing brain.* London: NFER.

Bronowski, J. (1973). *The ascent of man.* Toronto: Little, Brown.

Bruner, J.S. (1960). *The process of education.* New York: Vintage.

Chomsky, N. (1968). *Language and mind.* New York: Harcourt, Brace, Jovanovich.

Cole, M., & Bruner, J.S. (1971). Cultural differences and inferences about psychological processes. *American Psychology, 26,* 867–876.

Coleman, J.S., et al. (1966). *Equality of Educational Opportunity.* Washington, D.C.: U.S. Government Printing Office.

Connolly, K., & Bruner, J.S. (Eds.). (1974). *The growth of competence.* London: Academic.

Davie, R., Butler N., & Goldstein, H. (1972). *From Birth to Seven.* London: Longman.

Elkind, D. (1974). *Children and adolescents: Interpretive essays on Jean Piaget.* New York: Oxford University Press.

Erikson, E.H. (1963). *Childhood and society.* New York: Norton.

Gesell, A., & Thompson, H. (1938). *The psychology of early growth.* New York: Macmillan.

Halliday, M.A.K. (1973). *Explorations in the functions of language.* London: Edward Arnold.

Henderson, R.W., Bergan, J.R. (Eds.). (1976). *The cultural context of childhood.* Columbus, OH: Charles E. Merrill.

Kagan, J., and Moss, H.A. (1962). *Birth to Maturity.* New York: Wiley.

Lenneberg, E.H. (1969). On explaining language. *Science, 164,* 635–643.

Maslow, A.H. (1943). A theory of human motivation. *Psychological Review, 50*, 370–396.

Montessori, M. (1967). *The absorbent mind* (C.A. Claremont, Trans.). New York: Delta.

Olson, W.C. (1959). *Child development.* Boston: Heath.

Phillips, C.E. (1957). *The development of education in Canada.* Toronto: Gage.

Piaget, J. (1955). *The language and thought of the child* (M. Gabain, Trans.). Cleveland, OH: Meridian.

Piaget, J. (1971). *Science of education and the psychology of the child.* London: Longman.

Piaget, J. (1972). Equilibrium. In R.C. Smart & M.S. Smart (Eds.), *Readings in child development and relationships* pp. 514–517. New York: Macmillan.

Rutter, M. (1978). Early sources of security and competence. In J.S. Bruner & A. Garton (Eds.), *Human growth and development.* Oxford: Clarendon.

Ryan, T.J. (1972). *Poverty and the child: A Canadian study.* Toronto: McGraw-Hill.

Sears, R.R., Maccoby, E., & Levin, H. (1957). *Patterns of child rearing.* New York: Harper and Row.

Sister Valerie. (1972). *Primary program.* London, ON: London and Middlesex County Roman Catholic Separate School Board.

Skinner, B.F. (1957). *Verbal Behavior.* New York: Appleton, Century, Crofts.

Steiner, R. (1924). *The kingdom of childhood.* London: Steiner Press.

Watson, J.B. (1930). *Behaviorism.* New York: Norton.

White, R. (1959). "Motivation reconsidered: the concept of competence." *Psychological Review, 66*, 297–333.

7

The Child-Care Profession in Canada

Alan R. Pence

The Infant School Movement
The Victorian Family
In Search of Models for the 1990s
Conclusion
References

This chapter will address the question of child care's century and a half of "wandering in the wilderness." In the process of examining that history it will become clear that child care in North America has roots that are very different from those generally presented to the public and to our own budding professionals. Most early childhood texts fix the origins of North American child care in the day-nursery, creche, and settlement kindergarten programs of the latter half of the nineteenth century (see, for example, Feeney, Christensen, & Moravcik, 1987; Roopnarine & Johnson, 1987). Such an ancestry is hardly ennobling, let alone enabling of profession-building. Steeped in an atmosphere of moralistic paternalism and often self-righteous "assistance" to the poor and destitute, there is in these programs' tone, temper, or instruction little that we would like to see carried forward to the present. A more suitable and constructive ancestor for the challenges we face today is a movement with which far too few early childhood professionals are familiar—the North American Infant School Movement of the 1820s and 1830s.

Through understanding the forces that brought forth this much earlier "experiment" in early childhood care and education, we can obtain a clearer understanding of our contemporary problems, challenges, and possible futures. An understanding of the infant schools of more than 150 years ago can provide our budding profession not only with roots, but also with the capacity to develop strong wings that will carry us forward into the future.

THE INFANT SCHOOL MOVEMENT

Robert Owen and the British Program Models

Some might say that the New Lanark Mill had a serious problem. Its labour-force requirements were approximately double the number of men available in the small Scottish community. Robert Owen, the owner, had two options: he could either import more men and their families into the community (but that would entail the building of houses for the workers and additional related expenses), or he could employ the wives of the men already living in the community (but then he would need to address the workers' child-care needs). He chose the second route.

But Owen was not an employer of the 1980s; he was not even a twentieth-century employer. He faced his problem 173 years ago, and his solution ultimately led to the establishment of Canada's first child-care program more than 160 years ago. At that time, John A. Macdonald was only 14 years old, Upper and Lower Canada had a combined population measured in the thousands, and the Hudson's Bay Company was *the* economic force in most of the country. Today the Hudson's Bay Company is a department store, Confederation is 122 years old, and Canada has a population of over 27 million. But a strong, quality-based system of child care for children whose parents both work outside the home has yet to be established in Canada. Owen's private problem has become a public issue—arguably the policy issue of the decade.

Robert Owen was not simply an industrialist from the early period of the Industrial Revolution, he was also a philosopher and author in the progressive tradition of the Enlightenment. Child care may have been his motivation as an employer, but child *education* and the proper developmental *formation* of the child provided his inspiration as a philosopher and social activist. Indeed, Owen's major focus of concern is reflected in the name he gave his new program: "The New Institution for the Formation of Character." It was the first workplace child-care and education program in Western history. The date? 1816.

Owen had put much thought into the development of the New Institution. He had visited Pestalozzi's children's program and was very familiar with the writings of both Pestalozzi and Jean-Jacques Rousseau. Owen's theory of education, however, was probably in closest alignment with John Locke's theory of the child as *tabula rasa:* a blank slate to be written on for better or for worse. Owen's own rationalist (and environmentalist) position is stated succinctly in his *Book of the New Moral Order* (1842/1970): "The constitution of every infant ... is capable of being formed or matured, either into a *very inferior*, or a *very superior* being according to the qualities of the external circumstances allowed to influence that constitution from birth" (p. 1).

Owen took an active role in the definition of the New Institution. For the youngest children, (children were admitted from the "age at which they [could] walk"), he employed a male and a female teacher. The rules governing the program were established by Owen himself.

1st—No scolding or punishment of the children.

2nd—Unceasing kindness in tone, look, word, and action to all the children without exception . . . .

3rd—Instruction by the inspection of realities and their qualities, and these explained by familiar conversations between the teachers and the taught . . . .

4th—These questions always to be answered in a kind and rational manner . . . .

5th—No regular indoor hours for school; . . . [when minds are fatigued] change it for out-of-door physical exercise . . . .

6th—In addition to music, the children of these work-people were to be taught and exercised in military discipline to teach them the habits of order, obedience, and exactness . . . .

7th—But these exercises to be continued no longer than they were useful and could be beneficially enjoyed by the taught . . . .

8th—To take the children out to become familiar with the production of gardens, orchards, fields, and woods, and with domestic animals and natural history generally. (pp. 232–233)

Robert Dale Owen, Owen's son, who later taught at the New Institution, confirmed the tone established by his father in his own reflections on the program: "all rewards and punishments whatever except such as Nature herself has provided . . . are . . . excluded as being equally unjust in themselves and prejudiced in their effects" (Salmon & Hindshaw, 1904, p. 25).

News of Owen's experiment in pedagogy soon spread throughout Great Britain and beyond, to Europe and North America. Among the more frequent visitors to New Lanark was a group of gentlemen from London, who saw in Owen's experiment a very different potential purpose. Whereas Owen was motivated by his rationalist philosophy and a desire to create a new order in the world, as well as by his needs as an industrialist/employer, the London gentlemen were primarily concerned about the multitude of young street urchins in the city and the growth of juvenile crime. Their observations at New Lanark led them to believe that "planting a sufficient number of infant schools for training and instructing these classes of people [would] at once solve the problem of prevention" (Roberts, 1972, p. 155).

By the early 1820s, the infant schools had spread beyond Scotland and could be found throughout Great Britain. In their adoption by a variety of groups, organizations, and individuals, numerous adaptations and changes were made from Owen's original plans. In London the infant schools encountered monitorial or Lancasterial instructional methods, wherein great halls filled with young children were envisioned. Samuel

Wilderspin, the leading British proponent of that system, believed that "it [would be] possible to have two-hundred or even three-hundred children assembled together, the oldest not more than six years of age, and yet not have one of them cry for a whole day" (Albany Infant School Society, 1829, p. 7). Wilderspin became an active "evangelist" for *his* form of infant schools and toured throughout Great Britain, often accompanied by "demonstration children."

Infant Schools in North America

By 1825, infant schools had crossed the Atlantic and been established in North America. William Russell, founder and editor of the *American Journal of Education*, was an early proponent of the programs, noting that "[in England] these schools have hitherto been applied (primarily) to the amelioration of the conditions of the poor. There is no good reason, however, why they should be restricted to any one class, whilst they are so well calculated for the benefit of all" (1826, p. 6).

The desirability of infant schools was also noted by major political figures of the time. De Witt Clinton, then governor of New York State and a presidential aspirant, noted that

> the institution of the Infant Schools is the pedestal to the pyramid. It embraces those children who are too young for common Schools; it relieves parents from engrossed attention to their offspring, softens the blow of care and lightens the hand of labor. More efficacious in reaching the heart than the hand, in improving the temper than the intellect, it has been eminently useful in laying the foundation of good feelings, good principles, and good habits. (Fitzpatrick, 1911, p. 107)

Soon infant schools had spread to every major city on the Atlantic seaboard, from Halifax to Savannah. Church groups, schools, non-profit societies, and individual entrepreneurs had all joined in on what Russell referred to as "a favorable change on the subject of early education" (1826, p. 6).

One individual who became interested in this new educational venture was Amos Bronson Alcott, a philosopher and teacher perhaps better remembered as Louisa May Alcott's father. In 1828, Alcott accepted the position of instructor in one of the first infant schools in Boston. In preparation for assuming that responsibility, he visited two established programs, one in New York and the second in Philadelphia. The former he found "too mechanical and sectarian" and the latter "an engine of orthodoxy" (Jenkins, 1978, p. 154). Alcott returned to Boston to design his own approach to infant education. That approach, which emphasized a "simple, natural, and rational process," represented a further development of the humanistic, child-centred thread of pedagogy pioneered in Switzerland by Pestalozzi, in Great Britain by Owen, and subsequently in North America by Alcott and Russell.

We can gain a fuller sense of Alcott's revolutionary theory of infant instruction and its compatibility with Pestalozzi's and Owen's earlier work in an essay of Alcott's entitled *Observations on the Principles and Methods of Infant Instruction* (1830). In that essay Alcott called for the education of the "whole child," maintaining that "the affections, the conscience, and the intellect present their united claims for distinct and systematic attention. The whole being of the child asks for expansion and guidance" (Alcott, 1830, p. 4). While Friedrich Froebel (founder of the kindergarten) wrestled in Germany with the "Universal Laws" of childhood that would eventually lead him to place play at the centre of the kindergarten's activity, Alcott, working independently, but within the same Romantic, Rousseauian/Pestalozzian paradigm, declared that "play is the appointed dispensation of childhood; and a beneficent wisdom consists of turning this to its designed purpose" (1830, p. 4).

The keystone of the Romantically inspired, humanistic approach to the education of children that set Pestalozzi, Owen, and Froebel in Europe, and Alcott in the United States, apart from the didactic and rote practices of most teachers and programs of the period was an unflagging belief in the innate goodness and abilities of the child. These pedagogues of the Romantic period had rejected the determinist beliefs in original sin and those espoused by Calvin, and most had gone beyond Locke's *tabula rasa*.

The Romantic image of childhood espoused by Alcott was agreeable to William Russell. However, while Alcott sought to create a new and original pedagogy harmonious with his developing Transcendentalist beliefs, Russell focused on modifying and humanizing existing practices. Russell selected the Massachusetts Primary Schools as his focus for reform and the infant schools as his measure of success. Russell noted:

> The great moral defect in primary schools is, that in them the management of childhood is regulated by a few arbitrary rules, and a corresponding scheme of various stages of punishment. Let us turn to inspect for a moment, a primary school, taught in the common way, and we usually see a number of little sufferers, confined to one uncomfortable posture, for hours in succession; enduring the irksome restraint, as the conditions of an escape from penalties; conning mechanically a memory lesson which they do not understand, or reciting it as mechanically; controlled in every look and action by the aspect of authority the whole nature of the little beings put under a discipline of repression and restraint (1830, p. 125).

Russell's attack on the established institution of the Massachusetts Primary Schools did not go unnoticed. The gauntlet was picked up in the 1830 Bigelow Report prepared for the Boston Primary School Board:

> With regard to children from the 'Infant Schools,' it is the decided opinion of every instructress in the district who has had any experience on the subject, that it is better to receive children into the Primary Schools that have had no instruction whatever, than those who have graduated with the highest honors of the Infant Seminaries. It is stated that these children are peculiarly restless in their habits, and are thereby the cause of restlessness and disorder among the other children; and it does not appear that their previous instruction renders them, in any respect, particularly proficient or forward in the studies of the Primary Schools (Wightman, 1860, p. 125).

Sound familiar? Are these not the words of some schools and some research reports in the 1970s and 1980s? Is there not today a tension between the largely direct instruction practices of elementary education and the learning centres and interest areas of early childhood programs?

Truly the Infant school movement of the 1820s and 30s represents a rich, exciting, and profound period of early childhood care and education. The parallels with current issues and events are dramatic and conspicuous: from Owen's needs as an industrial employer to the dilemma of a "culture of poverty" that troubled the gentlemen of London; from Russell's attack on the Boston primary schools using the progressive pedagogy of "early education," to Wilderspin's promotion of "super babies"; from Alcott's emphasis on the whole child to the narrow purposes of sectarian programs. The Infant School era represents a rich, exciting, and dynamic period in early childhood programs posing problems, ideas, and rival ideologies not unlike those encountered today.

But where did it go? Why are we not aware that contemporary issues have such an extensive history? Why are we not aware that more than 160 years ago North American politicians had early childhood education and care for workers' children as part of their political platform? Why are we striving today to create a system of care that was already well on its way toward establishment and acceptance over a century ago? Why have we not consolidated gains and extended ideas that were discussed in Halifax and Montreal when John A. Macdonald was a youngster? Because we have lost our history and with it our perspective on social change. We have lost our knowledge of our roots. How can we plan and prepare for what lies ahead when we do not understand what has come before?

Understanding what happened to the North American infant schools provides a key to understanding where we are today.

THE VICTORIAN FAMILY

One infant school society of that era described the Infant School Movement as a "ray of millenial light" (Infant School Society of the City of Boston, 1833, p. 5). That ray of light was eclipsed in the 1830s in North America by the development of a very different system for the care of young children—the Victorian family (Strickland, 1983). The emergence of the Victorian family closely follows the emergence of industrialization and urbanization in North America. Prior to industrialization and major urbanization the typical family was rural, economically based in agriculture, and domestically centred. This domestically based model of the family was largely self-sufficient. Typically all members of the household (except for the very young—up to age two or two and a half) had *economic* responsibilities to the family, and in most cases that economic participation took place in or near the household, the domestic and economic centre of action. With the onset of industrialization the locus of employment shifted away from the home—father became the out-of-home wage-earner and mother became the keeper of the home, with all that such a role implied (Shorter, 1977).

The Victorian family was divided in its roles and in the locations wherein those rules were pursued. It maintained "separate spheres of influence" (Kraditor, 1968), which might overlap on occasion but which never merged. The Victorian family, and mother's role within that family, became the caregiving alternative to infant schools in North America.

Although women were needed as workers in the early days of industrialization in North America, their utility progressively diminished as immigrants swelled the pool of available labour. Immigrant men were a cheaper and more pliable source of labour than native-born North American women. An economic transition had precipitated the need for industrial labour, and labour-force availability modified that need as it related to women.

But the transition was not treated simply in economic terms. In fact, its economic underpinnings were obscured behind the screen of a new social ethic—an ethic that extolled the virtues of the new family form. Poems and sermons from the middle 1800s capture in no uncertain terms the duties of mothers within the Victorian family model. The lines and refrains are familiar to us all, for they are a part of our longstanding inheritance.

> The bravest battle that ever was fought
> Shall I tell you who and when?
> On the maps of the world you'll find it not;
> It was fought by the mothers of men.
>
> Joaquin Miller, "The Bravest Battle"

And the omnipotent, omnipresent power of motherhood is reflected in these lines:

> Don't poets know it,
>   Better than others?
> God can't be always everywhere; and, so,
>   Invented Mothers.
>
> Sir Edwin Arnold, "Mothers"
> (from Bernard, 1974, pp. 3 & 4)

Those words, that chant, the mantra of mother-care that we have memorized at the knees of generations of North American mothers totally suppressed the other-care movement, the child-care movement, for over a century and a half. It drove from our consciousness the fact that at one time the majority of people did not practise the ways of the Victorian family, maintaining separate spheres of influence; at one time fathers played a more active role in their children's development and education; at one time mothers and children were also breadwinners, contributors to the family's economic health. We forgot all that. At the same time, we were blind to the fact that most other peoples of the world do *not* emulate our revered family model with mother-care as a central pillar. In most other societies, mothers play a much less critical role in their children's care (Weisner & Gallimore, 1977).

It was because we could not see these other realities that we became so fearful when the era of the Victorian family began to come to a close in the late 1960s and 1970s. Fearfully, we looked for scapegoats, and found them in the women's movement. Fearfully, we waited for the increase in women and mothers in the labour force to level off, to retreat, but it did not. Fearfully, we watched a welfare system designed for the few expand and burst in attempting to care for the many. Fearfully, we opened the paper to see what children have suffered, even died, because we had been too fearful to act on their behalf in a changed world.

But ours is a time of fear and sorrow only if we choose to make it so—only if we turn away from the very real needs of today's children and families today and continue to grieve for an era that had a beginning, and has now reached an end.

IN SEARCH OF MODELS FOR THE 1990S

If we seek models to understand our task as child-care professionals in the 1990s, we will not find them in the welfare "day cares" of the 1950s, the progressive nurseries of the 1920s, or the day nurseries and creches of the late 1800s. These are all models for the children of the few, either the rich or the poor, furtively promoted in the shadow of mother-care. If we wish to understand the risks and the possibilities of other-care, away from the imposing presence of mother-care, we must turn either to our very recent history or to our distant history—of the 1820s and early 1830s—or to both. And if we want our young professionals to have a sense of pride in who they are and what they can accomplish, then they must be made aware that it is not they who have been despised these many years, but the threat they represent—a threat not only to the Victorian family, but to the structure of the socioéconomic system that lies behind the veil of our mother-care ethic.

Just as we should not turn to the creches, the day nurseries, and the settlement kindergartens as our most informative history, neither should we turn today to models of the education system or the social service system to construct the child- and family-care programs Canada so desperately needs. We must construct a system that puts *all* children and *all* families at the heart of the matter. We cannot afford the "one best system" approach that characterized the formation of public schools throughout North American, for not all children and not all families are the same (Tyack, 1974). We cannot afford the professional distancing and parent/professional rivalry that typify too much of our educational and our social service systems. We cannot afford the stigmatism and family-deficits orientation that characterizes our welfare programs.

We must create something better than what we could borrow from other systems. Our Canadian approach must focus on the child *and* the family, and we must recognize that no "one best system" can meet the range of needs presented by families today. We must recognize that for many parents, being able to stay home with a child or children without fear of losing their place in the work force is their preferred option. We must recognize that for others, having a caregiver in their own home works best; for others, a family child-care home; and for still others, a child-care centre. The system must allow for and be responsive to a multitude of needs. It must be supportive rather than restrictive of parents and their choices. And the care that children receive must be of the highest possible quality, be it from parents or from other caregivers.

CONCLUSION

The challenge for Canada is to never lose sight of the child even as we face the complexity of economic, social, and familial change. The challenge is to create something that has never before existed in North America: a system of quality child care with viable options that respect individual children's needs and their rights not only to a safe and secure environment, but also to an environment that builds and develops their strengths and empowers them for the future.

We must realize that while this challenge is unique in our century, it is not—and must not be construed as—unique across all time, nor should it be viewed as the Armageddon of the family. This is a time of social, economic, and familial transition. Such transitions have happened before in North America, and they will happen again. Ours is the excitement of being active professionals practising on the cusp.

When transitions not dissimilar to these took place in Western society in the early 1800s, there were individuals who did step forward on behalf of children and shared their vision of a better future for those children. Owen, Alcott, and Russell are but three who saw in their time of transition opportunities for the good and worked to create positive experiences for children. They are part of our strong and healthy roots. It is time now, in our own period of transition, for individuals, groups, and associations to step forward and lead the way on behalf of children and families. The times are challenging and we, as professionals, must rise on wings of our own creation to meet those challenges.

Editor's Note

This chapter was adapted from a research keynote address for the first Canadian Child Day Care Federation conference, held in Winnipeg in April 1989. Appreciation is extended to the conference organizers.

REFERENCES

Albany Infant School Society. (1829). *Proceedings*. Albany: Albany Christian Register.

Alcott, A.B. (1830). *Observations on the principles and methods of infant instruction*. Boston: Carter and Hendee.

Bernard, J. (1974). *The future of motherhood*. New York: Penguin Books.

Feeney, S., Christensen, D., & Moravcik, E. (1987). *Who am I in the lives of children?* Toronto: Merrill.

Fitzpatrick, E.A. (1911). *Educational views and influence of De Witt Clinton*. New York: Teachers College Press.

Infant School Society of the City of Boston. (1833). *Fifth annual report*. Boston: Perkins and Marvin.

Jenkins, J.W. (1978). *Infant schools and the development of public primary schools in selected American cities before the civil war*. Unpublished doctoral dissertation, University of Wisconsin, Madison.

Kraditor, A.S. (Ed.). (1966). *Up from the pedestal*. Chicago: Quadrangle.

May, D.L., & Vinovskis, M.A. (1976). A ray of millenial light: Early education and social reform in the infant school movement in Massachusetts, 1826–1840. In T. Harevan (Ed.), *Family and kin in urban communities*. New York: Watts. (ERIC Document Reproduction Service No. ED 111 530).

Owen, R. (1841). *Address on opening the Institution for the Formation of Character at New Lanark*. London: Home Colonization Society.

Owen, R. (1970). *Book of the new moral order*. New York: A.M. Kelley. (Original work published 1842)

Pence, A.R. (1980). *Preschool programs of the nineteenth century: Towards a history of preschool child care in America*. Unpublished doctoral dissertation, University of Oregon, Eugene.

Pence, A.R. (1986). Infant schools in North America. In S. Kilmer (Ed.), *Advances in early education and care* (p. 25–40). Greenwich, CT: JAI Press.

Phillips, C.E. (1957). *The development of education in Canada*. Toronto: Gage.

Roberts, A.F.B. (1972). A new view of the infant school movement. *British Journal of Educational Studies, 20*, 154–164.

Roopnarine, J.L., & Johnson, J.E. (1987). *Approaches to early childhood education*. Toronto: Merrill.

Rothman, S.M. (1978). *Woman's proper place*. New York: Basic Books.

Russell, W. (1826). Address. *American Journal of Education, 1*, 6.

Russell, W. (1829). Intelligence. *American Journal of Education, 4*, 462.

Russell, W. (1830). A lecture on the infant school system of education and the extent to which it may be advantageously applied to all primary schools. *Introductory discourse and the lectures delivered before the American Institute of Instruction*. Boston: Hilliard, Gray.

Salmon, D., & Hindshaw, W. (1904). *Infant schools: Their history and theory*. London: Longmans Green.

Shorter, E. (1977). *The making of the modern family*. New York: Basic Books.

Strickland, C. (1983). *Victorian domesticity*. Unpublished manuscript, Emory University, Atlanta.

Tyack, D.B. (1974). *The one best system*. Cambridge, MA: Harvard University Press.

Weisner, T.S., & Gallimore, R. (1977). My brother's keeper: Child and sibling caretaking. *Current Anthropology, 12* (2), 169–190.

Wightman, J.M. (1860). *Annals of the Boston primary school committee, from its establishment in 1818 to its dissolution in 1855*. Boston: G.C. Rand and Avery.

8

A Froebelian Perspective on Early Childhood Education

Barbara Corbett

Friedrich Froebel
Froebel's Influence in Canada
Froebel's View of Education for Young Children
Creativity
Play
The Kindergartner
A Day in a Froebelian Kindergarten
Conclusion
References

Friedrich Froebel has been called the "father of the kindergarten." In this chapter, his philosophy and pedagogy are described to illuminate the heritage of Canadian kindergartens. Froebel conceived his kindergarten for children aged three to seven. The word "kindergarten" (meaning "a garden of children") expressed his approach to child development, an approach that suggested nurturing, cultivation, and (where necessary) pruning. The years from three to seven were to be an integrated unit of education for each child and that unit would provide the foundation years for each child's future education.

Those who worked with these young children were called "kinder-gartners." They were nurturers and cultivators not of plants but of children. In the 1880s when Froebel's kindergarten was first introduced into Canada, the public objected to paying for the education of young children—who, they believed, should be at home with their mother. This attitude became even more set when parents and educators were presented with the Froebelian idea of educating children through their own play. So, in those early years only the one-year senior kindergarten experience was accepted and introduced into Ontario schools. Not until the 1940s did the kindergarten begin to extend downward to include three- and four-year-olds in what has come to be known as junior kinder-garten.

FRIEDRICH FROEBEL

Friedrich Froebel (1782–1852) was a German educator who followed in the same line of modern progressive educators as the Geneva-born Jean-Jacques Rousseau and Swiss educator Heinrich Pestalozzi. Froebel lived during the time of the great classical composers Mozart and Beethoven and was at one time a soldier fighting against Napoleon. In fact, it was while in the army that Froebel formulated and discussed his educational views with fellow soldiers. During the marches he made two lifelong friends who, after the war, worked with him to fulfil his educational dreams. A residential school for boys was established in Keilhau, Germany, in 1819; then, in 1837, the first kindergarten.

An interesting story surrounds the word "kindergarten." Apparently, Froebel was hiking with friends along a mountain trail; they had stopped to view the valley below, with the village tucked into the surrounding hills, when Froebel suddenly shouted, "Eureka, I have it. Kindergarten shall be the name of the new institution!" (Froebel, 1889, p. 137). Prior to that he had referred to the class for the youngest children as a "Kleinkinderbeschaftigungsanstalt"—meaning "a place where young children are occupied." This cumbersome title failed to express his child-development approach to education.

Froebel's own life had had both its joys and sorrows. His mother had died when he was an infant. Consequently, he had been brought up by his father, a Lutheran minister, and his step-mother. Possibly his most beloved relative was a maternal uncle with whom Froebel lived as a young teenager while attending school. He loved nature and trained as a forester. Later he studied architecture as well as mineralogy at university. Needing to work in order to pay his way at university, he began tutoring students. Eventually he accepted a post as a classroom teacher. He took to teaching readily.

His educational career was chequered, with both successes and failures. His work with children was exciting and productive, but his educational theories were too far ahead of his time to be understood by other educators. Near the end of his life, when he was in his late sixties, the Prussian government, controlled by the aristocracy, delivered the final blow to Froebel's educational dreams and professional career. Suspicious of his teaching because it was designed to educate all people—and, therefore, they felt, posed a threat to the established government—the government banned the kindergarten as a revolutionary activity. Froebel died while the kindergarten was still under that ban. Before his death, however, he expressed the belief that the kindergarten could best take root and thrive in North America.

Europe's loss was North America's gain. The first Froebelian public-school kindergarten was opened in 1876 in St. Louis, Missouri; the second, in 1883 in Toronto. By 1887, the Ontario provincial government offered grants to public-school kindergartens; it was one of the first government systems in the world to do so. Gradually the kindergarten flourished and spread across the continent to become a part of all public-school systems in American states and most of those in Canadian provinces.

FROEBEL'S INFLUENCE IN CANADA

Froebel's influence on Canadian education has been extensive (Phillips, 1957). All kindergartens in Canada can trace their roots to the one that was introduced into the Toronto public-school system in 1883. In these Froebelian-influenced kindergartens there were circles, singing games, art occupations, and other activities—all aimed at child development and at encouraging a child's inner motivation. Froebel's influence extended further, into the elementary grades, with the spread of his ideas that education is to be enjoyed, that schools can be cheerful places, and that the teacher should be a guide in the learning process rather than merely an authoritarian disciplinarian. Integrated courses such as social studies, as well as the introduction of manual training and home economics, were Froebelian contributions. From Froebel, too, came the idea of parent–teacher cooperation. Many parent–teacher associations grew out of the early kindergarten mothers' meetings, which aimed to unite the home and the kindergarten. Such alliances could only benefit the child.

FROEBEL'S VIEW OF EDUCATION FOR YOUNG CHILDREN

Two of Froebel's views are profoundly woven into the Canadian educational system; these views significantly affect the quality of early childhood education. The first is Froebel's concept of kindergartens as providing the foundation years of the educational system. The second is his method of education, child development through play. Both ideas are expressions of his view of the universe. To understand Froebel's metaphysical basis is to understand why he suggested certain practices in children's education. That understanding can provide a basis for flexibility in choosing appropriate educational ways and means.

The kindergarten, attended during the years from three to seven, provides a foundation for education. This foundation is built in at least two ways: first, by the *impressions* children receive as a result of their kindergarten experiences and second, by the *love* that surrounds the child.

Experience leads to impressions. Impressions are the subtle, deep-rooted feelings, thoughts, and attitudes that a child forms in the midst of experiences. It must be kept in mind that the word experience refers not only to the child's activity but also to the quality of the child's interaction with others, whether children or adults. A child's senses are alive to odours, tastes, sights, sounds, and touch; all of these contribute to the impressions the child forms. Froebel referred to the five senses as "the doors to the inner child."

Love is the quality of life that determines a child's self-image, leading to a sense of security as well as of freedom and becoming the springboard for creative expression. Parental love is essential in a child's upbringing, but we must never underestimate the quality of love and caring offered by the child's "kindergartner" and later teachers nor the value of harmony between parents and kindergartner in their approach to child development.

Foundations are the beginnings and, therefore, determine ends. It is important that there be a depth and breadth of experience offered to the young child in all areas of development, for in the kindergarten experiences are found the beginnings of all the school subjects. At this stage, ideas are "caught" rather than "taught." Therefore, the kindergartner must provide not only a loving atmosphere but also a stimulating environment, both indoors and outdoors, that will give the child a wealth of suitable experiences.

The key to child development, however, is found not in the environment but in the *quality of interaction* between the kindergartner and the children. By listening to and observing the children, the kindergartner comes to know them and their needs, and can ensure that the impressions they form are both clear and accurate.

Key terms that reflect Froebel's view of the universe are "unity," "harmony," and "balance." What did Froebel mean by these words? To Froebel, *unity* implied relationship and interdependence. Applied to education, this word suggested a quality of relationship between parents; between parents and children; between the child and the kindergartner or other people in the community; and ultimately, between the child and God. This spiritual dimension in Froebel's philosophy reflects his view of Christianity. Froebel believed in the idea of God as the Father, and in the brotherhood (or sisterhood) of humankind; he referred to Jesus as God's son, the "mediator" between heaven and earth. Froebel speaks of the "divine spirit" within each individual, a reference to the third element of the Holy Trinity. All life, to Froebel, was woven together in relationship for good or ill, whether this connection was recognized and acknowledged or not. Humankind and the natural world live in interdependence on each other and ultimate dependence upon God as Creator and Sustainer of all life.

Harmony implied the blend possible in dealing with diversity or individuality. Although each part of creation is unique, the very differences actually imply an original unity. For example, each family member is unique but together they form one family. Harmony, however, can only be achieved through effort, self-discipline, and self-sacrifice. It might help to picture the possible harmony of individual parts by thinking of a symphony orchestra with its pleasant blending of diverse sounds.

Since the essence of the child from Froebel's perspective is the divine spark within, the child bears a resemblance to God. And since God is the Creator of all, the child, too, is both creative and self-active. That creative spark and energy is within, and can give birth to an idea. Skill involves formulating a plan and working persistently to accomplish the task in order to make that invisible inner idea a visible outward reality.

CREATIVITY

Creativity is both an energy and an attitude. It cannot be limited to a set period on a timetable. The playing, active child is full of creative thoughts and expressions. Froebel believed that children have the potential to live creatively in all aspects of daily life, in the arts, and in relationships. Since the essence of a child is the creative spark within, in likeness to the Creator, creativity is the natural expression expected from every child in all circumstances.

During the early years at one Froebel kindergarten, kindergartners observed an interesting example of creative thinking and action. At the time, the kindergarten was using rented space in a church. There was a large upstairs room as well as a basement playroom. A rubber-backed rug had been placed on the downstairs floor to provide warmth underfoot. When trying to remove the rug, the kindergartners found that it was stuck fast to the floor. A five-year-old in the kindergarten who lived just across the street observed the dilemma and asked permission to dash home. In a few moments he returned with a shovel and began scraping and shoveling the carpet off the floor. His system worked!

Another time a small group of six-year-olds, who appreciated their own individual work spaces, were concerned that their kindergartner had no desk. She would do her various tasks at the round table shared by all. One day on their way to the kindergarten, the children managed to collect enough pieces of scrap wood from local curbside trash to place a flat piece on top of two box ends, thus providing a "desk" for their kindergartner. It was an act of creative caring. Froebel claimed that any creative thought felt first in the heart and then worked out by head and hand was one of the purest expressions of childhood and extremely beneficial in child development.

PLAY

Froebel wished to educate the whole child in relation to nature, to humankind, and to God, and to do so by using the child's own energy. Thus, his method of education emphasized the child's play. Play reveals not only the child's inner essence but also the child's inner potential—temperament, interests, abilities, and so on. Froebel noted that the entire future life of the child is revealed in his or her play.

> Play is the first means of development of the human mind, its first effort to make acquaintance with the outward world, to collect original experiences from things and facts, and to exercise the powers of body and mind. (Von Marenholz-Bulois, 1887, p. 67)

As an expression of the child's inner spirit, play is both imaginative and creative. It is a happy approach to all activity.

Play is the mediator between children and their world; it places the child in the centre of all that happens. Children become aware of the greater context when involved in an activity. Not only do they gain many impressions that form the foundation for later learning, but they are able to discover the relationships among things, as well as their right and proper use.

Through play, children exercise the inner gifts of creative energy and develop the skills of self-activity—for example, the skills of formulating and expressing feelings and thoughts and of learning how to plan out an idea in order to bring it to fruition. They learn to plan time, to think about the resources needed for the task, to plan the best use of energy, and to develop the required skills. Such an education involves the whole child.

Childhood is the time for play. Children learn how to live as they imitate the life and work of adults and life in nature. Through play, their powers of concentration are increased, as they learn to sustain their efforts. Furthermore, a child's play is the root of work; attitudes and habits formed in play are later applied to work. This is why playing children must learn habits of self-discipline and self-control as well as develop all the necessary skills. Self-activity can only be realized through self-discipline—children must learn that there is a time to begin and a time to end, a time to take out and a time to put away, a time to listen and a time to speak, and so on. It becomes both tedious and unpleasant for a youngster if these guidelines are always applied externally by the adult. If self-discipline is being developed, the play is happy and has the potential to lead to joy in work. The happy child becomes the joyous adult.

Froebel's play method and his belief that the kindergartner should be the children's guide have in the past met with distrust and misunderstanding as well as outright opposition. As early as 1913, Mary McIntyre, inspector of kindergartens for the province of Ontario as well as director of the Toronto Normal School Kindergarten, realized that the Froebelian play method was understood by only a very few educators and was therefore misunderstood by most parents. Even school inspectors in Ontario had little grasp of Froebelian views. It *was* difficult to introduce an active-play approach into a school system that was based on the work ethic—and on work that was often both difficult and unpleasant. How could the kindergarten, with its emphasis on play and the joy of learning, become the foundation of such a school system?

Kindergarten–primary classes were introduced into Ontario public schools in 1915 in an attempt to harmonize the primary grades with kindergarten education. It was hoped that the kindergarten–primary classes would be the means whereby the primary grades would adopt the kindergarten methodology of play. Instead, however, the new classes became the channel for two aspects of primary education to enter the kindergarten. One was the idea that kindergarten children should begin the serious business of school work as well as play; the other, the idea that the five-year-olds were to be introduced to the three Rs.

Most kindergarten teachers in the 1930s and 1940s saw the value of involving children in the learning process through the children's own activity, but that activity began to take different forms depending on how well the teacher understood Froebel's guided-play method. There were always those who provided the children with ideas, expecting these to be duplicated. This approach can still be seen in mathematics and reading-readiness activities as well as in arts and crafts.

The idea of "free play," which opposed directed activity of all kinds, came to Canada in the 1930s from the United States. An American group who called themselves Reconstructionists and who were very much influenced by new studies in child development, came to believe that Froebelian toys and methods were restrictive. They therefore discarded them all and introduced large floor blocks, outdoor play equipment, large paint easels, and the like. Children were encouraged to play freely in this open environment.

The path that lies between the broad roads of directed activity and free play is Froebel's *guided* play. Froebelian kindergartners work with small groups of children; the adult/child ratio is lower than that in many present-day kindergartens and child-care programs. For example, three-, four-, and five-year-olds are in groups of nine children, while six- and seven-year-olds are in groups of twelve to fourteen children. The kindergartner has time and energy for each child and can maintain a joyful Froebelian attitude and spirit in interacting with each one. The low adult/child ratio is important if we are to educate children through their own individual ideas, helping each one to plan and to do. All life skills are involved, as well as the three Rs!

THE KINDERGARTNER

Truly productive child development can take place only if the kindergartner is the child's guide and not the originator of every activity, or even the idea of it and the planning of how it should be carried out. The kindergartner is responsible for providing an atmosphere of love, freedom, acceptance, and encouragement; for providing an orderly environment both indoors and outdoors; and for creating opportunities for challenging and stimulating activities. What makes all the children's experiences educational is the interaction that takes place between the children and the kindergartner. The kindergartner guides the children by word and song in order to help them form clear and accurate impressions from their experiences. As a guide, the kindergartner leads the children through each experience, using words to encourage, make suggestions, and aid the children in their productive purposes but not to interfere with, direct, control, or manage the flow of the children's play. The Froebelian admonition to "follow the child" does not mean catering to the whims of children, but knowing each child so well that we can select and guide the child into those activities that will best further that child's development.

A DAY IN A FROEBELIAN KINDERGARTEN

What follows is a description of a typical day in the Froebel Kindergarten in Mississauga, Ontario.

Kindergarten Circles

The day begins with the Opening Circle. A mix of ages is involved from the three-year-old to the seven-year-old. Each child is greeted by the kindergartner in song and responds in kind; other songs are sung and comments exchanged. The kindergartner presents a Biblical or inspirational thought for the day—for example, "What does it mean to be a good Canadian/a good Samaritan?"; "Children obey your parents for this pleases God"; or "God created the universe and we, like God, are also creators; so what can we make today?" A child often begins by saying, "Do you know what?" The children give examples from their own understandings and experience: "I take out the garbage," "I help Daddy wash the car," "I always ask my Mom if I can go to a friend's house," "I'm going to paint a picture," or "I'm going to make a storybook." The children give shape and meaning to that 20-minute circle by their comments and sharing. The kindergartner's songs and words build on their thoughts.

The circle concept comes out of Froebel's view of unity. The children and kindergartner are one as they sit in a circle formation, everyone equal, having a share in the conversation and activity. Each one is respected when he or she speaks, including the kindergartner. It is not a "teaching" circle (as it has been interpreted in many early childhood programs) but rather a *nurturing* circle. As the ball is the child's first plaything and its shape represents an unbroken line, the children and kindergartner are one in relationship in the circle setting.

There is another Froebelian circle in the middle morning or afternoon: the Singing Games Circle. Froebel suggested that the play formation could also be an oval, a square, a triangle, or some other shape, depending on the play and the children's needs. Here the play consists of singing games that imitate the life and work of adults (for example, "Oats, Peas, Beans and Barley Grow") as well as life in the natural environment (for example, "Caterpillar Creeping Ever"). The play also helps build physical agility.

The Froebel Gifts

The Singing Games are frequently an outgrowth of the children's play with the Gifts, the Froebelian toys. The Froebel Gifts, of which there are ten, fall into four categories—solids (I to VI), surfaces (VII), lines (VIII), and points (IX). The tenth Gift is a combination of sticks and plasticine balls that permits the child to build dimensional constructions. The shapes include hand-sized balls, cylinders, blocks, tablets, sticks, rings, and points. The kindergartner and a group of eight or nine children, each child with his or her own container of the same Gift, play at a large round table. The children create their constructions with the materials of the Gift, using their own experiences and imaginations to reproduce the world they have internalized. Each child takes a turn at telling a story about his or her construction while the kindergartner and others listen. Afterwards the kindergartner weaves all the stories into one, uniting the play of each child in the group and thereby nurturing the group's unity. Each child's contribution is important, for it has become a part of the total story.

The Gifts are simple toys that allow children to express their impressions of the world they know and feel. They help in building language, mathematical understandings, and design patterns because the child is able to connect deed and word by using these concrete materials. From the Gift play, each child develops a greater awareness of the objects in his or her environment and their connections.

Activity Times

Other times in the kindergarten day are divided into activity blocks. The two activity blocks for the three-, four-, and five-year-old children are (1) Gift play at the table, then floor play with larger toys and equipment; and (2) art occupations and outdoor play. The six- and seven-year-olds have four activity blocks: (1) language arts; (2) theme studies; (3) mathematics; and (4) art occupations and outdoor play. As well, all the children enjoy snacks, story time, music, and playroom activities every day. Froebel's curriculum includes the beginnings of all traditional school subjects—science, social studies, language arts, French, mathematics, music, physical education, and art—as well as spiritual nurture through Christian teachings and the encouragement to be creative in discovering and solving problems. This curriculum was designed to develop the child fully—physically, mentally, emotionally, socially, and spiritually—in a rounded, balanced way in relationship to God, humankind, and nature.

CONCLUSION

Friedrich Froebel, a German educator, not only founded the kindergarten, but also, by focusing attention on young children, gave a heightened importance to the early years. By calling his educational institution a "kindergarten," he helped determine that our course in Canada would be education through child development. His method of education involved learning through play, with the kindergartner (the child-nurturer) serving as the children's guide in the learning process by providing professional, skilful interaction.

Play is an expression of the young child's energy. Froebel believed that every child possesses the creative spark in likeness to God, the Creator, and that this originality reveals itself in daily life, artistic expressions, and relationships. At the same time, children—through their own activity complemented by the kindergartner's guidance—can develop skills and habits of self-discipline. The ideas are the child's own; with guidance, the ideas are planned out and executed by the child.

The circles symbolize the unity between children and kindergartner. They provide a forum for the group to share equally in expressing ideas and recounting experiences, a forum in which everyone, including the kindergartner, learns from the others. The Gifts are table-size Froebelian toys in fundamental natural shapes; using these allows children to build a microcosm of their world and encourages language development, mathematical understanding, and a sense of design or proportion.

The kindergarten day is divided into activity blocks, in which the beginnings of all school subjects are experienced. Early childhood education is a most important part of the educational spectrum, for beginnings determine possibilities and end results. If education is to be viewed as a continuum from kindergarten or infant care, sensible and wholesome educational principles must be applied throughout.

We are fortunate in Canada that the Froebelian kindergarten is our heritage. While Froebel's ideas had changed the nature of Canadian education by the turn of the century, they have only begun to grow from those roots and to flourish. Certainly Froebel's philosophy and approach to early childhood education require reflective study, for they have more relevance for us today than they had in his own time. Knowledge of our Froebelian roots in Canada will give us the insights we need to nurture and cultivate our young children.

The kindergarten years, as an integrated unit of education, have a crucial role as the foundation of the educational system, the context in which the young child is developed through play. And the schools must continue that development with activities that use each student's creative energy, for it is the expression of energy that needs to be guided, with the child being taught the wisdom and skills of self-discipline. The kindergartner holds the sacred key to unlock that inner potential and free each child for productive, creative, helpful living.

REFERENCES

Corbett, B.E. (1980). *A garden of children*. Mississauga: Froebel Foundation.

Corbett, B.E. (1989). *A century of kindergarten education in Ontario, 1887–1987*. Mississauga: Froebel Foundation.

Froebel, F. (1889). *Autobiography of Friedrich Froebel*. E. Michaelis & H. Keatley, Trans.). New York: C.W. Bardun.

Hughes, J.L. (1899). *Froebel's educational laws*. New York: D. Appleton.

Ontario. Ministry of Education. (1985). *Report of the Early Primary Education Project*. Toronto: Ontario MOE.

Ontario. Ministry of Education. (1985). *Teaching and learning in the primary years*. Toronto: Ontario MOE.

Phillips, C.E. (1957). *The development of education in Canada*. Toronto: Gage.

Von Marenholz-Bulois, B. (1987). *Reminiscences of Friedrich Froebel* (Mrs. Horace Mann, Trans.). Boston: Lee and Shepard.

9

Multiculturalism in Early Childhood Education

Karen R. Mock

Background, Definitions, and Rationale
Multicultural Education for Young Children
Principles for a Multicultural Curriculum
The Successful Multicultural Educator
Conclusion
References

Multicultural education attempts not to eliminate differences but to build on cultural diversity as a strength in the classroom and in our Canadian society. The rationale for multicultural education at the early childhood level is to be found in the principles of child development—that is, what we know about how children develop cognitively, socially, and emotionally—and the implications of that development for effective teaching and learning. This chapter explores and explains these issues.

BACKGROUND, DEFINITIONS, AND RATIONALE

Canada will soon celebrate the twentieth anniversary of the federal government's policy of multiculturalism within a bilingual framework. The Royal Commission on Bilingualism and the Biculturalism (the "B. and B." Commission) was set up in 1963 as a response to the Quiet Revolution and the birth of separatism in Quebec. The Commission's primary mandate concerned the relations between English-and French-speaking people in Canada, but it was also charged with taking into account the contribution made by other ethnic groups to the cultural enrichment of Canada and the measures that should be taken to safeguard that contribution. An entire volume of the Commission's five-volume report was devoted to "the other ethnic groups"; in response to that volume, the federal government announced the policy of "multiculturalism within a bilingual framework" in October 1971.

Since then, the concept of multiculturalism has been entrenched in our constitution and in the Charter of Rights and Freedoms; many provincial governments have followed suit with similar official policies regarding multiculturalism, race relations, and human rights. It is important to note that since the "B. and B." Commission, it has been emphasized that, in a multicultural society, we must pay attention to race relations and to inclusive language (that is, it is inappropriate to marginalize people by referring to them as "other" groups), so that we may ensure that all groups have equal access to the rights and privileges of this country, and that barriers to equality are removed. But what does this—or *should* this— mean for educators across the country, and for early childhood educators in particular?

According to the definition adopted by the Canadian Council for Multicultural and Intercultural Education (CCMIE) in 1984, "Multiculturalism fosters a society and a Canadian identity in which people and groups of all cultures are accepted. Multiculturalism promotes human and group relations in which ethnic, racial, religious and linguistic differences are valued and respected."

Hohmann, Banet, and Weikart (1979), in *Young Children in Action*, offered the following definition: "Multiculturalism means understanding and functioning comfortably within more than one cultural context. It begins in the preschool with everyday experiences in play, language, art, music—not "lessons" about people and places remote from the child's experience" (p. 13).

In other words, multicultural education does not attempt to eliminate differences. It builds on cultural and racial diversity as a strength in our classrooms and in our Canadian society. Furthermore, multicultural education at the early childhood level is in keeping with the principles of child development and what we know about how children learn and how they develop cognitively, socially, and emotionally.

Teachers of young children know, and research has confirmed, that early experiences provide the foundation for later learning, and that during their preschool years children develop many basic cultural attitudes and values that will last a lifetime. Early childhood educators also know how important self-esteem and self-worth are to learning and development. It follows that if we are to raise children in an increasingly diverse multicultural and multiracial society, "in the daily classroom experience, schools must attempt to communicate a basic set of ethics aimed at instilling a sense of self-worth, validity of differences, pride in heritage and place—all within a framework of unity" (Herberg, 1977).

In writing about the implications of multiculturalism for early childhood education, an important distinction must be made between the learning needs of young children and the learning needs of their caregivers. The rationale for multicultural education for very young children is to be found in what we know about how children develop and how they learn. It is now generally accepted by early childhood educators in Canada that quality programming for young children requires a recognition of individual differences in order to design a program based on sound cognitive-developmental learning principles combined with humanistic strategies for fostering socialization. Thus a case can be made for infusing multicultural content throughout the curriculum in order to build on every child's background experiences and cognitive skills to enhance learning and to foster a positive self-concept. For young children, multiculturalism must be an integral part of all early learning as a reflection of the Canadian context, not lessons about people or places that are portrayed as exotic and removed from the child's experience.

However, the learning needs of those who teach and care for young children are very different from the learning needs of the children themselves. Practitioners crave more information about the cultures and practices of specific ethnocultural groups and need to know how and where to get that information. In addition, they must learn to understand their own cultural values and assumptions and how their assumptions about child-rearing, discipline, parenting, education, communication, and other important cultural variables affect their interaction with children and families. Early childhood educators must become intimately aware of the effects of immigration, stereotyping, prejudice, and racism on human behaviour; must know something of the historical developments in these areas in Canada; and must understand their impact on the education of young children. They must develop skills for recognizing cultural bias in their teaching activities, curricula, books, audio/visual aids, and even in the testing and developmental-assessment tools they use. Students and practitioners in early childhood education are recognizing the need for and requesting specific instruction in multicultural education in order to address both theoretical and practical issues with enough depth to ensure effective implementation in their classrooms.

The theoretical rationale for multicultural early childhood education has been elaborated in more depth elsewhere (Mock, 1982, 1984a). A course for early childhood student teachers has also been described at some length (Mock, 1983). In this chapter we will move from the theoretical rationale to the practical necessity for multicultural education for young children; we will then focus on the implications of multiculturalism for the early childhood curriculum; and finally, we will examine the characteristics of the successful multicultural early childhood educator.

MULTICULTURAL EDUCATION FOR YOUNG CHILDREN

A summary of the developmental literature on racism led the Urban Alliance on Race Relations (1984) to conclude that by age four, children have a well-developed conception of race and racial differences in terms of the consequences of those differences in our society (see also Goodman, 1964; Milner, 1975). For example, many children are aware, by the time they enter school, that different roles are usually ascribed to people of different colours. They learn this from seeing how groups are depicted in the first books they read—or even from an unconscious recognition that certain groups are not depicted at all in the primers, comics, pictures, and posters in their environment. Visible minorities are virtually invisible in much of the material available to young children. At a very early age, children have been exposed to a wide variety of media that teach them that certain groups are more important than others in our society. Curriculum guides and visual aids depicting our multicultural and multiracial Canadian society are simply not available for early childhood classrooms. Not only does this dramatically affect the identity and self-concept of children from minority backgrounds, who are made to feel less significant by not seeing themselves reflected in the environment; it also results in many children having already developed well-defined racist attitudes by the time they get to school. Unless early childhood programs are modified to reflect the multicultural and multiracial population of Canada, they will continue to be a part of the problem, when they could be part of the solution. Multicultural education today must be permeated by an anti-racist perspective in all subject areas and school practices. We must aim to eradicate racism in all its forms.

Ramsey (1982), in making a case for multicultural education in early childhood, cites compelling evidence that in order to influence children's basic racial and cultural attitudes, we must start with the very young. All early childhood educators are aware of the importance of the early years in shaping attitudes, values, and habits of social behaviour. Good preschool education has been shown to have a lasting influence on children's later social and emotional behaviour and even on their future life chances (Schweinhart & Weikart, 1984).

Most early childhood educators today consider a "good" program to be one that recognizes individual differences among children and builds on each child's experiences as the foundation for learning, while providing opportunities for physical, social, emotional, and intellectual growth in a safe and secure environment. However, those same early childhood teachers rarely reflect on the cultural biases inherent in currently accepted notions of good programming for even the very youngest children. Sources of bias include the curriculum, methods, and materials used; the assessment instruments and testing procedures; and the teacher's expectations for the children's behaviour. For example, one goal of a cognitively oriented curriculum might be to help the children to become independent learners. Another goal might be to encourage participation in discussion, planning, and "hands on" activities. How odd these goals must seem to parents who raise children to obey authority and wait to be told exactly what to do, to be seen and not heard (particularly in the presence of elders or teachers), and to learn from demonstration and didactic instruction rather than from active participation. Current views on the most effective early childhood curriculum stem from modern Western philosophy, psychology, and pedagogy. Ethnocentrism, a common human trait, leads us to believe that our theories and practices are the "right" ones or even the "best" ones, while those of others are deemed to be "wrong"—or at least not as good—and therefore in need of change. However, such a conclusion runs contrary to a very important aspect of currently accepted early childhood programming—that is, the concept of adapting the program to the child, not the child to the program. Cultural background, ethnicity, and race are all aspects of individual difference that must be taken into consideration when designing an educational plan for any child. A teacher who is trying to avoid being prejudiced and who therefore believes that all children should be treated the same, regardless of their cultural background, is paying mere lip service to the concept of individual differences. It is especially important for early childhood educators to attempt to meet individual needs, whatever they are, so that young children may have equal chances to learn, develop, and succeed in the system. Any attempt to give children equal opportunity in education necessitates treating them differently. Recognizing and building on cultural differences are essential components of quality early childhood education in Canada today.

PRINCIPLES FOR A MULTICULTURAL CURRICULUM

Multicultural education does not mean a set of activities tacked on to the curriculum. It is an attitude, an underlying ethic, a commitment to broadening the cultural base of curriculum, methods, materials, and assessment strategies. Simple examples include commemorating a wide variety of holidays, festivals, and celebrations, not just those with which the teacher is most familiar. The doll or house centre must include props and costumes that reflect all, not just some, of the children's home experiences. Snacks should include a diversity of foods so that all children have an opportunity to try new things as well as an equal chance of recognizing very familiar foods or treats. Different assessment tools must be used for different children, and each must be administered in the appropriate language (or at least by someone who is sensitive to the cultural biases inherent in most of the currently available instruments). Evaluators must be absolutely sure that the relevant developmental characteristic has been isolated and is being evaluated effectively—that is, that the child's cultural background or language experience are not unfairly influencing the assessment results. Books, posters, music, and all other curriculum aides must be selected with a view to ensuring that all the children can identify with at least some of the material being used, and that all children will be exposed to the unfamiliar, rather than the minority-group children always being the ones who must adapt to a novel, strange, and sometimes bewildering environment.

In keeping with what we know about how young children learn, multicultural early childhood education must not consist of lessons or information about exotic places or "other cultures" remote from the child's experience. This approach emphasizes differences, and the children have no context into which to place the information. All currently trained early childhood teachers understand that children do not learn best when information is presented out of context. A far more effective approach is to emphasize the shared experience of all people through an examination of similarities and differences in everyday, common experiences. This is the approach taken in the resource book *Multicultural Early Childhood Education* (McLeod, 1984) and in Chud and Fahlman's (1985) *Early Childhood Education for a Multicultural Society*.

To design an effective multicultural program, the early childhood educator must learn about the racial, cultural, and socioeconomic background of the children in his or her care, including what experiences they have had with people from other groups and their attitudes toward their own and other groups. Then the teacher must respond to these variations, both by enhancing the multicultural climate in the classroom through appropriate multicultural materials, displays, and teaching strategies, and also by striving to enhance cooperation and acceptance among the children. The teacher must take an active role, since these behaviours are too important to be left to chance or for the children to work out on their own. Some examples will illustrate this point:

"Recess"

Recently, during an assessment, a seven-year-old girl of Chinese origin explained that she had to go out for recess to help her friends fight back against some children who were calling them names. "They call us 'Chinky' and say nonsense sounds that they think sound like Chinese, and they say they don't like us because we're good in class. So I don't like them and we're trying to figure out how to fight back. It hurts our feelings. I wish we could be friends."

Discussion with the child revealed that nothing was being done to prevent this kind of behaviour in the schoolyard or in the classroom. Further, the child believed that "if we told the teacher, she'd get mad, and then they would hate us more." Rather than ignoring the situation or blaming the children for it, the teacher should have been in tune with the attitudes of the children in the class. She should have addressed these attitudes in a preventive manner with effective multicultural curriculum resources and intercultural communication techniques to increase awareness and sensitivity among the children and to foster more effective race relations within and outside the classroom.

"The Nutrition Lesson"

In the absence of relevant multicultural material or appropriate personnel, the teacher may not be aware of the important influence a child's background can have on classroom behaviour. The teacher may therefore misinterpret a child's reactions to the program. As part of an integrated unit on nutrition, the teacher is presenting a lesson on the classification of various foods into their groups (fruits and vegetables, meat and equivalents, dairy foods, bread and cereals, and extras). She is well prepared. Based on her knowledge of how children learn, she has included various audio/visual aids and several concrete props in an effort to motivate the children and enhance participation. In general she has succeeded, for most of the children clustered around her table are volunteering answers to her questions and participating enthusiastically in the discussion. Most are able to complete the follow-up classification activities successfully, and some even go beyond what she required by colouring pictures or working on a related creative activity.

But one little boy, a recent newcomer to Canada from the West Indies, does not respond as enthusiastically as the teacher had hoped. He stands at the back of the group, eyes cast down a great deal of the time. He does not volunteer answers or participate in the discussion. When called upon, he mumbles so that the teacher asks him to repeat himself and the other children either giggle or look perplexed. He does not seem to know what to do during activity time. After some encouragement, those activities he does attempt are done either incompletely or incorrectly. The teacher interprets his behaviour as shy, withdrawn, possibly even indicating delayed or slow development. Since this is his usual pattern in other parts of the program, she is likely to report to his parents that she believes he needs remedial help, English as Second Language (ESL) or English as Second Dialect (ESD) classes, special education, or whatever special programs are available in her Board. On the other hand, she may simply continue to face the daily frustration of trying to "get through" to the child and "bring him out" while working with approximately 30 other children.

For any teacher who has faced the reality of trying to integrate a newcomer or minority-group child into the regular classroom, it is not difficult to identify with this scenario. Rather than "shy, withdrawn, and slow," another child's behaviour might seem to be "aggressive, impulsive, and hostile," but the problem remains: How do I help this child adjust to my classroom and succeed in my program when I'm under such time constraints and can't give him the kind of attention I think he needs?

For any parents who have faced the reality of hearing their child described in a way that seems totally unfamiliar and is not fully understood, it is not difficult to identify with that nagging fear that the child will fail in a school system whose ways seem inappropriate to meet those important goals that they feel only education can secure. For the parents, the problem remains: How can I tell the teacher what my child is really like, what I expect from him, and why? And how can I learn what I need to know about Canadian schools when I'm under such personal constraints?

And for the child who faces the daily reality of unfamiliar faces, a strange language or accent, a different school system, and the insecurity of constant change, although he may not be able to articulate it, the terrifying problem remains: How can I learn what I have to know here and get through this system with some degree of self-esteem when I can't even make my teachers and parents understand me and what I'm going through?

The teacher here is well intentioned. From her extensive preparation of the nutrition lesson, it is clear that she is up-to-date on cognitive-developmental teaching strategies; from her concern for the little boy, it is clear that she is a sensitive teacher interested in the individuals in her class. However, had she known more about the child's language and experiences, she would have realized she was not using the appropriate materials to teach that particular child according to the cognitive-developmental approach she knew. For example, even though the child spoke English, what the teacher was calling a "pear" (Bartlett) looked nothing like any "pear" (avocado) he had ever seen; the teacher's "apple" (an Ontario McIntosh, so familiar to the other children) looked nothing like what this child knew as an "apple" (the sweet "star apple" of Jamaica). Most of the other fruits and vegetables shown in the lesson he had never seen, let alone tasted or eaten. How could he know whether they had seeds or not (a concept very important to one of the classification tasks to follow)? So the child's reluctance to participate in the discussion was not due to slowness or shyness (though he may have been embarrassed by the other children's reactions to his dialect). And his problem with the later tasks was certainly not due to lack of ability or motivation. The fact is that without any previous experience with these foods, which were so familiar to the other children, the higher-order classification tasks were impossible for him. How different and exciting it might have been for him had the teacher included a mango—a fruit that none of the other children could identify. And how interesting and exciting it might have been for the other children if a plantain had been included so that he could have corrected them when they called it a "big banana."

I could have chosen a child representing any culture other than the dominant group in any school or community, for the classroom situation described above is a common occurrence for the minority-group child. The minority-group child not only feels different but also feels confused, inadequate, inferior, isolated from the peer group, and often misjudged by the teacher. This inhibits the child's learning and also reinforces inappropriate stereotypes for the teacher and the other children. However, with some assistance to the teacher in the area of multicultural programming, the typical scenario can be turned around so that the child feels valued, has more positive self-esteem, and enjoys greater acceptance by the peer group and more accurate understanding by the teacher. The child's learning is enhanced because it is founded in his or her own experience; the teacher and the other children are enriched by learning something outside the realm of their usual experience.

Multiculturalism must be an integral and continuous part of the curriculum, just as it is a fundamental part of Canadian society today. However, there are some educators who labour under the misconception that multicultural education is only important in classes and neighbourhoods where a variety of cultural and/or racial groups are represented or where race or ethnicity is a source of concern to the teacher. Multicultural education is relevant to all Canadian classrooms and child-care centres, regardless of the ethnic or racial composition of the children, because it builds on the cultural diversity that is a strength of Canadian society. We know that early experience influences later development. If young children are exposed to diverse ethnic groups and multicultural materials as integral parts of their programs right from the beginning, they will learn at an early age that multiculturalism is an integral part of Canadian life. Regardless of their own race or ethnicity, this will facilitate their increased future participation as accepting, well-adjusted adults in Canada's multicultural society.

THE SUCCESSFUL MULTICULTURAL EDUCATOR

What are the implications of multiculturalism for preparing early childhood educators to teach and care for young children in Canada today? And what are the characteristics of a successful multicultural educator? In the United States, a study of multicultural education has become part of the compulsory requirements for teacher certification in every state, and several Canadian educators have emphasized the need for effective multicultural teacher education (Chud, 1983; Mallea & Young, 1980; Mock, 1982, 1983, 1984a; and Ray, 1980, among others). But recent surveys of multiculturalism in early childhood education programs (Mock, 1984b, 1986b) reveal that most provinces have a long way to go to ensure that early childhood educators are effectively prepared to meet the demands of teaching and caring for young children in our multicultural/multiracial Canadian society. There is consensus among those currently involved in multicultural education that there are certain key components that must be included in the preparation of today's Canadian educators. These areas of study may be summarized as follows:

- *Intercultural awareness.* This includes an examination of one's own ethnocultural heritage and identity, as well as a study of other communities. This increases teachers' awareness of their own values and assumptions and develops their understanding of how these values and assumptions affect interactions and relationships with other people.
- *Cross-cultural child-rearing practices.* This includes an examination of how culture shapes and influences the child's development, increasing teachers' awareness that universal values may be expressed in very different parenting practices and that there is no one "right" way to raise or teach children.
- *Family and community resources.* This includes a study of various family structures and dynamics from a cross-cultural perspective; of the way immigration and resettlement affect families; and of what resources are available in the ethnic and minority communities to assist families and teachers.
- *Language development.* This includes a study of the developmental stages of language acquisition, including psycholinguistic and sociolinguistic perspectives; a study of the effects of second-language learning and of dialect differences; and knowledge of current issues and programs (for example, ESL/D, Heritage Languages, Bilingualism, and so on).
- *Multicultural curriculum development.* This includes a collection of programming suggestions for enhancing the multicultural nature of the classroom environment and activities, and an introduction to diverse curriculum resources.
- *Historical aspects of immigration and multiculturalism.* This includes an awareness of Canada's immigration patterns and policies and their impact on child care and schooling, along with various approaches to resettlement and integration (for example, assimilation, absorption, acculturation, and multiculturalism).
- *Stereotyping, prejudice, and racism.* This includes a study of definitions, theories, and research; an increased awareness of prejudice, racism, and discrimination as they occur in education and society; the development of skills for dealing with related problems and issues as they arise in the educator's personal and professional life; and an increased understanding of the real effects and dynamics of racism.

- *Interpersonal experience.* This includes a practicum or other opportunity for direct contact and interaction with members of a variety of cultural, racial, or ethnic groups; ample opportunity for discussion and personal involvement in an atmosphere that minimizes feelings of being threatened or inhibited; opportunities for teachers to come to terms with their own feelings, values, attitudes; and opportunities for personal growth and awareness.

The above list suggests that effective multicultural teacher education is interdisciplinary and multidimensional. Multicultural education must involve experiential learning and skill development or training, as well as material presented in a more traditional academic style. Community colleges and teacher education faculties are particularly well suited for integrating the theoretical foundation with the very practical strategies that have been found to be most successful in multicultural education. It is important to maintain a flexible and eclectic approach to such material. Experienced multicultural educators find that it is not unusual for some students to demonstrate a lack of understanding and lack of empathy (sometimes bordering on overt bigotry or hostility) at the beginning of a course. Many of those same students, however, develop considerably more insight and apparent understanding and are less affected by stereotypes after completing a required practicum. Student teachers should be required to work in a multicultural setting—such as an inner-city school, parent/child drop-in centre, ethnic community centre, an ESL or ESD program, an alternative school, or a parochial school—in order to have first-hand experience with children from a cultural background other than their own. One student teacher summed up her practicum experience as follows:

Multiculturalism is not merely a proposition to be considered by the people of Canada; it is a reality. Canada is a country of many languages, religions and traditions. As equal Canadians we must strive for harmony within this diversity. One of the most effective vehicles for realizing this goal is through education. Teachers within the system, early childhood inclusive, must be aware of and sensitive to the cultural components of the "mosaic." The teacher's understanding and acceptance of the multicultural facet of our country will facilitate the learning process and will promote positive attitudes in the children. In order to develop the teacher's awareness, multicultural training is essential. Within that training, the multicultural placement is invaluable. My own experience has helped me develop a working understanding not only of another culture but also of the role of multiculturalism within the educational process. It has been a very positive and most meaningful learning experience. (E. McIntyre, 1981).

Mallea and Young (1980) ask, "What does the ideal teacher in a system committed to multiculturalism look like?" To answer that question, they offer a three-dimensional teacher profile:

1. *Personal Characteristics.* The belief in cultural pluralism as a worthy goal of Canadian society, and a commitment to that goal; a recognition that in the past, minority cultures have generally been regarded as inferior to the dominant culture and that this has contributed to a negative self-image in many minority children; a commitment to enhance the minority child's positive self-image; a respect for the culturally different child and the culture that he or she brings to the school; the conviction that the culture a minority child brings to school is worth preserving and enriching; an awareness that cultural and linguistic differences are positive individual differences; a confidence in culturally different minority children and their ability to learn; a belief in his or her ability to contribute to a multicultural program; a willingness to learn more about multicultural education; flexibility in human relations and an ability to contribute and share ideas.
2. *Professional Characteristics.* Effective experience in a multicultural school environment; a knowledge of areas such as English or French as a second language related to bilingual and multicultural education; literacy in the minority language or dialect of the target population; an awareness of the implications of culture [for] learning; an interest in continuing to seek out better ways to reach culturally different students in the school; the ability to adapt materials to make them culturally relevant and to design relevant curricula; the knowledge of the research in multicultural education and its relevance; a commitment to the objectives of the program; a facility in applying modern approaches to the teaching of concepts, skills and performances; a readiness to participate in team teaching and other innovative staffing patterns and to co-operate with other adults in a classroom setting (i.e., teacher aids, parents, community resource people).
3. *Community Orientation Characteristics.* A recognition of the legitimate role of the parents in the educative process; a readiness to participate in a variety of minority community activities; a desire to involve minority parents and community residents in school community programs; an understanding of the dynamics of the minority community; a willingness to receive guidance and support from members of the minority community regarding the special needs of their children; organizational ability in sponsoring community service projects and programs to benefit a target community; a genuine sensitivity to the desires and needs of the minority communities which his or her school serves.

Parents of children in child-care programs corroborate that these are indeed the qualities, sensitivities, and skills they look for in caregivers. The need for parent and community involvement in early childhood education and child care and the need for increased sensitivity and awareness from staff were cited frequently in a recent cross-Canada study of the child-care needs of cultural minorities (Mock, 1986a). This study offers many personal examples in which families unknowingly lost their child-care space or subsidy because they did not know how to fill out the required forms or did not know that proper notice was required before taking a child out of child care temporarily for a holiday or to be cared for by relatives. The bureaucratic "culture" of child-care services delivered in English presents insurmountable obstacles to many immigrant and minority families. We need qualified interpreters with detailed knowledge of the child-care system in Canada, as well as qualified translators who can translate the system's documents, brochures, and questionnaires accurately. Where numbers warrant, linguistically diverse staff should be hired. Centres should at least have access to a pool of qualified personnel who can be hired on an *ad hoc* basis. Most parents surveyed pointed out the need for at least one person in a centre—more than one if possible—who could communicate effectively with parents and children from a minority cultural, linguistic, or racial background. First Nations peoples recommended that Native Indian children should be cared for and educated by qualified Native workers who can help strengthen their language skills and their familiarity with cultural customs and many black parents stressed the need for more black early childhood teachers so that black children could receive care in an environment that includes surrogate parents of their own race. Most of the people interviewed stressed not only that minority-group children need role models but also that all young children need to see a variety of ethnic- and racial-group members in positions of power and authority. It is important that we consider the characteristics of successful multicultural educators and also hire more teachers from racial- and ethnic-minority groups. We must adopt multicultural and anti-racist curricula in all early childhood settings, regardless of the ethnocultural composition of the client group. Indeed, child-care settings must examine all their policies and practices to see that the basic tenets of multiculturalism and harmonious race relations are upheld.

In summary, what we know about children's learning and development dictates that staff members in child-care and early childhood programs should not deal with cultural or racial minorities as if they come from foreign lands, but rather as integral to Canadian society. If this attitude is reflected in the curriculum and the environment created by educators and caregivers, then children at a very early age will learn that cultural diversity is the norm for Canada, that all cultural and racial groups are to be respected, and that no group should be treated with suspicion or in a discriminatory fashion.

Parents and child-care workers from ethnic communities do not necessarily prefer separate, culture-specific care and education; they do stress that centres serving a multicultural population should have staff members fluent in a variety of languages and skilled at cross-cultural communication, to ensure that children receive sensitive and empathic treatment. To be consistent with their beliefs about how children learn, all early childhood centres and child-care agencies in today's Canadian society must develop guidelines and implement employment equity programs. Incentives should also be offered to encourage racial- and ethnic-minority students to enter early childhood education training programs. In keeping with current needs and trends, colleges should recognize the credentials of immigrants with prior teaching or child-care experience and provide retraining or updating programs leading to certification as teachers or teaching assistants. Those who are responsible for hiring and promotion in early childhood settings should give special consideration to those with knowledge, skill, and experience in multiculturalism and race relations, and provide in-service training opportunities for staff members to gain such experience.

Clearly the policy and philosophy of multiculturalism in Canada has implications and ramifications at every level of the system of early childhood care and education. The student or practitioner who is interested in going into greater depth in this area will find the following resources helpful: the Canadian Council for Multicultural and Intercultural Education (CCMIE); the National Heritage Languages Resource Unit; Early Childhood Multicultural Services (Vancouver); Multiculturalism Canada; the Secretary of State; provincial ministries of Education, Citizenship, Culture, and Community and Social Services; provincial and local multicultural associations; and school boards with departments of multiculturalism and race relations. There is now a wide range of resource material and personnel to assist early childhood educators to develop the characteristics essential for providing culturally sensitive service to young children and their families in Canada today.

CONCLUSION

The purpose of this chapter was threefold: to emphasize the importance of providing multicultural education for young children, to suggest some practical principles for multicultural curriculum development, and to provide some guidelines and additional resources to enable teachers of young children in a multicultural society to develop the characteristics that will enhance successful multicultural teaching and child care. We must provide young children with multicultural education as early as possible because of what we know about cognitive development, attitude formation, identity, and self-concept. We must also continue to work at developing multicultural teacher-training programs. Colleges and universities must send their graduates out into classrooms and child-care centres well prepared for the multicultural/multiracial realities of Canada. And they must provide ongoing professional development to increase the ability of all early childhood personnel to provide equitable service to all children in their care.

Equality Now!, the report of the Special Committee on Visible Minorities in Canadian Society (1984), highlighted early childhood education as an area worth the attention of the proposed Ministry of Multiculturalism. Specifically, the recommendations of the parliamentary committee regarding early childhood education called for the following:

1. minimum standards for working in early childhood education;
2. multicultural teaching materials for use in training programs; and
3. curriculum materials that would positively influence attitudes and values during the period of early childhood education.

The inaugural meeting of the CCMIE National Multicultural Early Childhood Network (held in Ottawa in April 1989) revealed that since the publication of *Equality Now!*, strides have been made in all three of the recommended areas across the country. It is now important to ensure that the materials that have been developed are published and widely disseminated to practitioners, students, and teacher educators. By doing so, we can move toward celebrating the twentieth anniversary of the Canadian policy of multiculturalism feeling confident that this important and unique aspect of the Canadian context will have a firm foundation where it can make the greatest impact—in the care and education of our young children, who will grow up understanding, accepting, and believing in the rich cultural, ethnic, and racial diversity that is now and always has been an integral part of their Canadian identity.

REFERENCES

Canadian Council for Multicultural and Intercultural Education. (1984). Principles of multiculturalism [Poster].

Chud, G. (1983). Working with ESL preschoolers: Meeting the needs of the whole child. *TEAL Occasional Papers, 7*, 61–68.

Chud, G., & Fahlman, R. (1985). *Early childhood education for a multicultural society*. Vancouver: Wedge.

Dotsch, J., & McFarlane, J. (1981). *The newcomer preschool*. Toronto: Ontario Ministry of Culture and Recreation.

Goodman, M.E. (1964). *Race awareness in young children.* New York: Collier.

Herberg, E. (1977). Multiculturalism in education: A different kind of conference. *Multiculturalism, 1* (2), 22–24.

Hohmann, B., Banet, B., & Weikart, D. (1979). *Young children in action.* Ypsilanti, MI: High/Scope.

Mallea, J., & Young, J. (1980). Teacher education for a multicultural society. In K. McLeod (Ed.), *Intercultural education and community development,* (pp. 87-93). Toronto: Faculty of Education, University of Toronto.

McIntyre, E. (1981). Personal Communication.

McLeod, K. (Ed.). (1984). *Multicultural early childhood education.* Toronto: Guidance Centre, Faculty of Education, University of Toronto.

Milner, D. (1975). *Children and race.* London: Penguin.

Mock, K.R. (1982). Early childhood education in a multicultural society. *Multiculturalism, 5*(4), 3–6.

Mock, K.R. (1983). The successful multicultural teacher. *The History and Social Science Teacher, 19* (2), 87–97.

Mock, K.R. (1984a). Multicultural education at the early childhood level: A developmental rationale. In K. McLeod, (Ed.), *Multicultural early childhood education,* pp. 7–14. Toronto: Guidance Centre, Faculty of Education, University of Toronto.

Mock, K.R. (1984b). *Status report on multicultural education in early childhood education.* Ottawa: Secretary of State, Multiculturalism Directorate.

Mock, K.R. (1985). *Multicultural preschool education: A resource manual for supervisors and volunteers.* Toronto: Ontario Ministry of Citizenship and Culture.

Mock, K.R. (1985). Multicultural early childhood education: The best place to start. *Canadian Children, 10*(1/2), 31–41.

Mock, K.R. (1986a). *The Child care needs of cultural minorities.* Ottawa: House of Commons Special Committee on Child Care.

Mock, K.R. (1986b). *Multicultural early childhood education in Canada* (Vols. 1 and 2). Ottawa: Multiculturalism Canada, Secretary of State.

Ramsey, P. (1982, January). Multicultural education in early childhood. *Young Children,* 37(1), pp. 13–23.

Ray, D. (1980). Multiculturalism in teacher education. In K. McLeod (Ed.), *Intercultural education and community development,* pp. 79–86. Toronto: Faculty of Education, University of Toronto.

Schweinhart, L.J., and Weikart, D.P. (1984). Changed lives: The effects of the Perry Preschool Program on youths through age 19. Ypsilanti, MI: High/Scope.

Special Committee on Visible Minorities in Canadian Society. (1984). B. Daudlin (Chair). *Equality Now!* Hull, PQ: Queen's Printer.

Urban Alliance on Race Relations. (1984). Brief. Quoted in special Committee on Visible Minorities in Canadian Society, *Equality Now!* Hull, PQ: Queen's Printer.

10

Children of Native Indian and Other Sociocultural Backgrounds

Anne Lindsay

Language Use from the Sociocultural Background
Discourse and the Sociocultural Background
Discourse of Young Children
Significance of Sociocultural Differences for Discourse Style
Implications for Early Childhood Programs
Conclusion
References

An appreciation for the intricate and significant role of language in the development and education of young children is often well developed already among early childhood educators. However, especially when faced with the numerous demands of daily practice with young children, we may begin to use language as a tool that, while indispensable, is also invisible. Language in this context can be seen rather like water, a sort of universal solvent—critical but taken for granted. There are often few opportunities in the average day while working with young children to listen to and reflect on the language we use and hear used by children.

This invisible nature of language is basic to the concerns in this chapter. However, this invisible quality does not result simply from a deflection of our attention from the use of language itself. It also reflects the level at which we tend to focus on children's language. Our attention to children's language frequently concentrates on its information-carrying capacity or on the development of phonetic, semantic, and syntactic structures. This approach to language involves viewing it at the level of words and sentences. Here, however, language and its organization will be discussed at another level—the level above the sentence or clause, which is known as the level of *discourse*. Explorations at this level involving children and language development have not been done until recent years.

This chapter is specifically concerned with the relationship between children's discourse and their sociocultural background—with a particular emphasis on Native Indian children—and the implications of this relationship for children in early childhood settings in Canada. An understanding of discourse tells us that even when language is being used merely as a convenient tool to achieve some non-language-related goal, its significance does not in fact disappear. The ways in which language is organized and presented, or not presented, all carry meaning. In addition, work with cross-cultural communication has indicated that the structures that carry this meaning are deeply embedded in the sociocultural conventions of the speaker. Similarly, the audience's interpretation of meaning is rooted in knowledge acquired from their sociocultural background. The processes of acquiring this knowledge are part of the young child's language socialization.

LANGUAGE USE FROM THE SOCIOCULTURAL BACKGROUND:

Heath (1983) described the use of language in three English-speaking communities located in a small region of the southeast United States: Roadville, a white mill community; Trackton, a black mill community; and Maintown, a racially mixed middle-class town-oriented community. In these communities, Heath observed children from birth to the early school years, as well as the adults around them. She described the social and physical context of language use, the patterns of language use made available to the children, and the values and significance of different patterns of language use within the children's lives. She was able to provide strong evidence that the development of children's patterns of language use depends on the children's cultural background and the patterns of language socialization practised within this culture. From this study emerged a picture of three contrasting communication networks or language communities. Heath described these contrasting language communities in rich detail. Some examples of these descriptions will illustrate the extent of the contrasts between the three communities.

One such contrast involved adults' conceptions of their role in children's language development. In Roadville, this process was described as "teaching how to talk" (Heath, 1983, p. 113); in Trackton, as "learning how to talk" (p. 73). Children in Trackton were not seen as information givers or as answerers; in both Roadville and Maintown, adults frequently used questions to elicit information from children that was already known to adults.

Another difference among the three communities was reflected in the various approaches to contextualization and children's language. Children in Trackton compared and connected ideas from one situation to another by seeing similar patterns in the situations, not by labeling specific details. Heath described this view of a situation in which specific ideas are not separated from their context, as a gestalt. In Roadville, however, labeling items and their features was of central importance in language learning. In Maintown, children were also encouraged to practise labeling, but as part of a more complex interaction in which parents focused children's attention first on a scene, then on individual objects or events, then on labeling these, incorporating a turn-taking discourse pattern throughout. In Heath's view, this process allowed parents to "freeze" a scene, thereby helping children to observe and decontextualize objects and items and to practise related verbal strategies.

A third, and perhaps the most graphic, difference among the language socialization patterns in the three communities was apparent in the varying conceptions of "good children's stories":

> Children in Roadville are not allowed to tell stories, unless an adult announces that something which happened to a child makes a good story and invites a retelling. When children are asked to retell such events, they are expected to tell non-fictive stories which "stick to the truth". Adults listen carefully and correct children if their facts are not as the adult remembers them. In contrast, fictive stories which are exaggerations of real-life events, modeled on plots or characters children meet in story-books, are not accepted as stories, but as "lies", without a "piece of truth". (Heath, 1983, p. 158)

In Trackton, however, a "good story," while usually based on a real event, is a work of creative fiction:

> The content varies widely, and there is "truth" only in the universals of human experience. Fact is often hard to find, though it is usually the seed of the story. Trackton stories often have no point—no obvious beginning or ending; they go on as long as the audience enjoys and tolerates the storyteller's entertainment. (Heath, 1983, p. 68)

In Maintown, it is fantasies, structured in a story format, that are reinforced. Frequently these are requested and expanded on by adults. There is also wide variation in the use of the fantasy story by Maintown families to entertain their children.

The contrasts among these three communities illustrate how language socialization patterns can vary relative to their sociocultural context, even among three communities that speak the same language and are in close geographic proximity to each other. Heath (1983) argued that children's patterns of language use within their sociocultural context were "interdependent with the habits and values of behaving shared among members of that group" (p. 11).

DISCOURSE AND THE SOCIOCULTURAL
BACKGROUND

Other studies have focused on more specific patterns of language use—in particular, oral narrative discourse. Oral narrative discourse can be simply described as discourse, related orally in a narrative form, with narrative being understood to mean a relating of a past or ongoing experience (Heath, 1986). Studies focusing on adults from different cultural backgrounds have described different models of adult oral narrative discourse. These models provide further illustration of relationships between patterns of language use and the sociocultural context of the speaker. In these models of adult oral narrative discourse it can be seen that although the narrative task differs somewhat, they all depict a contrast to a model of mainstream North American speech in a similar narrative context.

One such model was described by Cooley and Lujan (1982). In discussing the public speeches of North American Indian speakers, they explained that to white North American listeners, these seemed unorganized and rambling. The speeches, however, were in fact organized, but using a different framework. According to Cooley and Lujan, the speeches presented a number of topics all related to a central theme, but with the relationship between these topics left implicit. A white listener, however, would expect this relationship to be made explicit. Furthermore, Cooley and Lujan explained that such lack of explicit intertopic information is rooted in cultural concepts of the role of the speaker, who is not expected to provide these intertopic relationships. It is considered instead the audience's role to make intertopic connections and interpretations.

Scollon and Scollon (1981), in their work with Athabaskan speakers in northern Alberta, described a similar contrast between Athabaskan Indian narrative discourse and that of white North Americans. They also described how features of inexplicitness in the Indian discourse conflict with the white listener's expectations. Moreover, they observed, the Indian narratives were organized into four units, rather than the three typical in mainstream North American discourse. As Cooley and Lujan (1982) had, Scollon and Scollon also interpreted these features of narrative discourse as expressions of the speakers' sociocultural values.

These models of adult oral narrative discourse support Heath's (1983) depiction of distinctly different language communities related to the sociocultural background of the speakers. Heath's work illustrated how three different communities practised distinctively different patterns of language socialization with distinctively different patterns of language use emerging in their children. Together this work suggests that young children who grow up with different sociocultural backgrounds could be developing distinctively different patterns in their use of language, and in particular, in oral narrative discourse—a form of discourse that, as discussed below, plays a central role in early childhood education programs.

DISCOURSE OF YOUNG CHILDREN

Heath's (1983) work described how children in their early years learn a wide variety of language strategies to use in varying situations within their broader sociocultural contexts. Although Heath's work was founded on a broad-based, long-term ethnographic study of three communities, she focused primarily on "the effects of the preschool home and community environment on the learning of those language structures and uses which were needed in classrooms and job settings" (p. 4).

Upon entry into mainstream school systems, some specific language strategies become especially significant. Although much emphasis has been paid to children's story-telling, children's ability to simply *talk about* or *tell about* something is a common and important element in these settings. This narrative task may be used in group sharing activities, discussions of books, and much of the informal discussion between adults and children about objects and events. It is also the narrative task that forms a common pattern for early writing tasks and for work within a language-experience or whole-language approach to early reading and writing. The importance of this particular narrative task in young children's development of language use has been emphasized by Heath (1986), Preece, (1985), and Scollon and Scollon (1981). In this open-ended narrative task, a child is both presenting certain information on a topic and presenting it to an audience. The audience's comprehension of the information the child is presenting depends on the child's ability to present it in a form that is comprehensible to an audience.

Other researchers have focused on the role of this "talk-about" form of oral narrative discourse in the early school years and on its relationship to children's sociocultural backgrounds. At this point, the comprehensibility of children's language to their audiences becomes intertwined with its acceptability, according to the conventions of the settings in which children find themselves.

Young Black and White Children in U.S. Schools

Michaels and Cook-Gumperz (1979) investigated black and white children's oral narrative discourse in the particular setting of the "sharing time" component of grade-one and grade-two programs. They argued that the teacher was using a very specific model of "good" oral narrative discourse in this activity—a model involving simple descriptive prose that incorporated an explicitly decontextualized approach to a clearly defined topic. Such a decontextualized approach, they said, assumed a minimum of shared background knowledge and context.

Michaels and Cook-Gumperz (1979) examined similarities and differences among the children with respect to the teacher's model of good oral narrative discourse. Through this process they identified two distinctly different narrative styles—two different sets of discourse characteristics among the oral narratives. A style they called *topic-centred* was described as "tightly organized, centering on a single topic or series of closely related topics" (p. 154). In this style, children explicitly stated connections between items. Combined with other techniques, such statements contributed to an overall sense of topic continuity in their narratives.

The other style Michaels and Cook-Gumperz (1979) called *topic-chaining* (and later, *topic-associating*). Here the children changed topics frequently, without explicitly stating connections between the topics. These narratives were described as giving "the impression of having no beginning, middle or end and hence *no point* at all" (p. 657). Michaels and Cook-Gumperz explained that a continuity of theme could, in fact, be found in these narratives. This continuity, however, depended not on explicit connections, but rather on intonation patterns and the listener's inferences based on shared common knowledge.

In an extended study of these oral narrative discourse styles, Michaels and Cazden (1986) argued that the preferred style for black children is the topic-associating style, and for white children, the topic-centred style. They found strong support for their findings in other descriptions of black narrative style and they concluded that "black children's ST [sharing time] narratives fall within a highly developed narrative tradition and that these children are approximately a well-formed adult standard" (p. 149).

As well as describing distinctively different oral narrative discourse styles for black and white children in the tell-about type of narrative task, Michaels and Cazden (1986) also described how these styles interacted with the teacher's model of good discourse in this context. With the black children's topic-associating style, the teacher had difficulty collaborating constructively with the narratives. The activity did not allow the teacher to help these children expand their narratives or to use more explicit language to help the children develop toward the teacher's model of good narrative discourse. In fact, her interventions often seemed interruptive. With the children using the topic-centred style, however, the teacher could collaborate constructively in helping children to develop and practise closer approximations to the model of good narrative discourse. In this way, Michaels and Cazden illustrated how these two oral narrative discourse styles not only differed from each other, but also seemed to be differentially effective in teaching and learning in this narrative task. In addition, Michaels and Cazden also described how the topic-associating narratives were much more likely to be evaluated negatively by adults (although not by black adults).

Michaels (1981) termed this conflict in the collaborative exchange between children and the teacher an unintentional mismatch. Factors of incompetence, prejudice, and lack of pedagogical responsibility were not seen as contributing to this mismatch. In addition, Michaels and Cazden (1986) also suspected that as this same narrative task was found in other activities in the program, this same mismatch was likely to be occurring in these other activities.

Although no researchers have examined this point as widely as have Michaels and her colleagues, others have contributed supporting points of view. Harris (1985) argued that inappropriate assessment of American Indian children's use of English can be founded in these children's discourse patterns—which, in turn are based in the children's sociocultural background. In New Zealand, Clay (1985) also indicated that there appeared to be "some kind of difference in the communication of Maori children and teachers" (p. 34). The point Clay identified as vulnerable in cross-cultural communication between teachers and children seemed to be similar to that identified by Michaels and Cazden (1986).

In summary, it would appear that young children from differing sociocultural backgrounds, at least by age four or five, may be using oral narrative discourse styles that differ from the style expected by their teacher. Apparently, a mismatch in styles may also seriously affect the quality of teachers' oral intervention in narrative exchanges and increase the possibility of negative assessment of children's narratives. The likelihood that this mismatch occurs in a type of narrative exchange common in many programs for young children increases the possible significance of such a conflict.

Native Indian Children in a Canadian School

The work of Michaels and Cook-Gumperz (1979), Michaels (1981), and Michaels and Cazden (1986) was used by Lindsay (1988) to examine the oral narrative discourse style of young Carrier Indian children in a British Columbia school. Using the descriptions of topic-centred and topic-associating narratives developed by Michaels and her colleagues, Lindsay described a small minority of these Indian children's narratives as topic-centred. The majority were using a third style, which incorporated some features of the topic-associating style.

This third style typically involved a series of units of approximately equal value in the narrative, with no clear beginning, middle, or end, and all related to a single topic. Explicit relations between the units were not observed. Instead, prosodic devices, especially the repetition of a characteristic intonation pattern, indicated the structure of the units of the narratives. Because of its dominance in the children's narratives, Lindsay (1988) termed this pattern the "common intonational contour." The pattern was characterized by a slight fall and then a rise in pitch at the beginning of the unit, with a fall and then a rise over the last few syllables. The beginning syllables were slower and more unevenly paced, while the ending syllables were more smoothly paced and contained the stress in the unit. The repetition of this intonational unit was emphasized by the repetition of syntactic and semantic structures in each unit, providing an overall rhythmic effect.

Lindsay (1988) suggested that this third style, which she labeled the *common narrative style*, may represent a distinct cultural style of narrative discourse among these children. This possibility was supported by descriptions of North American Indian narratives. For example, Cazden (1988) described Arapaho story-telling as serial and with no clear ending. Harkin (1988) also described a serial attribute in narratives of the Heiltsuk Indian people (a subgroup of the Kwakiutl people of the Northwest coast). The non-topic-centred narrative style used by the Carrier Indian children in Lindsay's (1988) study might also have been interpreted as disorganized by white listeners, just as Cooley and Lujan (1982) reported was the effect of North American Indian speeches.

Lindsay (1988) also suggested that the rhythmic repetition in the common narrative style seemed to make it more closely resemble a poetic rather than a prosaic style. This observation has been made elsewhere regarding North American Indian narratives (Hymes, 1982; Tedlock, 1983). Another connection between a cultural style and the children's narratives was made by Indian adults. Like the black adults commenting on the black children's topic-associating narratives in Michaels and Cazden's (1986) study, Indian adults did not judge Indian children's narratives negatively, but remarked that the children were using a familiar narrative style such as parents and elders used for story-telling.

The possibility that the style used by the majority of the children in Lindsay's study is also a cultural style is also supported by the resemblance of this common style to a style Heath (1986) described for this same type of narrative task in many societies or cultures. Heath explained that in the mainstream community, adults shape or coach children's narratives to include explicit connections between ideas. This comparison emphasizes one point about the common narrative style described for these Indian children: the style may differ most distinctively in comparison to the narratives of children who have grown up in mainstream, school-oriented communities. It may differ less from narratives in language communities that are not mainstream and school-oriented. This would be possible if, in mainstream, school-oriented language communities, adults were attempting to develop in young children a particular distinctive style of oral narrative discourse, at least in specific narrative contexts. This does not mean that the narratives of children from cultural backgrounds other than the mainstream, school-oriented one need be the same. Rather, as Cazden (1988) explained; "What seems similar about black and Arapaho stories is probably only their contrast with the topic centred stories told primarily by white middle-class children" (p. 12).

Lindsay's (1988) study suggested that at least one group of Native Indian children in a Canadian school was using a distinctive style of narrative discourse in the tell-about type of narrative task. This style was neither topic-centred nor topic-associating, but a third style that Lindsay suggested may well be based in these children's sociocultural background.

SIGNIFICANCE OF SOCIOCULTURAL DIFFERENCES FOR DISCOURSE STYLE

The work described so far suggests that differences in sociocultural background may be expressed through children's oral narrative discourse styles. This possibility provokes two observations about the relationships of sociocultural background, language, and young children's development. First, it suggests the degree to which children's sociocultural background may pervade their development. Frequently, multicultural programs for young children involve costume, food, song, and dance. Although these are undeniably aspects of cultural background, it also seems likely that children's sociocultural background may be integral to and expressed in much more complex and less tangible ways.

Second, this work suggests the need for awareness of the subtlety of language and its capacity to carry information far more complex than the meaning of the words and sentences used. The tendency to see language as a transparent medium (Cazden, 1988) or as transparent to fact (Gee, 1985), and the limitations of this point of view should be of concern to all educators, but particularly to those in cross-cultural situations involving young children in their first encounters with educational settings.

Preparation For Literacy

The above observations may suggest some possible directions for early childhood educators. However, to date the work in children's oral narrative discourse style and sociocultural background has concentrated on considering its significance for the acquisition of literacy, especially in the first years of school.

Literacy as a concept has received much attention in recent years.

However, one particular conception of literacy is of significance to educators, especially those involved in cross-cultural settings. Holdaway (1979) described a model that treats literacy as a language style, closely resembling that of books, and also as the language of schooling. He also emphasized that for many children coming to school, this language of schooling is foreign.

Scollon and Scollon (1981) also described a model of literacy—the model around which, they said, educational issues tend to orient. According to this model, literacy involves being able to understand and construct "essayist prose," a style of writing built from the discourse patterns and the underlying sociocultural conventions of the mainstream English-speaker. They argued that for children from such homes, the essential ingredients of this form of literacy are mostly complete before the age of school entry.

Heath (1983) described literate patterns of language use in the three communities of Trackton, Roadville, and Maintown. She emphasized the variation among these patterns and the fact that only the Maintown families prepared children for success in the type of language activities likely to yield further success in school.

These school-related conceptions of literacy define it as a narrow range of discourse patterns conducive to success in mainstream educational settings and closely approximating the written form of discourse known as expository prose. Understanding the existence of such a model suggests the need for schools and society to re-examine its appropriateness.

A number of researchers have examined the relationships between children's ways of using language, those expected by the school, and school success or failure (Genishi, 1987; Halliday, 1973; Heath, 1983; Wells, 1985). However, the specific mechanisms by which these relationships function have remained unclear. One approach to understanding these relationships better involves exploring how a mismatch between the oral discourse styles of teachers and children may affect the quality of teacher/child verbal interaction in key learning activities. Michaels (1981) argued that such activities as sharing time were an opportunity for young children to practise oral discourse skills that were required by what she called the "implicit literate standard" (p. 72) of the mainstream school. Michaels (1985) also argued that teachers seemed to feel that children "first need to gain control over simple 'topic-centred' forms of discourse as a *transition to literacy*; only then can they proceed to tackle more complex rhetorical and literacy texts" (p. 82). This process was termed an oral preparation for literacy by Michaels and Cazden (1986). Michaels (1985) emphasized that it is not the children's own narrative styles that affect the children's acquisition of literate discourse patterns, but rather the reduction in quality in the teacher/child interaction in these key learning activities (that is, those designed for practising the prose-like oral discourse style).

IMPLICATIONS FOR EARLY CHILDHOOD PROGRAMS

Although these studies are limited to specific populations, teachers of young children should consider the possible implications of this work. Children from non-mainstream sociocultural backgrounds, such as the black children in U.S. schools in Michaels and Cazden's (1986) work and the Carrier Indian children in the Canadian school in Lindsay's (1988) study, can be seen as more vulnerable than children from mainstream communities when entering mainstream educational settings. First, they may be less likely than children from mainstream backgrounds to have optimal access to teacher assistance in the kind of learning activities seen as important to literacy acquisition. Second, if oral narrative discourse styles do in fact represent the sociocultural background of the children who use them, this has implications for the children's cultural identity in the school system. For Native Indian children in Canada, both these implications are in direct conflict with the aims for their education as stated by the National Indian Brotherhood (1972)—namely, to optimize Indian children's opportunities for success in mainstream settings in Canada, while also protecting and nurturing the children's Indian identity.

How does a teacher of young children integrate these considerations into daily practice with children from differing sociocultural backgrounds? Perhaps the most important step to meeting these children's needs better lies in early childhood educators' willingness to continue to develop their awareness and understanding of how sociocultural factors may be blended into the composite of influences forming children's identities, whether the children are from a different sociocultural background or from the mainstream. As educators of young children, we also need to be constantly aware not only of the sociocultural patterns that they bring to us, but also of those we bring to them.

Among teachers of young children, the use of the topic-centred discourse style as a standard of reference needs to be clearly understood. For example, materials for early language programs often incorporate teaching suggestions and evaluation materials based on stories with a beginning, middle, and end. An awareness of this standard of reference and its limitations, especially in children's earliest encounters with educational settings, underscores the need for an alternative to the school standard. Montgomery (1982) advocated the use of the "natural text" rather than an "artificial text" for teaching Native American languages. She argued that a natural text has an inherent capacity to attract students' attention and interest. She also argued that a natural text retains the appropriate sociocultural linguistic information, which can then be used by the students. One of the earliest advocates of the use of the "natural text" (or what has become known as "language experience") was Sylvia Ashton/Warner (1963), who developed this practice in her work with Maori children in New Zealand. Language-experience approaches may have special merit for programs involving children from varied sociocultural backgrounds.

Finally, educators working with young children and using the non-traditional approaches discussed above may want to consider a further possibility, at least for children from North American Indian backgrounds. Traditionally, children's language—including narratives—has been recorded in conventional prosaic form. However, as was observed in Lindsay's (1988) study, Indian narratives seem to resemble a poetic rather than a prosaic style.

What follows is a sample of one of the children's stories from Lindsay's (1988) study, transcribed first in a prosaic style such as might have been used in a dictated-story activity, then in the format that emerged from Lindsay's study of the children's discourse style.

> I played and we played not it. And I played cops and robbers and I was the robber. They put me in jail and after that I played baseball and I batted first and I ran home free. And last night we were playing gunfight and my cousin won and my cousin won a control car. I let him have it and I went to town with my mother and dad. We bought groceries and she bought me a gun and I went back to home and we went to town and after that we went hunting. We shot a moose. Then we played not it and hide and seek and we're playing fight. This morning we're all playing next to Bernie's cars and we ate rolled oats. We went outside. After that we had fun after school and that's the end.

I played
and we played not it
and I played cops and robbers
and I was the robber
they put me in jail
and after that I played baseball
and I batted first
and I ran home free
and last night we were playing gunfight
and my cousin won
and my cousin won a control car
I let him have it
and I went to town with my mother

and dad
we bought groceries and she bought me a gun
and I went back to home
and we went to town
and after that we went hunting
we shot a moose
then we played not it and hide and seek
and we're playing hide and seek
and we're playing fight
this morning we're all playing next to Bernie's cars
and we ate rolled oats
we went outside
after that we had fun after school
and that's the end

The structure of the second transcription seems to match the flow of the child's thought more accurately. It also seems to express the child's meaning more clearly. Teachers of young children may want to consider such alternative forms of transcription for children's dictated narratives and other language. This may also present other possibilities for choosing written material to present to young children.

CONCLUSION

The role of the early childhood educator extends beyond superficial knowledge of a particular cultural group—knowledge, for example, like that described by Lee (1985) of the group's sociocultural status, child-rearing practices, family roles, and views of technology. As Kleinfeld, McDiarmid, Grubis, and Parnett (1983) discovered, it also extends beyond the realm of standard competencies such as subject knowledge and discipline, and beyond political skills such as relating to the culture: in their study, teachers identified as "good teachers" in Inuit and Indian communities were most often described in terms that emphasized strong affective qualities.

If teachers of young children of varying sociocultural backgrounds are going to accept the responsibility to educate these children, they must consider sociocultural determinants such as those described in this chapter. But such a commitment also requires something more fundamental—that early childhood professionals must value cultural identity as highly as they value individual identity. The early childhood educator is therefore faced with a humanistic, rather than a purely academic issue.

There remains much to be discovered about how our sociocultural backgrounds influence the ways we live in, understand, and describe our world. Young children of Native Indian, as well as other, sociocultural backgrounds in Canada depend on the willingness of early childhood educators to assume responsibility for the quality of their early experiences in educational settings. As we have seen, this task requires not just a deeper objective understanding of children, their language, and their sociocultural background, but also a reflective process by which we as early childhood educators come to better understand what we bring to them.

REFERENCES

Ashton-Warner, S. (1963). *Teacher*. New York: Simon and Schuster.

Cazden, C. (1988). *Classroom discourse*. Portsmouth, NH: Heinemann.

Clay, M. (1985). Engaging with the school system. *New Zealand Journal of Educational Studies, 20*, 20–38.

Cooley, R., & Lujan, P. (1982). A structural analysis of speeches by Native American students. In F. Barkin, E. Brandt, & J. Ornstein-Galicia (Eds.), *Bilingualism and language contact* (pp. 80–92). New York: Teachers College Press.

Gee, J. (1985). On the narrativization of experience in the oral style. *Journal of Education, 167*(1), 9–35.

Genishi, C. (1987). Acquiring oral language and communicative competence. In C. Seefeldt (Ed.), *The early childhood curriculum* (pp. 75–101). New York: Teachers College Press.

Halliday, M.A. (1973). Relevant models of language. In M. Halliday (Ed.), *Explorations in the functions of language* (pp. 9–21). London: Arnold.

Harkin, M. (1988). History, narrative and temporality: Examples from the Northwest coast. *Ethnohistory, 35*, 99–130.

Harris, G.A. (1985). Considerations in assessing English language performance of Native American children. *Topics in Language Disorders, 5*(4), 42–52.

Heath, S.B. (1983). *Ways with words*. Cambridge, MA: Cambridge University Press.

Heath, S.B. (1986). Taking a cross-cultural look at narratives. *Topics in Language Disorders, 7*(1), 84–94.

Holdaway, D. (1979). *The foundations of literacy*. Sydney: Ashton Scholastic.

Hymes, D. (1982). Narrative form as a grammar of experience: Native Americans and a glimpse of English. *Journal of Education, 164*, 121–141.

Kleinfeld, J., McDiarmid, G., Grubis, S., & Parnett, W. (1983). Doing research on effective cross-cultural teaching: The teacher tale. *Peabody Journal of Education, 61*(1), 86–108.

Lee, M. (1985, November). *Making child development relevant for all children: Implications for teacher education*. Paper presented at the annual conference of the National Association for the Education of Young Children, New Orleans, LA. (ERIC Document Reproduction Service No. ED 265929)

Lindsay, A.C. (1988). *A study of the oral narrative discourse style of young Indian children in a school-related activity.* Unpublished master's thesis, University of Victoria, British Columbia.

Michaels, S. (1981). Sharing time. *Language in Society, 10,* 423–442.

Michaels, S. (1983). The role of adult assistance in children's acquisition of literate discourse strategies. *Volta Review, 85*(5), 72–86.

Michaels, S. (1985). Hearing the connectives in children's oral and written discourse. *Journal of Education, 167*(1), 35–56.

Michaels, S., & Cazden, C. (1986). Teacher/child collaboration as oral preparation for literacy. In Schieffelin, B., & Gilmour, B. (Eds.), *The acquisition of literacy: ethnographic perspectives.* Norwood, N.J.: Ablex.

Michaels, S., & Cook-Gumperz, J. (1979). A study of sharing time with first-grade students. *Proceedings of the Fifth Annual Meeting of the Berkeley Linguistics Society, 5,* 647–660.

Montgomery, J.A. (1982). Natural texts and delayed oral production: An indigenous method for the teaching of American Indian languages. In F. Barkin, E. Brandt, & J. Ornstein-Galicia (Eds.), *Bilingualism and language contact* (pp. 241–250). New York: Teachers College Press.

National Indian Brotherhood. (1972). *Indian control of Indian education.* Ottawa: National Indian Brotherhood.

Ong, W. (1982). *Orality and literacy.* London: Methuen.

Preece, A. (1985). *The development of young children's productive narrative competence in conversational contexts.* Unpublished doctoral dissertation, University of Victoria, British Columbia.

Ramsey, Patricia. (1982). Multicultural education in early childhood. *Young Children, 37*(2), 13–23.

Scollon, R., & Scollon, S. (1981). *Narrative, literacy and face in interethnic communication.* Norwood, NJ: Ablex.

Tedlock, D. (1983). *The spoken word and the work of interpretation.* Philadelphia: University of Philadelphia Press.

Wells, G. (1985). Some antecedents of early educational attainment. In G. Wells (Ed.), *Language, learning and education* (pp. 74–99). Berkshire: NFER–Nelson.

PART 3

A CANADIAN CURRICULUM FOR EARLY CHILDHOOD EDUCATION

Understanding the dynamics of the Canadian child and the Canadian context is an empty exercise unless we apply that understanding. This part provides that opportunity for the reader, and forms the core of this volume. The contributors present questions, concepts, and challenges about the design, development, and implementation of a Canadian curriculum for early childhood programs and services.

In Chapter 11, Isabel Doxey provides a framework for the discussion by exploring some curriculum perspectives, purposes, and organizational principles. Next, Patricia Dickinson and Ellen Regan—in Chapters 12 and 13, respectively—focus on the key curriculum element, the early childhood educator. A curriculum needs appropriate environments, and the directions for providing these follow in Chapter 14, by Steen Esbensen. In Chapter 15, the focus shifts to a specific child population for whom appropriate care and education must be provided—infants and toddlers. Finally, Chapter 16, by Catalina Ferrer and Joan Gamble, demonstrates how the current concern for peace and human rights education can have application in an early childhood curriculum.

11

A Basic Canadian Curriculum?

Isabel M. Doxey

Curriculum Perspectives
Curriculum Approaches
A Curriculum Purpose
Curriculum Organization
Conclusion
References

When we involve children in early childhood education programs—in child-care facilities, nursery schools, kindergartens, or early primary classes—we assume and even assure that the children will benefit. But there is no consensus about what form early education should take or about what children should be doing in an early childhood program environment to gain the maximum benefit. This chapter explores some issues surrounding the early childhood curriculum. Perspectives about curriculum elements will be linked to clients and to context—that is, to young Canadian children and to Canadian society in the 1990s—to support the conclusion that there is indeed a "basic Canadian curriculum" for early children education.

CURRICULUM PERSPECTIVES

The essence of education is intervention. In the early years, care and education aim to influence the direction and scope of children's developmental processes. The curriculum is the design and delivery of this intervention. In much of the early childhood education literature, the term *program* is often used interchangeably with curriculum. In this chapter, however, program refers to how a curriculum is made available to the child in a nursery school, a child-care facility, a kindergarten, or an early primary class. Curriculum, on the other hand, refers to all that happens to the children who attend the program.

The early childhood curriculum may be intended or unintentional, narrow or broad, flexible or rigid, spontaneous or systematic, emergent or predetermined. However characterized, it is a critical element in program quality, for it is the curriculum that "defines and clarifies so many other issues" (Weikart, 1986, p. 8).

There have been many trends and patterns in the evolution of curriculum perspectives and models for early childhood. Although the search for one perfect curriculum seems simplistic and unrealistic today, the search continues (Seefeldt, 1988, p. 272). The current dominant theme promotes a "whole" curriculum—that is, a curriculum designed for the "whole" child rather than a separate-subject approach with a skill-development focus. The whole-child approach calls for the integration of intellectual, emotional, social, and physical capabilities, with development and learning in any one of these domains necessarily involving the others. This theme "reflects a rich tradition of comprehensiveness that has characterized early education from its beginnings" (Williams, 1988, p. 1).

In the 1980s, a new curriculum development movement appeared, resulting from a reassessment of children's needs and responses, and the roles of process and play in their education. According to a growing number of early childhood professionals, the curriculum in Canadian care and education programs should recognize the distinctive needs of Canadian children within the context of Canadian society.

Canadian society provides the context for the evolution of curriculum designs for early childhood programs: "Designing a curriculum is a value-saturated and culture-bound task" (Egan, 1983). In the introduction to this book, some qualities of Canadians and of the Canadian context were identified. In this chapter, this context will be the filter for interpreting some universal principles and characteristics of curriculum development.

Diversity, for instance, is something we respect, treasure, and strive to protect in this democratic, pluralistic country. Early childhood educators in particular have typically attempted to respond to the culture, values, and desires of parents and the community. In our search for curriculum options and a context for Canadian early childhood programs and services, we must continually look to our society and to the values that are its foundation.

CURRICULUM APPROACHES

Curriculum development must be a rational, conscious, and intentional procedure. Weikart (1986) has commented that "the big dividing line between effective programs and ineffective programs is that the staff of the latter have not made a decision about the curriculum" (p. 8).

There is also a difference between an intended curriculum and the received curriculum (Dowling, 1988). While we might intend to affect a child's knowledge base, creativity, imagination, moral value system, and social skills, the child instead may receive, learn, and develop in ways neither planned for nor intended. This can happen despite the expertise of curriculum-developers, teachers, support staff, administrators, and policy-makers. The challenge is not only to have a curriculum plan, but also to be sensitive to its impact on children and to appreciate their perspective and participation.

Traditionally, the process of curriculum development has proceeded from identifying outcome aims and objectives through selecting and sequencing the most appropriate learning experiences to achieve those aims and objectives (Taba, 1962). What is much more currently appropriate is a process approach—a naturalistic curriculum. Knowledge becomes not the object of mastery, but a means to an end: a vehicle for passing on our social and physical realities. Teachers design and sequence activities to provide children with the opportunities to try, to practise, and to master, not merely to memorize. It is the process that is the priority in an early childhood curriculum, not merely the measurable outcomes or products of the process. When children are painting, for example, it is the process of experimenting with running colours on paper, and trying to understand how and why changes happen when yellow and green mix, rather than the product—"a picture" for parents—that is the essence of the experience. It is through processes of trying on, taking apart, putting together, planning, doing, observing, and testing that children come to understand the relationships within their physical and social worlds.

As a plan, a curriculum has many components. In the traditional curriculum literature, the four most common components are aims and objectives; the selection and organization of learning experiences; teaching and learning strategies; and evaluation. In the balance of this chapter, the two curriculum components most relevant to early childhood settings in the Canadian context will be considered. First, what should be the purposes of the early childhood curriculum for Canadian children? Second, what principles could direct the selection and organization of the learning experiences?

A CURRICULUM PURPOSE

The purposes of a curriculum may be stated in terms of goals or outcomes to be achieved. Four major goals are frequently argued for in the early childhood literature. First, many believe that the early childhood curriculum ought to prepare children for *academic success* in later schooling.

Second, others maintain that the early childhood curriculum ought to be *developmental*, providing experiences that either compensate for deficits in or enrich and extend the developmental process in all areas: affective, social, physical, moral, cognitive, aesthetic, character, and personality. These two perspectives may be pictured as opposites—hence, the "academic instruction versus enrichment" debate described in Chapter 12 (Elkind, 1987).

Two other goals are often championed. One view—a primarily American outlook (Braun & Edwards, 1972), although it also underpins early education intentions in other countries—holds that early childhood education can be a tool for *social reform*. By intervening in children's lives when they are young and most susceptible, it is thought possible to shape their attitudes and their future potential as adult citizens, thereby compensating for some of the deprivations related to poverty, lack of parental education, level of intelligence, and low socioeconomic status.

The fourth goal is espoused by those who operate from the children's rights perspective (Gross & Gross, 1977). The early childhood curriculum, they maintain, ought to reflect the child's right not just to an education *per se*, but to a particular kind of education: one that guarantees support for the child's unique personal and cultural identity.

Each of these perspectives will be discussed to identify its source, strength, validity, and relevance to Canadian early childhood care and education.

Academic Preparation

Rooted in the tenets of behaviourism and the work of education theorists of the 1930s and 1940s, academic preparation was and is an explicit and primary aim for many early childhood programs. This perspective stresses acquiring predetermined skills and information along traditional subject lines as an end in itself—for example, number facts in mathematics.

Elkind (1987) notes many disadvantages to concentrating on academic preparation, particularly when children are exposed to formal instruction that involves the "inculcation of symbolic rules" and emphasizes producing correct answers and paper-and-pencil tasks. Demands for proficiency and correctness can result in unacceptable levels of stress for young children. Children's motivation to learn may be adversely affected; they may become too dependent on adult direction and instruction, and not take enough initiative in their own learning. There is also increasing evidence that the pressures of an academically oriented curriculum, particularly in the early years, represent a major contributor to failure and frustration (Bredekamp, 1986).

Current trends in Canada indicate strong support for academic-preparation aims in early childhood. There is an increase in availability of junior kindergarten and all-day senior kindergarten programs, with many teachers emphasizing the abilities to follow directions and to sit attentively as indicators of school readiness. In early primary programs, teachers design "lessons" to ensure subject-matter learning and skill mastery. Nursery schools offer guarantees for academic achievement: "superlearning," claims one recent advertising brochure. Many childcare directors use reading-readiness workbooks as evidence of the extent of academic preparation provided by their program. Parents and principals look to test results for evidence of academic progress in the early years.

Certainly in Canada, academic preparation has as many supporters as critics. Many parents demand academic preparation from early childhood programs. They want their children to achieve, to succeed—and they believe that the best path to a bright future starts with learning to read and to "do" arithmetic. If such skills are acquired early, parents are even more elated. The debate between the critics and supporters of academic-preparation goals for early childhood programs will undoubtedly intensify.

As other chapters in this volume indicate, an emphasis on academic skills and formal instruction is based on misconceptions about early learning. As a perspective for a Canadian curriculum for young children, academic preparation constitutes a narrow and short-sighted aim. We need children who know how to get and use knowledge, not children who merely have it. Academic success will come to children who are emotionally and socially healthy, and motivated to achieve. The Canadian early childhood curriculum needs a broader scope than academic preparation.

Developmental Perspective

In the early 1960s, many people in the field began to believe that early education should exist primarily to nurture and stimulate development and to help children become more competent and autonomous (White, 1963).

This curriculum objective was grounded in stage theory, which holds that development progresses in a definite order. At each stage in this progression, children have special abilities and specific needs that provide the framework for educational planning (Weber, 1984).

This perspective, too, has had its critics. Parents often do not trust that appropriate learning happens when children follow their natural inclinations to learn through play. A group of concerned parents recently demanded the removal of toys from the kindergarten of a local school, and a return to "real teaching."

Egan (1983), among others, has attacked the use of psychological theory in developing a theory of curriculum. He claims that knowledge of child development does not directly answer the question of how children should be educated. Chapter 13 elaborates this view.

Yet compelling evidence from child-development research indicates that learning through play is powerful and effective. Numerous studies have concluded that social learning is as essential for children as academic achievement, and that the personal satisfaction a child gets from working with other children is a powerful motivator for further learning. Chapter 5 analyzes in greater detail the role of the child's self-image in the learning process.

The developmental perspective sets learning goals for children's progress, not performance goals by which to measure outcomes (Katz & Chard, 1989). It is more important for children to search for answers as to how the caterpillar weaves its cocoon than it is for them to know the fact that the caterpillar does so.

The developmental perspective is an appropriate emphasis for the Canadian early childhood curriculum. It is respectful of children as individuals. It permits educators to emphasize interactive learning. This approach to curriculum design best permits the use of the multicultural and non-stereotyping materials and activities that are necessary for and relevant to the Canadian cultural context.

Social Reform

An early childhood curriculum cannot be value neutral: it will reflect socially valued norms. Sometimes there are conflicts between what society needs and what some parents want for their individual children. Parents may prefer young children to be obedient and conforming, to be "seen and not heard." One of Canada's distinctive communities, the Hutterites, for instance, intentionally structures the environment and education system for its young to promote communal living and obedience to elders (Sinclair, 1988).

The social reform approach has been seen as an endorsement for activities and experiences designed to compensate young children for deficits in their social circumstances. Indeed, this perspective provided the main rationale for the development of the "Head Start" programs in the United States during the 1950s and 1960s. This compensatory intent contradicts the Canadian multicultural perspective with its tolerance for diversity. As a curriculum development aim, social reform needs a different interpretation for the Canadian context.

One starting point for curriculum development should be a value statement about "what we want children to become" (Spodek, 1988). Canadian society needs initiators, entrepreneurs, risk-takers, visionaries, and leaders. We need future citizens who are sensitive to environmental concerns, more ecologically conscious. We want citizens who are cultured, who appreciate the visual and performing arts. We want citizens who are tolerant and free from attitudes and behaviour that are disrespectful of others. If we expect to have these qualities in our adult citizens, we must begin by nurturing them in our early education programs.

It is this broad mandate, then, rather than a belief that "deficits" must be compensated for, that provides the more appropriate basis for social reform objectives in the early childhood curriculum.

Children's rights

The British North America Act (1867) made no attempt to define the place of the child in our social or political structure: indeed, there are no references to children in the entire statute. The first international declaration of children's rights came after World War I—when, in 1920, the League of Nations adopted the Geneva Declaration of the Rights of the Child. In 1948, the United Nations General Assembly adopted the Universal Declaration of Human Rights in which the rights and freedoms of children were implicitly included. This was followed in 1959 by the adoption of a separate document, the Declaration of the Rights of the Child. In 1979, the International Year of the Child was declared in hopes of significantly raising the level of services for children worldwide. In 1989, the UN is expected to act on behalf of children, by approving the Declaration as a Convention. Canada and the other signatories will thus be legally mandated to enforce the rights of children in their respective countries.

What is the relationship of children's rights, either legal or moral, to the development of a Canadian early childhood curriculum? First, safeguarding one such right—a child's right to have his or her individuality recognized—should be a curriculum objective. Adults should not impose unrealistic expectations for performance, or make accusations about inferiority or worthlessness. Second, early childhood educators are responsible for ensuring that children develop in an environment of respect, affection, and stimulation. Third, we must ensure that each child has access to an education appropriate to the critical learning and development periods. The curriculum should therefore provide balanced and integrated educational opportunities for all developmental areas. Furthermore, we must recognize the rights of children with special needs to accessible educational opportunities and experiences that are appropriate for their circumstances (see also Chapter 19).

From the children's rights perspective, another implication for curriculum development involves recognizing and supporting each child's personal heritage. Canadian society is becoming increasingly multicultural, with recent immigration patterns intensifying cultural, religious, and linguistic differences (see Chapter 9 for a more detailed discussion of these issues). Franco-Ontarians make up about eight percent of Ontario's population. Native Canadians also need relevant educational options. In Vancouver and Toronto, the extent of the linguistic diversity in schools is considerable and increasing. In early childhood programs, each child's personal heritage must be valued as an essential part of that child's uniqueness and as a significant factor in his or her development and educational achievement. Assuring the rights of children must be a conscious and explicit goal for the Canadian early childhood curriculum.

All children have the moral, as well as legal, right to expect their needs to be met. The goals and purposes of the early childhood curriculum, therefore, should incorporate an understanding of these needs. Pringle (1974) categorizes children's needs as primary or secondary. The primary needs are universal: food and shelter. The secondary needs are for love and security, praise and recognition, new experiences, and responsibility. Satisfaction of these secondary needs in particular calls for a focus on the relationships that are important and significant for the child. Furthermore, stresses Pringle, all these needs are inextricably linked. No matter how we conceptualize children's needs, it is how we see children in relation to need fulfilment that is most influential in curriculum planning. Children may, for example, be considered imperfect, incomplete, underdeveloped, deficient, or immature, albeit appealing and lovable. From this viewpoint, one philosophical position would contend that children therefore need opportunities in their early childhood education experiences to overcome their imperfections and move toward the "perfection" of adulthood.

Yet another view suggests that children are just fine as they are, that they have their own forms of perfection. The purpose for a curriculum according to this view is to provide for the continuation and cultivation of the child's existing perfections (Egan, 1988).

None of these purposes by itself is truly complete or totally adequate for curriculum planning. We need to find a consensus in our beliefs about children—one that accommodates the developmental nature of childhood, respects the rights of children, and blends the desires for fulfilment and for achievement of potential.

CURRICULUM ORGANIZATION

The early childhood curriculum must be designed and delivered so that its purposes clearly underpin its organization. The main elements of curriculum organization are scheduling; allocating space; establishing the system of rules and routines; and selecting and sequencing learning opportunities. Three principles can provide a foundation for decisions about organizing these four elements: naturalness; personalization; and democracy. All three reflect the approaches prioritized in the previous section for a Canadian early childhood curriculum.

Naturalness

An early childhood curriculum with the characteristic of naturalness is one that respects children's rights and needs within a flexible and adaptable organization.

Time, for example, does not have the same meaning for children as for adults. Traditionally, time in early childhood settings has been blocked by adults into subject-matter or activity segments. Usually, for example, the early childhood teacher determines when activities begin and end, and how long each should last. This contrived arrangement often results in unnatural transitions for the children. Furthermore, adult decisions about time may not be functional for individualized programming.

Schedules, routines, and other strategies for structuring time are necessary. They offer children security and help them to know what is expected. But schedules and routines should be designed to reflect the natural rhythm of children's behaviour, and to permit a natural flow from one activity segment to another. If children, for instance, have not finished a play episode, they should not be required to finish in order to satisfy an adult's demand for schedule obedience. In some infant and toddler programs, children are permitted to sleep only after lunch, even though some become so tired that they cannot keep their eyes open to finish eating. But this scheduling is necessary to accommodate lunch breaks for the program staff. In other programs, the end of outdoor play is determined by the clock rather than by the quality and flow of the play. Such time decisions may suit the adults, but they are unnatural for the children.

It is natural for children to be messy, untidy learners—to know something one day or one minute, and forget it the next. Children are naturally curious. To satisfy their curiosity and to arrive at genuine understanding, they must have opportunities to make connections, to mix and match things and ideas in different ways. (Chapter 3 cites some memorable illustrations of children's naturalness. Chapter 2 also furthers our understanding of the naturalness in children's play.) Our curriculum ought to permit and respect the "messy" and "playful" ways young children learn best.

It is also natural for young children to be aggressive (Marion, 1987): unsocialized, immature, and with limited self-control. They need time to test, and to practise turn-taking, sharing materials, and negotiating with words.

The organization of space should also match the natural rhythms of children's behaviour and learning. Elsewhere in this volume, Esbensen details concepts of space organization that can help early childhood educators design more natural playscapes.

Adults who want to repress, control, direct, and manage children tend to be those with limited training and limited understanding of children. They often do not appreciate or respect children's natural developmental patterns and learning styles. Early childhood educators who have studied and understand child development generally have higher levels of tolerance for children's natural immaturity.

When selecting and sequencing learning activities we should consider children's interests, experiences, and aptitudes and blend these with our societal values. For instance, many children are fascinated by bugs. This fascination could lead to a major project about bugs, including some consideration of their ecological value. Early childhood educators in Canada need not look much farther than the challenges of coping with our changing seasons and developing a nurturing respect for our natural environment when planning for the selection and sequencing of children's activities.

Personalization

Personalizing a curriculum means organizing time and space in a way that permits each child to respond individually and to find a sense of belonging.

To begin with, space should be organized so that each child has his or her own storage area and/or a place to display finished work. There should also be a place where a child may go to be alone. In addition, children need a chance to influence the space, to make decisions about where things belong and how they are kept.

The sequencing of learning experiences should also be personalized. Children with a rich cultural heritage of music and dance could use their heritage as a springboard for reading, writing, computing, constructing, and creating. Personalization also involves ensuring that children have choices about what to do, who to do things with, how to carry out an activity, when to begin and end it, and how to use materials. Each planned activity should offer a chance for some level or type of success by all children who participate. If writing materials are provided, for example, some should be usable by children at the scribbling stage, while others should present a challenge to those who can already print words with some accuracy. More complex and difficult tasks need to be balanced with simpler ones, so that each child may make a positive contribution. Some may pour the juice, others pass the napkins. Some may read parts of stories, others merely follow the illustrations.

Democracy

If we want children to develop independence and initiative, they need to practise tasks that involve problem-solving, delegating, making decisions, and organizing their thinking. Canada's government is a democratic system that permits individuals to be represented. The Charter of Rights and Freedoms and our constitution are based on principles of consensus-building, rather than autocratic leadership.

The organization of our early childhood programs can reflect, in microcosm, our larger governmental systems. Children should be represented in curriculum-planning. Such involvement gives them some ownership, some control over their learning. Participation in short- and long-term planning helps them think about the present, the past, and the future within the range of their developmental abilities. Children's planning must be sincere, legitimate, and relevant.

Even the youngest children can be involved in planning. A toddler can make a commitment to go to the lunch table, then proceed to do so, avoiding distractions and deterrents. Older children need even more opportunities to be involved in all parts of the curriculum-planning process. They can discuss what materials might be needed to change the house-play area into a hospital. They can delegate the tasks of getting some of these materials and arranging them. They can help establish the rules for turn-taking. They can also individually plan to be involved in a given area chosen from among the available options.

Older children may also be involved in establishing and revising the program's rules and routines. Children themselves will often voluntarily take responsibility for monitoring obedience to rules they have helped to frame.

The youngest children can be helped to accept responsibility for their own behaviour within the program's established rules and routines. If, for instance, a child does not help put away supplies and toys after an activity period, the teacher can help that child think about what he or she could be doing and how to do it as a member of the group, rather than merely ordering the child to obey or conform. The "democratized" early childhood program offers children opportunities to make decisions, negotiate, accept the consensus of the majority, and act responsibly.

CONCLUSION

Whether the curriculum for our early childhood program is intended or unintentional, narrow or broad, flexible or rigid, spontaneous or systematic, emergent or predetermined, as early childhood educators we have a responsibility to ensure that it clearly reflects and respects the children's rights and needs as present and future Canadians.

REFERENCES

Braun, S. J., & Edwards, E. P. (1972). *History and theory of early childhood education*. Worthington, OH: Charles A. Jones.

Bredekamp, S. (1986). *Developmentally appropriate practice*. Washington, DC: National Association for the Education of Young Children.

Denholm, C., Ferguson, R. & Pence, A. (1987). *Professional child and youth care: The Canadian perspective*. Vancouver: University of British Columbia Press.

Donaldson, M., Grieve, R., & Pratt, C. (Eds.). (1985). *Early childhood development and education*. Oxford: Basil Blackwell.

Dowling, M. (1988). *Education 3 to 5: A teacher's handbook*. London: Paul Chapman.

Egan, K. (1983). *Education and psychology: Plato, Piaget and scientific psychology*. New York: Teachers College Press.

Egan, K. (1988). *Primary understanding: Education in early childhood*. New York: Routledge, Chapman and Hall.

Elkind, D. (1986). *The miseducation of children: Superkids at risk*. New York: Alfred Knopf.

Elkind, D. (1987). *Miseducation: Preschoolers at risk*. New York: Alfred Knopf.

Evans, E. (1982). Curriculum models and early childhood education. In B. Spodek (Ed.), *Handbook of research in early childhood education* (pp. 107–134). New York: Free Press.

Gross, B., & Gross, R. (1977). *The children's rights movement*. New York: Anchor Press/Doubleday.

Kamii, C. (1985). Leading primary education toward excellence. *Young Children, 40*(6), 3–9.

Katz, L. (1987). *What should young children be learning?* (ERIC Document Reproduction Service No. ED 290 254).

Katz, L. G., & Chard, S. (1989). *Engaging children's minds: The project approach*. Norwood, NJ: Ablex.

Marion, M. (1987) *Guidance of young children*. New York: C.V. Mosby.

Pringle, K. (1974). *The needs of children*. London: Hutchinson.

Regan, E., & Weininger, O. (1988). Toward defining and defending child-centred curriculum and practice. *International Journal of Early Childhood, 20*(2), 1–10.

Seefeldt, C. (1980). *A curriculum for preschools*. Columbus, OH: Merrill.

Seefeldt, C. (1988). Conclusion. In C. Seefeldt (Ed.), *The early childhood curriculum: A review of current research*. New York: Teachers College Press.

Sinclair, L. (speaker) (1988, June 14). *Ideas* [Radio program]. Toronto: Canadian Broadcasting Corporation.

Spodek, B. (1988, November 5). *Curriculum perspectives.* Presentation to Conference of the National Association for the Education of Young Children., Anaheim, CA.

Taba, H. (1962). *Curriculum development: Theory and practice.* New York: Harcourt, Brace and World.

Weikart, D. (1986, Winter). What do we know so far? *High Scope ReSource: A Magazine for Educators,* p. 8.

White, R. (1963). *Ego and reality in psychoanalytic theory.* New York: International Universities Press.

Williams, L. (1988). Determining the curriculum. In C. Seefeldt (Ed.), *The early childhood curriculum: A review of current research* (pp. 1–12). New York: Teachers College Press.

12

The Early Childhood Professional

Patricia Dickinson

The History of Programs
Categories of Early Childhood Professionals
Historical Roots of Early Childhood Professionals
Conclusion
References

This chapter will explore the philosophical and historical roots of various early childhood professionals in Canada—specifically, educators working in child-care, nursery-school, and elementary (kindergarten and grade-one) settings.

Perceived differences among these groups of educators have impeded progress in achieving consistency and coordination across these settings. In this chapter we will examine the nature of any actual similarities and differences that exist across these educator groups. A case will be made that differences among these professional groups may be more bureaucratic than philosophical. Differences that are noted will be viewed as strengths that could lead to greater consistency, rather than as impediments to coordination.

THE HISTORY OF PROGRAMS

Child-Care and Nursery-School Programs

Child-care centres have traditionally provided care for children from infancy to school age in response to the needs of working parents. The first child-care centres were established in the middle 1800s in Montreal; at the turn of the century, others came into existence in Toronto, Ottawa, Winnipeg, and Vancouver. The economic need for child care was particularly great during World War II, when women were needed to work in the wartime arms industry. When the war ended, however, women were encouraged to leave the work force. Consequently, many of these wartime child-care centres were closed.

Child care is now regulated in all provinces and territories, with the exception of the Northwest Territories, where, according to a 1984 survey, there are still no child-care regulations (Rosenstock & Rosenstock, 1985). Various provincial ministries and agencies across Canada assume responsibility for regulating and supervising licensed child care (Council of Ministers of Education, Canada [CMEC], 1986).

Nursery schools, which provide privately run preschool programs for three-, four-, and five-year-olds, were the most recently developed of the four models considered in this chapter. The nursery-school movement originated within departments of psychology and faculties of education in various North American universities—for example, the University of Toronto's Institute of Child Study. St. George's Nursery School, associated with the Institute of Child Study, opened in 1926.

Nursery schools were based on the philosophy that a scientific approach to child care and education could help ensure optimal development and eliminate social inequalities. This is the same philosophy that promoted the early-intervention movement of the 1960s. Large-scale programs, such as "Head Start" in the United States, increased public awareness of the benefits of early education. This awareness resulted in considerable expansion of private nursery schools in Canada as well as the promotion of public-school kindergartens for four-year-olds. Nursery schools in Canada are usually regulated under the same legislation as child-care centres.

Kindergarten and Grade-One Programs

Although child-care centres, nursery schools, and kindergartens have existed nearly as long as elementary schools, they have for the most part not become universally available and have remained largely within the private sector. The obvious exception to this is the public-school kindergarten; however, kindergarten education did not expand significantly in Canada until after World War II (Austin, 1976).

The first Canadian kindergarten was established in Toronto in 1883. In Quebec, kindergartens were initiated in 1892. Many Canadian provinces have had some privately and publicly funded kindergartens since the 1900s; however, in no province or territory is it compulsory for a child to attend school before age six. Kindergarten is now offered by education ministries across Canada except in New Brunswick and Prince Edward Island, where privately run kindergartens are sponsored by other ministries (Canadian Education Association [CEA], 1983; Council of Ministers of Education, Canada [CMEC], 1986).

Public-school kindergartens have also expanded to include four-year-olds. These programs are often called junior kindergartens. The first junior kindergarten was established in Ottawa in 1940.

Egerton Ryerson began the public elementary-school system for six-year-olds in Ontario in the middle 1800s. At the time, public schools were viewed primarily as a means of providing more educated and reliable workers for Canada's growing industrial economy. Ontario's system provided the model for much of the later development in the western provinces (Titley & Miller, 1982). In Quebec, the Roman Catholic church provided the early impetus for universal schooling. As a result of these initiatives, most provinces had established universally accessible, tuition-free, compulsory elementary schools by the late 1800s.

CATEGORIES OF EARLY CHILDHOOD PROFESSIONALS

According to Spodek and Saracho (1982), the preparation and certification of early childhood personnel is in a state of confusion regarding such basic issues as the minimum qualifications needed and the types of personnel that should be staffing early childhood programs. Historically, role definitions among early childhood professionals have differentiated between people who provide care and people who provide education. Those more involved with care have been called "caregivers" or "child-care staff"; those more involved with education have usually been called "teachers." These functions are often undertaken "by staffs with different training, remuneration and objectives" (van der Eyken 1982, p. 88).

Katz (1984) asserts that the majority of people teaching children under five years old (in some countries, under six years) have had no preservice education at all. According to one international study, pre-school teachers (as compared to other teachers) often are recruited younger, need lower entry qualifications, receive shorter training, enjoy lower status, and receive lower salaries coupled with longer hours of work (Woodhead, 1979). In Canada, in 1983–84, educators involved in preschool programs were paid from $8,000 to $19,272 a year, while those involved with kindergarten and primary programs received from $24,000 to $38,000 (CMEC, 1986).

Despite the many similarities in practices and objectives between kindergartens and child-care programs, Biemiller (1982) suggests that a gulf occurs between teachers on the one hand and child-care staff on the other because they are educated in different programs and at different institutions. In many provinces, kindergarten and primary teachers need university degrees combined with teaching certification from faculties of education, whereas child-care and nursery-school teachers may hold only a diploma from a two-year community college. Certification of kindergarten and primary teachers has traditionally been the responsibility of provincial departments of education. Child-care and nursery-school certification is less clearly regulated and specified.

Esbensen (1982) supports a need for more specialized programs in faculties of education, since the generalist approach in faculties has resulted in kindergarten teachers who lack an adequate knowledge of child development. In contrast, an Ontario-based study found that teachers certified in early childhood education from two-year community-college programs had very strong backgrounds in child development and care, but were not as well-equipped as teachers with degrees in dealing with "hard" course content in the learning skills (O'Bryan, Kaplowska, & O'Bryan, 1975).

Several studies and reports have addressed the issues raised by these distinctions (LaPierre, 1980; Mayfield et al., 1981; O'Bryan, 1986; O'Bryan et al., 1975; Ontario Ministry of Education [MOE], 1985). Recommendations include a differentiated staffing model in which teachers with university degrees teach in public-school programs, while non-university-qualified graduates teach in nursery schools and child-care centres, or work as teacher's aides in public-school programs (O'Bryan et al., 1975; Ontario MOE, 1985). Several studies recommend further specialization in early primary education that would require advanced postgraduate degrees and/or in-service training (LaPierre, 1980; Mayfield, et al., 1981; Ontario MOE, 1985). Others suggest bridging mechanisms across the two training programs, so that the benefits of each could become more accessible to all educator groups (O'Bryan, 1986; Ontario MOE, 1985, 1989).

O'Bryan (1986) suggests caution in two areas when considering training and certification requirements for early primary teachers. Universities tend to over-professionalize the role of the teacher of young children. The child gets lost in an ever-increasing focus on cognitive growth and development. However, there is an equal danger in community colleges of over-romanticizing the nurturing role of early childhood educators. Practicum and direct involvement with children are too heavily emphasized, at the expense of theory. O'Bryan favours an integration of these two approaches.

We need an integrated approach not only in certification but also in the type of programming we provide across these various settings. Since young children are more likely than ever before to spend a considerable part of their formative years in child care, nursery school, and kindergarten before entering grade one, we must consider program consistency and coordination among the various educators and agencies involved with young children.

Historically, distinctions among preschool, kindergarten, and grade-one philosophies have been reported for nearly 100 years (Gregory, 1908; Holmes, 1907). Contemporary concerns are embedded in these historical and traditional differences (Spodek, 1985). Basically, there are two debates: "care" versus "education," and academic "instruction" versus "enrichment." These traditional dichotomies were probably intensified in North America by the interest in early compensatory education, as exemplified by the Head Start preschools. In Canada, they were further complicated by a depressed economy and declining enrolment in the 1970s (Regan, 1978). As a result of a surplus of teachers, and of increasing numbers of women with young children working outside the home, a controversy began to develop regarding the best setting for meeting the young children's needs for care and education.

Very few studies have attempted to address the issue of conflicting orientations among early childhood professionals. Those that have been done have produced controversial and somewhat discouraging results. Langdon (1933) found very little consistency among nursery-school, kindergarten, and grade-one teachers in their approaches to various teaching "acts." Jacob and Peters' (1971) study of preschool, kindergarten, and grade-one teachers concluded that "there were few opportunities for continuity of experiences in intellectual development, individuation, and socialization that would provide for building on early school gains." However, Mayfield et al. (1981) found preschool, kindergarten, and grade-one teachers more similar than different. A study of child-care, nursery-school, kindergarten, and grade-one teachers by the author (Dickinson, 1988b), confirmed the Mayfield et al. (1981) findings and concluded that differences may be greater *within* than *across* the various professional categories.

Previous attempts at coordination across these educator groups and their respective agencies have not been especially encouraging (Dickinson, 1987). The final report of a coordinated program in the United States (Project Developmental Continuity, [PDC], 1982) outlined how differences in the values and attitudes held by child-care and elementary teachers impeded communication: "Regardless of physical proximity the social distance between these two groups, resulting from professional and socio-economic differences, remained an obstacle to substantive linkage between the two programs" (p. 19). After surveying these issues in Europe, van der Eyken (1982) suggested that the division between care and education has created "a hierarchy of power and resources, in which the younger, less skilled and most poorly paid are locked into the caring function, while status, training resources, higher salaries and career structures are reserved for the educational sector" (p. 89).

This background illustrates the complexity involved in conceptualizing the role of the early childhood professional. In the historical account that follows, the evolution of this complexity will be traced.

HISTORICAL ROOTS OF EARLY CHILDHOOD PROFESSIONALS

Child Care

From their very beginnings, child-care centres have responded to two types of needs. The first centres in Quebec, for example, were of two types: the *crèche* and the *salle d'asile*. Crèches were primarily custodial, providing care for the children of poor women who worked outside their homes. Salles d'asile were primarily educational, providing structured lessons for the children from both poor and more affluent families in which both parents worked outside the home (Schulz, 1978). The greatest support for child care during this early period was dispensed in the form of charity by volunteer, philanthropic women's organizations. At first, child-care workers were largely untrained nurses and nannies whose work was viewed primarily as a domestic service. According to Schulz, the centres gradually began to hire trained personnel (kindergarten teachers and social workers). The Institute of Child Study was established at the University of Toronto in 1926; it provided both information and personnel for these early child-care programs. Although child-care programs were somewhat influenced by the nursery-school movement, a distinction has generally been made between the care function (assigned to the child-care worker) and the educational function (considered the domain of the nursery-school teacher).

Professional requirements for child-care workers vary across Canada, depending primarily on the province's level of industrialization (CMEC, 1986; Schulz, 1978). No training is required in Newfoundland and Alberta, for example, while in other provinces child-care workers must complete some type of preservice program (which range from one-year training programs to graduate degrees). Only British Columbia requires all child-care staff to have early childhood training (CMEC, 1986, p. 83).

In 1965, when the Colleges of Applied Arts and Technology were proposed for Ontario, they seemed the obvious institutions to handle the growing demand for qualified staff in the province's rapidly expanding preschool and child-care facilities. Diploma and postdiploma programs at these colleges provide a range of specialties—for example, students may specialize in infant care; in working with children who have special needs; or in program administration.

In an analysis of the salaries and work experience of child-care workers in Ontario's Hamilton–Wentworth region, educational level was among the variables considered (Association for Early Childhood Education, Ontario [AECEO], Hamilton Branch, 1986). Of the 177 workers, 13 percent had completed grade 12 or less; another 8.5 percent held at least one university degree; and 70 percent had a two-year early childhood diploma or the equivalent. Another Ontario-based study (Dickinson, 1988b) surveyed 34 child-care workers and found that 97 percent had an early childhood diploma, while 6 percent had a university degree.

Recently attempts have been made to link child care more closely with public-school systems in order to facilitate continuity for children while providing more convenient arrangements for parents (CEA, 1983; Ontario MOE, 1985, 1989). Levine (1978) suggests that this trend has heightened the controversies between care and education and has exacerbated the debate as to which professionals have the most appropriate qualifications for providing child care and what these qualifications should be. The results of the National Day Care Study in the United States (Ruopp et al., 1979) suggest that specialized training appropriate to the developmental needs of young children is the critical factor in providing high-quality early childhood care and education. It is not the number of years of formal education, but whether or not that education focuses on child development, that seems to be the key.

For the most part, child care has been viewed primarily as a response to the basic health and care needs of the children of working parents or to the recipients of social assistance, rather than as an outgrowth of either educational ideology or psychological theory. But a study of the professional perspectives of various early childhood educators (Dickinson, 1988b) reflects considerable ideological controversy among child-care workers. They reported a conflict in overall philosophy between an interpersonal, affective, child-centred orientation and the need to be professionally accountable. They also reported considerable constraints arising from philosophical differences among colleagues within the child-care field. Case studies of two child-care workers, chosen because of their "typical" child-care profiles highlighted such differences clearly: one subject reflected a custodial view of child care, while the other reflected a more educative view of the early childhood professional's role. The latter said;

> "I feel that a big part of my job is my program, and program means the curriculum for the year, and the week-to-week themes, a monthly report that I do on children, how they progress from one month to another, and how their skills develop.... I'm looking at the long term in the toddler program, long term development."

Clearly this child-care worker did not view herself only as a provider of young children's health and care needs. This changing perception of the role of the child-care worker is reflected in *Good Care Educates, Good Education Cares*, the AECEO's (1985) response to the Ontario Ministry of Education's Early Primary Education Project:

Our philosophy of education for the young child, as well as our practical experience, leads us to firmly believe that care and education for young children should be integrated if we are to ensure that the programs meet the needs of the whole child and his/her family. . . . The active learning which is characteristic of the early school years . . . cannot be arbitrarily confined to the brief period of time called "school" with the remainder of the time spent outside the home designated as "care"—and requiring only a custodial function from the caregiver.

It is clear from these comments that many child-care workers consider themselves educators as well as caregivers. This viewpoint blurs the traditional distinctions that have separated the child-care worker from other early childhood professionals.

Nursery-School Teachers

In the early days, nursery schools were often linked to the child study movement (Spodek, 1972) or were begun as an alternative to what was considered the dogmatic and ritualized approach of many kindergartens. The link between nursery schools and the parent-cooperative movement distinguished the former from both the public-school tradition and from child-care programs that were intended to supplement rather than complement the influence of the home. These distinctions are best expressed by the terms "care" and "education"—or, more specifically, *custodial care* and *enrichment*. Day nurseries assumed responsibility for the custody of children when parents were unable to do so; nursery schools were organized to enrich and possibly alter children's lives by enhancing or expanding on experiences already provided by the home environment and on natural patterns of growth in order to promote optimal growth and development.

Despite the historical distinctions in conceptualizing the roles of child-care workers and nursery-school teachers, they are often educated in the same manner and are usually regulated and licensed by the same agencies or ministries (CMEC, 1986). Almy (1975) suggests that nursery-school teachers in North America originally had more education than other early childhood educators. Because of nursery schools' early association with universities, nursery-school teachers in the 1920s and 1930s often had graduate degrees, when elementary teachers had only undergraduate degrees. However, this situation has gradually changed. "Preparation for nursery school teaching could range from experience in babysitting or with one's own children, to a master's degree (Almy, 1975, p. 31). In an Ontario-based study (Dickinson, 1988b), among 28 nursery-school teachers, 94 percent had early childhood diplomas and 25 percent had university degrees.

Omwake (1971) suggests that events in the 1950s and 1960s created a further dichotomy among people working *within* the nursery-school field. In discussing two models, the academic preschool and the modern American nursery school, Omwake says that "the academic preschool is concerned with the child's ability to deal with the demands of his later school experience . . . [while] the nursery school is involved with helping him to develop skills, abilities and attitudes with which to cope with the demands and meet the challenge of everyday life" (p. 29).

The "academic instruction versus enrichment" conflict was illustrated in the behaviour of two nursery-school teachers who were studied by Dickinson (1988b). Observations of the instruction-oriented nursery-school teacher showed that 30 percent of her interactions with children were focused on success and productivity, as compared with none of the interactions in which the enrichment-oriented nursery-school teacher was involved. Conversely, only 2 percent of the instruction-oriented teacher's interactions were related to affective, interpersonal goals; a full 37 percent of the enrichment-oriented teacher's interactions fit that description.

These two teachers were aware of the distinctions between them. The academically oriented teacher said:

> "Children should know that they have to do something correctly and not incorrectly. Not for the sake of showing the parents that this is something that is right or correct, but for the sake of the child. I think if they learn how to do something wrong, then they're going to do it wrong again. . . . I'm not so concerned with the finished product, but I am concerned with work habits."

In contrast, the teacher with an enrichment orientation said,

> "I'd like to see myself as a facilitator, both with the parents and the children . . . helping them make their own decisions. I try very hard not to make them for them. . . . I think [children] will learn competence by learning they can do things for themselves, in solving problems."

Omwake (1971) elaborates this dichotomy and concludes that "we do not know in precise terms which educational style provides the greater services to the individual's long-range educational needs."

Kindergarten Teachers

The beginnings of the kindergarten movement were closely linked both with the philosophy of Friedrich Froebel (see Chpater 8) and with North

American social reform. In the initial stages in the United States and Canada, kindergartens were promoted as a preventive measure that would counteract the evils of poverty and neglect. This approach led to a confusion between education and philanthropy (Spodek, 1982). Many early social reformers viewed kindergarten as a step toward creating a new social order through nurturing the natural unfolding of children's minds, while public-school administrators saw kindergarten as a way to provide children with an early start in the process of adjusting to society and the world of industry.

Froebel considered the ideal kindergarten teacher to be a woman who embodied the ideals of motherhood and sensitivity, and was also intellectually active (Ross, 1976). Ross suggests that young women from the upper class and from the rising middle class could see themselves in these criteria, and therefore found in kindergarten teaching a socially acceptable outlet that satisfied their desire for learning and adventure.

The differences in length between two-year community-college early childhood programs and three- and four-year university degree programs have caused considerable controversy as to which program most adequately prepares educators to work with young children, particularly children in junior and senior kindergartens. In some instances, graduates of four-year programs in child study or early childhood education are not considered qualified to teach kindergarten unless they have also attained teacher certification at a faculty of education.

This seems a questionable approach, since the National Day Care Study in the United States (Ruopp et al., 1979) found that training in child development was the most critical need for those working with three-, four-, and five-year-old children. In a British Columbia study (Mayfield et al., 1981), kindergarten teachers identified a need for more child-development studies in their preservice education. These controversies over qualifications are also related to philosophical issues. One of the kindergarten teachers studied by Dickinson (1988b) said, "You're in a bit of a dilemma, because you do want to move this educational process forward and not to stay static. On the other hand you want children to have this freedom of choice."

The dichotomy reflected here involves two basic educational philosophies: the belief that the holistic, child-centred philosophy of the kindergarten should be extended into the primary grades (that is "enrichment") and the idea that the kindergarten should do more to ease the child's transition into the formal academic program of the primary grades by providing more structure and more teacher intervention in the learning process.

Primary Teachers

The concept of free, universally accessible, and compulsory schooling, based on a standardized curriculum taught by state-trained teachers, provides a sharp contrast to the three early childhood settings outlined so far. It was at one time believed that the school's role was to manipulate young minds in the right direction so as to guarantee a responsible, informed citizenry that would perpetuate the morals and traditions of the culture (McDonald, 1978). This view—the acculturation model of education—remains paramount in many elementary schools in Canada today.

However, the progressive education movement, which developed in some western Canadian provinces in the 1930s, was founded on a quite different concept of the school's role. In this view the self-directed creativity of the individual was seen as a better means of achieving the ultimate goal of social progress.

The dichotomy between the acculturation and the progressive models of education is reminiscent of the instruction versus enrichment debates that have characterized the histories of child-care, nursery-school, and kindergarten teachers. This dichotomy, and the inner conflict it causes for primary teachers, was well articulated by two grade-one teachers in the Dickinson (1988b) study. The first teacher subscribed to a more progressive view of education:

> "All the academic drilling in the world won't help them if they don't feel good about themselves.... You often wonder, though, am I doing the right thing? Should I be drilling more? ... But I think the end result there is a joy for reading, a joy for learning and I think that is important. It doesn't matter about the pace."

The other grade-one teacher had experimented with the "newer" methods, but still basically held an acculturation model of education:

> "I've used a freer approach with them than I've used in the past, with less of the old fashioned teacher instructed classes.... But the new approach worries me too and that's why I have to go back to some of my old "bad habits" for my own peace of mind. By the end of the year I don't think the children will be as academically ahead as we would expect them to be. Maybe creatively they would be further ahead.... But I feel my job is to teach them how to read and do arithmetic. That's what you're hired to do. When it comes down to the standardized test at the end of the year, [the question will be] 'Did I do my job or not?' "

This teacher's students were all required to take standardized tests at the end of grade one to determine their placement for the next year. Her philosophy was influenced by the reality within which she functioned. When asked if she would enjoy teaching at any other level, she said,

> "I'd really like nursery school . . . because I think I would have less responsibility as far as productivity is concerned. I would really like to have days that you could play with kids and enjoy the children and let them do what they wanted to do and talk to them and encourage them. . . . It's a wonderful philosophy if you've only got five children."

This woman was teaching 28 children in a room less than half the size of the kindergarten across the hall. Her philosophy of education may have developed as much from the realities of the setting in which she worked as from any preconceived notion about how children should be taught.

CONCLUSION

The above description of the four early childhood professional groups should help clarify that philosophical disputes regarding the most appropriate methods for the care and education of young children have developed historically from *within* each professional category.

This chapter has also attempted to show the complexity and diversity that exists within the field of early childhood education. This diversity is not particular to any one group of educators. Moreover, we can now see that the distinctions often made between educator groups are actually universal, common within all four educator groups. These distinctions and debates have historically been present in each of the four professions, and may even have developed simultaneously in each. This realization challenges the common idea that key differences in history, training, philosophy, and approach have developed *between* the groups. This inaccurate notion has created the illusion of differences where perhaps none exist.

The implications of this misperception are significant. If there is as much disparity between two child-care, nursery-school, kindergarten, or grade-one teachers as there is across these professional classifications, what hope do we have for creating consistency and coordination in the lives of young children? How can two colleagues hope to work together if each has a significantly different viewpoint of what constitutes appropriate early childhood care and education?

The answer to these questions may be found in a greater appreciation of the value of diversity in professional perspectives, rather than in an attempt to create sameness. Encouraging coordination and cooperation— rather than strict conformity—both within and across settings may prove to be a more fruitful approach (so long as differences are not vastly illogical or abrupt). All those responsible for implementing a coordinated system of early education need to address how best to cooperate in using this diversity. The important issue is not whether all professionals involved in the care and education of young children have the same perspective; rather, it is whether we are all willing to try to understand and appreciate one another's different perspectives.

This emphasis on differences may come from a particularistic, rather than a wholistic, view of early childhood professionals. Admittedly, there are specific areas in which educator groups differ. However, when these groups are considered as total entities, in all their human complexity, the similarities across groups predominate. If we look for differences, for ways to separate ourselves from each other, we will always be able to find them. What seems more productive is to try to find areas of commonality from which we can mutually grow and develop as educators, and thus improve the lives of young children.

REFERENCES

Almy, M. (1975). *The early childhood educator at work.* Toronto: McGraw-Hill.

Association for Early Childhood Education, Ontario. (1985). *Good care educates, good education cares.* Toronto: AECEO.

Association for Early Childhood Education, Ontario. Hamilton Branch. (1986). *A regional analysis of Canada's national child care subsidy system: Salaries and work experience in the municipality of Hamilton-Wentworth, Ontario.* Hamilton: AECEO, Public Policy Committee.

Austin, G. (1976). Early childhood education in Canada. In G. Austin (Ed.), *Early childhood education: An international perspective.* New York: Academic.

Biemiller, A. (1982). Research on early childhood education: Some observations on the problems and possibilities in Canada. *Canadian Journal of Early Childhood Education, 2*(2), 9–14.

Canadian Education Association. (1983). *Day care and the Canadian school system: A CEA survey of child care services in schools.* Toronto: Canadian Education Association.

Cook, K., London, J., Rose-Lizee, R., & Edwards, R. (1986). *Report of the federal task force on child care.* Ottawa: Ministry of Supply and Services.

Council of Ministers of Education, Canada. (1986). *Early childhood education/services: A report prepared for the Council of Ministers of Education, Canada* Toronto: CMEC.

Dickinson, P. (1987, September/October). Day care in the schools: Linking care and education. *FWTAO Newsletter.*

Dickinson, P. (1988a, January). Linking care and education: Educators take action. *FWTAO Newsletter.*

Dickinson, P. (1988b). *The many faces of ECE: Similarities and differences in various educators of young children.* Unpublished doctoral dissertation, University of Toronto, Ontario.

Esbensen, S. (1982). A comment on Nos Enfants. *Canadian Journal of Early Childhood Education.* Toronto: Association for Early Childhood Education, Ontario.

Gregory, B.D. (1908). The necessity of continuity between the kindergarten and the elementary school: The present status illogical and un-Froebelian. In the *Seventh yearbook: The National Society for the Scientific Study of Education, Part II.* Chicago: University of Chicago Press.

Holmes, M.J. (Ed.). (1907). Kindergarten and its relation to elementary education. In the *Sixth yearbook: The National Society for the Scientific Study of Education, Part II.* Chicago: University of Chicago Press.

Jacob, A.S., & Peters L.R. (1971). *A field study of articulation and continuity of experience from prekindergarten through first grade.* Unpublished doctoral dissertation, Columbia University, New York, NY.

Katz, L.G. (1984). The education of preprimary teachers. In L.G. Katz, (Ed.), *Current topics in early education* (Vol. 5, pp. 209–227). Norwood, NJ: Ablex.

Langdon, G. (1933). *A study of similarities and differences in the teaching in nursery school, kindergarten, and first grade.* Published doctoral dissertation, Columbia University. New York: John Day.

LaPierre, L. (1980). *To herald a child: The report of the Commission of inquiry into the Education of the Young Child.* Toronto: Ontario Public School Men Teachers' Federation.

Levine, J.A. (1978). *Day care and the public schools.* Newton, MA: Educational Development Centre.

Mayfield, M.I., Dey, J.D., Gleadow, N.E., & Liedtke, W. (1981). *British Columbia kindergarten needs assessment: Summary report.* Victoria: British Columbia Ministry of Education.

McDonald, Neil. (1978) Egerton Ryerson and the schools as an agent of political socialization. In McDonald, N. and Chaiton, A. (Eds.), *Egerton Ryerson and his times.* Toronto: Macmillan.

O'Bryan, K.G. (1986). *Requirements for the training and certification of teachers in early primary education: A review of the literature.* Toronto: Ontario Ministry of Education.

O'Bryan, K., Kaplowska, O., & O'Bryan, M. (1975). *The junior kindergarten study.* Toronto: Ontario Ministry of Education.

Omwake, E. (1971). Preschool programs in historical perspective. *Interchange, 2*(2).

Ontario Ministry of Education. (1983). *Provincial review report, 1983 #1: Report of the junior kindergarten, kindergarten, grade one task force.* Toronto: Ontario MOE.

Ontario Ministry of Education. (1985). *Report of the early primary education project.* Toronto: Ontario MOE.

Ontario Ministry of Education. (1989, January). *Proposed ministry of education direction for child care: Draft.* Toronto: Ontario MOE.

Project Developmental Continuity. (1982). *Evaluation/Final Report/Executive Summary.* (DHEW contact No. 105-78-1307). Ypsilanti, MI: High/Scope Educational Research Foundation.

Regan, E. (1978). *Early childhood care and education.* Toronto: Commission on Declining School Enrolments in Ontario.

Rosenstock, J., & Rosenstock, E. (1985). *Child care: Options for working parents.* Toronto: Methuen.

Ross, E.D. (1976). *The kindergarten crusade: The establishment of pre-school education in the United States.* Athens, OH: Ohio University Press.

Ruopp, E., Travers, J., Glantz, F., & Coelen, C. (1979). *Children at the centre: Summary findings and policy implications of the National Day Care study* (Vol. 1). Cambridge, MA: Abt Associates.

Schulz, P.V. (1978). Day care in Canada, 1850–1962. In K.G. Ross (Ed.), *Good day care: Fighting for it, getting it, keeping it.* Toronto: Women's Educational Press.

Spodek, B. (1972). *Teaching in the early years.* New York: Prentice-Hall.

Spodek, B. (1982). The kindergarten: A retrospective and contemporary view. In L. Katz (Ed.) *Current topics in early childhood education* (Vol. 4). Norwood, NJ: Ablex.

Spodek, B. (1985, July). Early childhood education's past as prologue: Roots of contemporary concerns. *Young Children, 40,* 3–7.

Titley, E.B. & Miller, P.J. (1982). *Education in Canada: An interpretation.* Calgary: Detseling Enterprises.

van der Eyken, W. (1982). *The education of three-to-eight-year olds in Europe in the eighties.* London: NFER-Nelson.

Wahlstrom, M.W., Delaney-Donahue, S., Clandinin, J., & Oltaney, J (1980). *Early childhood education: Perceptions of programs and childrens' characteristics.* Toronto: Ontario Ministry of Education.

Woodhead, M. (1979). *Preschool education in Western Europe: Issues, policies and trends.* London: Longman.

13

Child-centred Programming

Ellen M. Regan

Conceptualizing Child-Centredness
Exploring Perceptions of Child-Centredness
Child-Centredness—A Meaningful Construct?
Conclusion
References

A traditional as well as contemporary goal of early childhood practice is to provide child-centred care and education. Because it is the program of the early childhood setting that can be talked about in concrete terms, it is not surprising that program is widely perceived as the measure of child-centredness. In fact, some argue that specific activities or experiences are by their nature more or less child-centred. But teachers sometimes experience difficulty in defending a child-centred orientation to planning and delivering programs and services for young children.

This latter experience provided the motivation for a study investigating practitioners' perceptions of appropriate practice in the early school years. This investigation is part of a longer-term effort to develop a conceptual framework that might facilitate the evaluation of child-centredness in various settings. This chapter analyzes findings from one study of practitioners' perceptions (Regan & Weininger, 1988) and suggests some first steps in constructing such a framework. To provide some context for reporting and interpreting practitioners' perceptions, we begin with the researchers' perceptions and understanding of child-centredness.

CONCEPTUALIZING CHILD-CENTREDNESS

It is generally acknowledged that the field of early education lacks a sturdy theoretical base. Montessori's work is an exception, since she developed a theory of pedagogy to parallel her theory of child development. Although theories of child development can and do influence curricular and instructional decisions, the thrust of these theories is to explain development, not to explain or prescribe practice. Nevertheless, many practitioners define and defend classroom programs with reference to child development theories. With respect to such claims, Kamii's comments are instructive: "When early childhood educators speak of child development, they are referring not to descriptive or explanatory theories but to a philosophy or approach to education" (1985, p. 3).

What Kamii refers to as "philosophy" seems to be what Spodek (1982) refers to as "ethical considerations" when he comments on the foundations of early childhood education (pp. xvii). If a practitioner's interest in child development constitutes a philosophy, the same can surely be said for the notion of child-centredness. In fact, on historical and rational grounds, child-centredness is perhaps best conceived of primarily as a philosophy or point of view.

Placing the child at the centre of the care and education process reflects a long-standing concern with the nurture of the child. Such concern is reflected in the thinking, over several generations, of those prominent in the field. Pestalozzi's belief that the teacher should model the sensitivity of the good mother and Froebel's claim that the kindergarten day must provide some freedom for the child to follow his or her own lead are examples of this tradition of thought. Similarly, Patty S. Hill's discussion of kindergarten functions, written in 1926 and recently reprinted, urges the kind of attention to young children's needs that makes it relevant 60 years later. Early education, from its beginning, has seen nurturing the individual's growth and development, through caring and sensitive means, as essential to its mandate.

Against this background of traditional thought and practice, the notion of child-centredness in programming emerges as an interaction between goal and method, or between ends and means. Although its proponents experience little difficulty in defending child-centredness as a goal or philosophy, it is more difficult to define or defend the methods and means of achieving it. This has been a long-standing problem. The height of the progressive education movement, for example, acknowledged the difficulty in implementing a child-centred philosophy. Interpreting this philosophy in the real world of practice continues to present problems for practitioners. These problems tend to be associated with different interpretations of what, in a given setting, represents a child-centred program. On the one hand we find those who claim that with the help of developmental theory we can define a comprehensive set of appropriate experiences for children of a particular age or stage of development. On the other hand we find those who claim that individual differences are so great that even within a given age or stage it is these differences that must determine what is more or less appropriate for individual children. Unfortunately, these differing perspectives sometimes result in a polarization that divides early educators and leads to debates about process versus product and the kind of either/or thinking about programming that Dewey (1938) criticized.

It should be noted that, within these major frameworks, individual teachers bring their own beliefs and experiences to the interpretation of child-centredness. This fact raises the question of how much we can generalize about child-centred programs. At the same time, it argues for research that seeks to discover any shared beliefs among teachers espousing a child-centered philosophy and any programming patterns associated with putting this philosophy into practice. These concerns constitute the thrust of the research discussed in this chapter.

In order to guide the selection of teachers and classrooms for study, the investigators proposed that child-centredness is revealed when there is "evidence that the program of activities, experiences and teacher-child interactions in the classroom is continually responsive to, and adapted for, the needs of children in that particular group at that particular time (Regan & Weininger, 1988, p. 3). It was further proposed that this view of child-centredness is consistent with both historical concerns within the field and data addressing program effects.

EXPLORING PERCEPTIONS OF
CHILD-CENTREDNESS

Following the selection of six child-centred primary teachers for participation in the study, the investigation proceeded through three phases. The first phase involved eliciting the six teachers' beliefs about learning. Beliefs refer here to what Sigel (1987) described as "truth statements held by an individual which are at the core of much of our actions" (p. 216). Each teacher prepared a written statement of her beliefs. Analysis of these statements revealed a marked similarity of beliefs among the six teachers.

The second phase included videotaping the ongoing program in three of the teachers' classrooms, followed by preparation of a voice-over sound track recording the three teachers' descriptions and discussion of what was portrayed on the tape. The resulting commentary was seen as representing teachers' perceptions of their practice—the lens through which they looked at children and program.

The third phase of the investigation involved responses to the tape by seven graduate students in a seminar course conducted by one of the investigators. Each graduate student had experience at some level of preschool or primary education and all were asked to view the videotape twice. For the first viewing, without the sound track, students were asked to identify what they perceived as evidence of child-centredness in the classrooms portrayed. During the second viewing, with the sound track, students were asked to compare their perceptions with those of the teachers in the videotape.

Data collected included the written statements of the six teachers, the videotape and sound track, and the written and recorded comments of the graduate students. Phase Two and Phase Three data, in particular, provided evidence of the points at which both the three teachers on video and the graduate students saw a match between what was observed in the classroom and what constitutes child-centredness. A more detailed description of study methods and of the findings from initial data analysis appear elsewhere (Regan & Weininger, 1988).

This chapter reports a further analysis in which sets of beliefs and features of practice appear to cluster in configurations that suggest the interaction of the two. When the beliefs, perceptions, and practice descriptions of both teachers and graduate students are combined, the configurations that surface suggest connections between beliefs about children's learning and programming. However, these suggest more about the nature of appropriate programming than about individual activities and experiences *per se*. For clarity of communication in the ensuing discussion, "teachers" will refer to the combined group of primary teachers and graduate students. Although the combined sample is small, the belief/practice configurations that emerge because of the consistency of certain responses do suggest particular features of child-centredness as practised and/or perceived by these teachers.

Analysis to date suggests three configurations combining belief and practice that, for purposes of discussion, are labeled "choice," "play," and "balance," respectively. Each label suggests the conceptual glue, or main idea, that organizes that particular configuration. However, as a group, the configurations suggest an overlap or interdependency in terms of programming. All three configurations are rooted in the same shared beliefs: that each child is *unique*; that each child learns in his or her own *individual way*; and that different children *learn at different rates*. As expressed by teachers in this study, these beliefs are at the heart of their perception of children and of their programming needs.

The "choice" configuration revolves around the claim that children, as learners, *need choices, opportunities for self directed learning*, and opportunities for *discovering* on their own. "Choice" surfaces here as the anchor, the prerequisite, for self-initiated learning and subsequent discovery. In program terms, these teachers see choice as dependent on the *number and variety of [worthwhile] activities* available to children. Planning must result in a sufficient number of appropriate activities from which children can choose, each with the potential for supporting children's *decision-making*.

The "play" configuration has at its centre the belief that *children learn through play*. Not only do *children develop concepts and skills through play*, but play activities also develop *pride* and *self-confidence* by providing opportunities for the child to *work at his or her own level*. Such opportunities are described as ensuring success or reducing the possibility of failure. Play as an approach to classroom learning is perceived as having much potential for accommodating different needs and abilities. It becomes an avenue for children's expression and experimentation that can be carefully, if often unobtrusively, monitored by the teacher. With respect to monitoring, these teachers expressed the view that, in order to assess play—or, for that matter, any activities—*the teacher needs to have an end in view for development*. Similarly, they claimed that *teacher direction is sometimes necessary to extend or initiate an activity* and that *teachers should build on children's experiences through questions, comments, and discussion*. This kind of teacher involvement is seen as important in facilitating both learning and the enjoyment of learning. Implicit here are two complementary ideas relevant to the teacher's role vis-à-vis play in the classroom. First, these teachers cautioned against activity for activity's sake in program planning. Second, they believe that the amount and nature of the teacher's involvement in learning must depend, at any given time, on what developmental end the teacher has in view and on the needs of the child or the group.

The "balance" configuration suggests that teachers see a need to create balance—both from day to day and from year to year—in programming the educational experiences of young children. Concerning day-to-day programming, the term balance is frequently used when referring to the nature of activities and to the initiation of activities. They claim, for example, that programs should provide *a balance of large- and small-group activity*, of *directed and non-directed opportunities for talk and work*, and of *routines* as well as *open-ended* activities. At another level, programs are seen as requiring a *balance of child-initiated and teacher-initiated activity*. What teachers perceive as necessary and appropriate balance is illustrated in their view that while *hands-on experiences and child-initiated activity are an appropriate beginning for learning*, teacher intervention is sometimes required *to help students learn from their experiences*. With respect to both day-to-day and year-to-year programs, the notion of balance is very much tied to what teachers call the *developmental* or changing nature of programming, from kindergarten through the primary level. Both teacher/child interaction and the educational experiences available must change constantly to accommodate the developmental changes in the children. The rate of change these teachers advocate and support is subtle and gradual, but renders impossible a static approach to programming characterized by much sameness of activity and expectation. Examples of developmental programming provided include gradually *decreasing solitary child play* and gradually *increasing teacher-initiated activities* across the kindergarten-to-primary spectrum. Implied here are great demands placed on teachers as program-developers who must continually balance sensitivity to children's needs with a sense of educational purpose.

CHILD-CENTREDNESS—
A MEANINGFUL CONSTRUCT?

As we may see from the configurations described, child-centredness is best viewed as a goal or end achieved through attention to particular program features. These particular features do not involve a specific set of activities or experiences, but rather pertain to the overall nature of the programming. As a result, this view of child-centredness falls short of the expectations of those looking for "pat" answers or solutions to programming needs. The teacher seeking to pin down *the* kindergarten or *the* first-grade program will find this concept of child-centredness of little value. In contrast, the teacher who sees programming as a continuing effort to effect a match between the child's needs and the objectives of care and education should find this concept useful and reassuring. In the current language of teaching, it is the "reflective" teacher who is likely to be attracted to this view of child-centredness.

Although the choice, play, and balance configurations provide some direction for those responsible for early education, we do not propose that they constitute a comprehensive framework for the development and assessment of child-centred programs. Rather, we suggest that continuing study of early education settings and continued discussion with thoughtful teachers are likely both to refine the current configurations and to suggest others that will inform our understanding of the demands of child-centredness. As noted earlier, this research is only a first step toward that goal. Nevertheless, what has emerged in the study is important, because it reveals the complexity of designing and delivering child-centred programs.

CONCLUSION

The notion of putting the child at the centre of care and education owes much of its appeal to its deceptive simplicity as well as to its inherent common sense. Certainly this research has demonstrated that the means to this common-sense end are far from simple or easy to define. However, the present investigation suggests that the teacher who believes in the uniqueness of the individual child, and accepts the implication of this belief for practice, will think about programming in terms of *what* is appropriate for *whom*. This kind of thinking encourages the search for alternatives, not for pat answers, and thus reflects a genuine effort to put the child at the centre of the care and education process.

REFERENCES

Braun, S.J., & Edwards, E.P. (1972). *History and theory of early childhood education*. Worthington, OH: Charles A. Jones.

Dewey, J. (1938). *Experience and education* (The Kappa Delta Pi Lecture Series). New York: Macmillan.

Hill, P.S. (1926/1987). The function of the kindergarten. *Young Children, 2*(5) 12–19.

Kamii, C. (1985). Leading primary education towards excellence: Beyond worksheets and drill. *Young Children, 40*(6), 3–9.

Regan, E.M. & Weininger, O. (1988). Toward defining and defending child centred curriculum and practice. *International Journal of Early Childhood, 20*(2), 1–10.

Sigel, I.E. (1987). Does hot-housing rob children of their childhood? *Early Childhood Research Quarterly, 2*, 211–225.

Spodek, B. (Ed.) (1982). *Handbook of Research in Early Childhood Education*. New York: The Free Press.

14

Designing the Early Childhood Setting

Steen B. Esbensen

Environment and Behaviour
Designing the Environment
Zoning the Indoor Environment
Moving Outdoors
Zoning the Outdoor Classroom
Conclusion
References

This chapter offers a framework for establishing both an indoor and outdoor physical setting that is effective for children and teachers of young children. The framework presented is based on practical experience, research, and theory, derived, respectively, from working with young children, from observing them, and from reading about their development. The design framework is ultimately one that provides the individual early childhood educator or team with an opportunity to exercise flexibility in working within the allotted play space.

Numerous studies on the impact of space on behaviour patterns in children have been reported in the course of the last two decades. Children are known to react to their environment in a more energetic and immediate way than adults. Children are curious and seek out new experiences in the environment. Studies have increasingly reported on the importance of providing natural elements for early childhood experiences and have emphasized the play potential of sand, water, mud, trees, bushes, rocks, and fire in the outdoor play environment (Moore, 1985). Indeed, the findings of numerous studies from the network of researchers involved with the International Association for the Child's Right to Play have been built into the municipal and residential design guidelines for children's play environments. In a previous publication, Esbensen, (1987) suggested that a playground attached to an early childhood education program should be considered an outdoor classroom. It should be a learning environment that meets curricular objectives by encouraging child-initiated, teacher-supported play activities that are both stimulating and safe.

In the indoor setting for young children, space that challenges children to interact should be provided since the spatial arrangement will affect the children's behaviour. Rosenfield, Lambert, and Black (1985) found that desk arrangement in the elementary-school classroom significantly affects pupil behaviour. While such studies are concerned with a more traditional classroom arrangement, it is nonetheless worth noting that Fraser and Fisher (1983) reported that affective and cognitive results in the classroom might be enhanced by an attempt to change the classroom environment in ways more congruent with the preferences of the class.

ENVIRONMENT AND BEHAVIOUR

In addition to affecting the cognitive and behavioural development of children, classroom arrangement provides immediate information about how teachers perceive children. Getzels (1974) presented the relationship between the classroom arrangement and the teacher's perception of the student's role in the following way: a classroom with fixed desks in a rectangular arrangement with the teacher's desk in front implies a perception of the child as a learner to be filled with knowledge by the teacher; a circular arrangement of desks implies a perception of the child as a social learner; and an "open classroom" organized around learning centres indicates a perception of the child as an active problem-solver.

The way in which a team of early childhood educators organizes the child-care centre, nursery-school, or kindergarten environment provides a good indication of the team's philosophical orientation. Observations made in the following situation provide an example. In a nursery school, a small climbing frame had been placed in a large open space at the entrance to the classroom. Eight children played almost exclusively on or around this climbing frame for several weeks, and all efforts to redirect the children were unsuccessful. The teachers were asked why they had chosen to place the structure close to the classroom entrance. They reported that they believed that young children needed to have an outlet for their abundant energy as soon as they arrived in the morning. However, after several weeks of living with the noise level generated by this active play, the staff decided to make a change. They moved the climbing frame close to the area dedicated to building with large hollow blocks and to dramatic play, which was at the opposite end of the classroom and away from the quiet-activity areas (where there had previously been a conflict between quiet and active play). As a result of the change, the eight children altered their play patterns, taking more time to interact with other children and eventually beginning to play with children in other areas of the room. There was also a dramatic decrease in the noise level of the classroom.

On the basis of subsequent observations and discussions with the teachers, it was possible to report that the teachers in this setting had changed their philosophical stance from a perception of play as a means of dealing with surplus energy to a more integrative, whole-child approach.

DESIGNING THE ENVIRONMENT

The design of the classroom environment is important and can have a direct impact on the quality of the experiences available to the children. The design criteria for an early childhood facility deviate substantially from those used to design a school building. Designing early childhood education facilities commissioned by private corporations, municipal governments, or non-profit community groups poses multiple challenges for the architects, landscape architects, and the groups sponsoring such projects. Only in recent years have architects begun to acquire significant experience in this field.

The ideal building for young children should be a low-rise building, preferably of a bungalow style. The height and style of such a building will allow young children between the ages of two and six to feel that the environment is scaled to their needs. The building should also have windows at children's eye-level so that the children can see outdoors, observe the changing weather conditions, and appreciate the natural environment adjacent to the indoor play environment. These are clearly ideal general design principles for creating a child-centred environment for a child-care centre, nursery school, or kindergarten.

ZONING THE INDOOR ENVIRONMENT

Once the basic space requirements for children have been defined and the appropriate provincial licensing requirements have been met, we can address the pedagogical considerations related to the organization of the space.

The early childhood education environment should set the stage for a variety of developmentally appropriate experiences. With the aid of Parten's social participation scale (1932), the following criteria for the organization of the learning environment have been developed (Esbensen, 1987, pp. 12–14):

> The environment should offer the young child:
> *A place to observe*—to stand, sit, or walk around looking at what is going on, without getting involved.
> *A place to play alone*—to use toys or natural materials alone, without physical or verbal interaction with other children.

A place to play alongside—to play with toys or materials like those of other children, such as blocks or single-user swings. There may be verbal interaction but it does not influence or change the play activity of others nearby. *A place to play with*—to associate with other children, to use materials or equipment and to discuss the play activity. There is peer involvement in the play experience, but roles are randomly assumed without a planned focus. *A place to play together*—to play together with another child or group of children to achieve a common goal. The roles taken in the play activity are no longer random and they may change as the play evolves. Material and equipment that require cooperation enhance such play opportunities.

Historically, the early childhood classroom has been equipped with a variety of play materials, neatly arranged on low shelves, with areas defined by the materials and the play experiences they stimulate. The arrangement of early childhood classrooms according to the philosophy and learning objectives of the teachers makes working and playing in the environment more agreeable for all. The degree to which teachers develop the physical space reflects the way in which they perceive the child as a learner; in turn, the spatial organization determines the degree of structure and responsiveness available to the children. The use of physical space in the early childhood program gives signals to the children about what they can do and how active they can be. The extent to which the space is furnished with materials and the disposition of those materials will also influence the way in which an area is used.

A framework known as the *design-zone framework*—which consists of the transition zone and four basic design zones (emotional, intellectual, social, and physical)—can be used to organize the indoor play space for young children. While some of the play areas are specific to a particular zone, others may overlap two or more zones. The flexibility of the design-zone framework allows it to be used by teachers working with various curriculum theories and in a wide variety of indoor spaces. The design-zone framework is particularly useful in setting up or reviewing the setup of the classroom facilities found in school buildings, church basements, and other rectangularly styled buildings. These spaces offer early childhood educators the challenge of placing the play areas in a logical and coherent arrangement. When the space being offered for use is designed to accommodate a child-care centre, the rooms will vary enormously. Some child-care centres will have indoor space in the conventional rectangular-room style described above; however, as new buildings are erected, there is greater diversity in the architecture. All facilities pose design challenges for early childhood educators, and this framework has been shown to help teachers of young children to organize space for activity.

We suggest that the design of the classroom be based on the premise that children learn through play and that the emotional, intellectual, social, and physical development of children all benefit from their play experiences. The classroom space should be organized to reflect all the developmental needs of young children, but the primary consideration should be to provide for their emotional needs.

The Emotional Zone

There are specific ways in which the classroom environment can be organized to meet the emotional needs of young children—by providing a reassuring, comforting, and cozy space. As young children's emotional needs should be a priority of the entire program, a design zone known as the *emotional zone* should be the first zone to be created in the classroom. It is highly recommended that this zone be relatively close to the *transition zone*, that is, close to the point of first contact or entry into the classroom. The space should be furnished so as to provide children with an opportunity to sit alone, with, or alongside of, either another child or an adult. A rocking chair or a small sofa on a carpeted area with a good selection of books organized on an adjacent shelf unit would serve to facilitate such opportunities and thus respond to the emotional needs of young children. This area can clearly double as the library corner where a language-arts program can be initiated, and the decor in this zone can provide the calm atmosphere appropriate to a library corner for young children. In addition to the language arts component, it is sometimes possible to include plants and small animals and to develop the science area on the periphery of the emotional zone.

The Intellectual Zone

The *intellectual zone* is another area that is included in the design-zone framework. This zone provides a variety of possible experiences. Children receive the message from the materials that this is an area in which they can manipulate concepts, solve problems, inquire about cause and effect, pose questions, and try out new strategies and words to understand what is going on. Several traditional play areas can be grouped within this zone: the science area and the various fine motor manipulative areas (which may include areas for drawing, colouring, cut-and-paste activities, and working with plasticine, clay, small blocks, cubes, Cuisinaire, Lego, and puzzles). These activities commonly involve young children in intense concentration. They generate some noise but, for the most part, the activity level is such that verbal exchanges are calm. The intellectual zone and the emotional zone are quite compatible in terms of the energy level of activities that occur within them; they should therefore be placed next to each other.

The Social Zone

A third design zone that should be included in the organization of the classroom is the *social zone*. The play areas that can be grouped within this zone include the sand table, the painting easels, the water-play area, the large building blocks, the wooden train set, and the dramatic-play area (kitchen, shop, clinic, office, and so on). This zone is characterized by the intensity of play and interaction that occurs both among the children and with the materials. As the activity level in this zone is more intense, it is inevitable that the noise level will be consistently higher, but the arrangement of the furniture can help to keep the noise within comfortable limits. Placing carpeting under block areas and positioning the sand and other tables so as to limit the number of children who can use them at a given time are examples of ways to keep the noise level comfortable. When furnishing the dramatic-play area as a kitchen, shop, or clinic, drapes, carpeting, and other soft materials can serve as acoustic buffers. The children playing in these areas within the social zone move around actively and coordinate some play experiences with others. It is a zone in which the children share, communicate, and experiment socially, and use physical dexterity. The quality of the detail given to setting the stage for each of the play areas will have an impact on the quality of the play activities.

The Physical Zone

A fourth design zone is the *physical zone*. The play areas that could be grouped within this zone include the woodworking bench, the large hollow block area, and the dance and movement area (which may include musical instruments and hoops). The physical zone may also contain an indoor climber, as described in the nursery-school example earlier in this chapter. Given the incredible variety of buildings and classrooms used, it is conceivable that some will have ample room for all the play areas that have been identified in the physical zone. However, it is also possible that some facilities will be short of space.

Transitions and Routines

The indoor classroom should have direct access to the outdoor play yard, and on arrival teachers should be able to greet children at the entrance. Immediately inside the building, a clothing-change space should be provided—a *transition zone*. Such an area should ideally be adjacent to a bathroom and a mud room where dirty or wet winter clothing can be changed and hung to dry. In the mud room, equipment can be provided to rinse off raincoats, boots, and snowsuits and to help speed up the process of drying the clothes. The facilities in the children's bathroom should be scaled to the age and size of the children who will use them and should include changing-tables if the children scheduled to use the facility are not toilet-trained. Locating the bathroom close to an exit to the play yard allows children flexibility to play outside in wet weather and enter the building to use the bathroom without having to track dirt through the whole classroom. The bathroom facilities should offer the children a sense of privacy but also allow teachers ease of supervision.

The design of the interior activity areas should provide numerous possibilities for meeting the needs of children. Some rooms may be small and cozy, but it is important that there are other rooms designed to allow children to use wheeled toys, to build with large blocks, and to play indoor cooperative games requiring abundant space.

As the program develops and resources become available, it is possible to consider creating multilevel platforms. This is particularly sensible if the space has very high ceilings that allow the platforms to be comfortably used to create a second-storey play area—for example, a cozy reading corner on top of a well-lit play space. Once again, in analyzing the placement of the play areas on, under, and close to a platform unit, it is useful to apply the design-zone framework to determine the extent to which the space will blend with the overall program objectives.

It is not only necessary to provide a stimulating environment for play; requirements for the daily routines of eating and resting also need to be considered. Young children need to have positive eating experiences. They can participate by setting the table, serving themselves, and calmly conversing with others during a pleasant meal. Eating routines in the early childhood program should ideally occur in small groups with an adult present at the table. Children should be encouraged to serve themselves and, at the end of the meal, be involved in clearing the table. This routine can take place in the various learning centres set up in the classroom and thus emulate the use made of dining-room tables in the home.

In much the same way, nap time can be organized in the playroom. Once again, children can be involved in bringing out their cots and getting them ready for nap time. Clearly, programs that have an additional room available for the rest period are at an advantage, especially when the children in the program typically rest for only a few minutes over the course of a full day.

MOVING OUTDOORS

Historically, the outdoor space has been perceived as providing an opportunity for children to get active physical exercise and replenish their lungs with fresh air. While there is nothing inherently wrong with this perception, it limits the play and learning experiences offered to children. The amount of time young children spend outdoors when attending early childhood programs varies according to the teacher's perception of the merit of outdoor play experiences and the amount and quality of the space available. Recommendations from the cooperative nursery-school movement and health practitioners state that young children should spend half of the duration of the program in outdoor play. Unfortunately, this amount of time is rarely allocated to outdoor play in urban child-care centres, where children often spend the major part of the eight-hour day indoors.

The challenge for early childhood educators is twofold: to allocate a substantial quantity of time to outdoor play experiences, and to ensure that a high-quality outdoor play environment is available to the children. The outdoor play space should provide opportunities for the child to develop not only physical dexterity but also social, emotional, and intellectual skills through interaction with other children and the environment.

Young children need experiences playing outdoors as well as within an exciting, well-planned, indoor environment. For decades, teachers of young children have been reminded of the importance of providing plenty of outdoor play space and equipment since these offer children essential living and learning experiences. If these are not available, the teacher may find that the children will not want to go outdoors. Space is the first and most essential requirement. Without ample space, children will have no desire to go out and there will be no possibility of developing the outdoor classroom according to child-centred design principles.

In the 1940s, early childhood educators grew concerned with the number of children growing up in apartment buildings, in crowded housing units, and on narrow city lots. These housing arrangements were seen as having negative effects on their growth and development. In the 1990s, this concern is even more critical since the majority of Canada's young children are growing up in an urban environment. Furthermore, the half-day cooperative playgroup experiences common for children growing up in the 1940s are now rare: more than 62 percent of mothers with young children are now actively involved in the work force and must therefore place their young children in the care of others, either in family child-care arrangements or in supervised early childhood programs. The need for more than the minimum amount of space is crucial for these young children. Outdoor space for play and recreation is most vulnerable in an urban housing development plan and early childhood programs need to be vigilant to ensure that their facilities have sufficient outdoor play space available.

The most desirable use of outdoor space occurs when the indoor space and the outdoor space are directly accessible, with a door from the classroom opening directly onto the outdoor play environment. It is most desirable that the two play and learning environments be adjacent to each other, as this reduces the time spent supervising the children as they flow back and forth between the two areas.

Unfortunately, these recommendations, which date from the early years of the nursery-school movement in Canada, have only recently begun to be incorporated into the design criteria for new child-care facilities. The present scenario in which increasing numbers of children are being cared for in facilities designed initially to accommodate school-age children means that thousands of children frequent facilities where they have to be constantly supervised by the caregivers: to change their clothes, to wait in line, to visit the toilet before going out to play, and to wait for the others before walking along the corridor, down the stairs, and out along the asphalt yard until they eventually arrive at their outdoor play setting. In these settings, which are less than ideal pedagogically, the environment must be as inviting, well equipped, and stimulating as possible through the provision of a comprehensively designed play and learning environment that is based on the needs of young children. The following design framework for the outdoor classroom, an environment for play and learning, is offered to provide guidance for the development of space directly outside the indoor play area, as well as to assist early childhood educators who are faced with the dilemma of having to create a stimulating child-centred environment in less than ideal circumstances.

Young children must not be exposed to the dangers of cars in a parking or drop-off area. A fence must surround the play area, as well as any outdoor space that young children can enter directly from the building. A fence that is sufficiently high, and constructed so as to discourage children from climbing over or through it will reduce risk and enhance the quality of teachers' lives. The fence can also serve as a screen to reduce the force of winter winds. Evergreen hedges and trees can also be used to modify the impact of changing weather conditions and to create microclimatic conditions that make outdoor play tolerable in cold weather.

A variety of surfacing textures should be provided. The children should be able to play on grassy areas, in sand, on gravel, at different heights, and on surfaces that allow for the use of wheeled toys. Soft, impact-absorbing surfacing material such as sand should be used underneath equipment from which children might have hazardous falls, including swings and climbing equipment.

In recent years, various materials have been used for surfacing playgrounds. Sand, pea gravel, granulated pine bark, rubber matting, and shredded rubber all have a relatively satisfactory shock-absorbing ability. However, they must be used selectively to produce a safe playing surface around each piece of playground equipment. To help in the selection of appropriate surfacing, the results of comparative tests concerning the relationship between height of fall and force of impact for various surfacing materials should be consulted. Several recent studies conducted in the United States indicate that sand has the highest shock-absorbing quality. If a synthetic surfacing is preferred, it should be selected only where tests are available to indicate that its shock-absorbing capabilities are acceptable. It is essential to remember that most impact surfacing used around playground equipment will not provide effective shock absorption if it freezes over during the winter months.

Water-play facilities can be provided in playgrounds in a variety of safe ways, depending on budget and site location. A water pump adjacent to the sandbox enables children to combine play with the two elements. Hoses that can be turned on or off as the play requires, or a water table, can also provide simple solutions. If standing water is chosen, a water container that can be emptied and cleaned each day is the most trouble-free approach. In some areas, it may be possible to develop ponds or shallow streams where children can explore organic growth in the water. Such water experiences, however, must be carefully supervised.

It is nature that is most at risk of disappearing from the experience of a young child growing up in an urban Canadian setting. The climatic conditions of a site for an early childhood play environment can be affected by the presence of trees, bushes, and hedgerows. The space will ideally have a variety of non-toxic vegetation so that the outdoor environment can be used all year. This should include a source of water that the children can use for play. An area for digging, a pile of either soil or sand, or a more generous garden area where children can dig and plant to their hearts' content, should also be available in the outdoor classroom. It is also necessary to have several storage spaces for the tools, assorted play materials, wheeled toys, and garden utensils that should be available for the children.

ZONING THE OUTDOOR CLASSROOM

Now that we have outlined the variety of play experiences we hope to offer, we can begin to organize the outdoor classroom with a zoning format similar to that proposed for the indoor classroom. The following zones "map" should help in planning the site:

Transition Zone

Manipulative/Creative Zone   Projective/Fantasy Zone

Focal/Social Zone

Social/Dramatic Zone   Physical Zone

Natural-Element Zone

This zoning format has been used to assist numerous child-care centres, nursery schools, and kindergartens in Canada and the United States to establish stimulating and safe outdoor classrooms. The following framework for conceptualizing the use of space in the outdoor classroom will help set the stage for play. For a detailed list of criteria for outdoor furniture and play equipment, we recommend *The Early Childhood Playground: An Outdoor Classroom* (Esbensen, 1987).

The Transition Zone

This zone covers the area close to the building from which the children enter the outdoor classroom. From here, they can look out over the space and size up the opportunities available to them. In this area, there will ideally be a choice of experiences. There may be a painting area with easels, a table with benches (perhaps for working with clay), a water table, or some wheeled toys ready to go. The transition zone offers activities that are essentially calm or that require quiet concentration, allowing children to move from indoors to outdoors at their own speed. As with all the zones, the transition zone may partly overlap with others, such as the three that are described next.

The Manipulative/Creative Zone

The playground cannot accommodate all the materials usually found indoors (blocks, puzzles, beads), but it is important to consider providing a zone with some outdoor activities that can help children develop their fine motor skills. Such a zone might be located close to the building, to facilitate storage and supervision. Outdoor manipulative/creative materials that have been successfully provided in many programs include clay, plasticine, playdough, and an easel with paints. The zone can also contain carpentry or construction materials. When such activities are provided outdoors, children can concentrate on the creative processes without undue concern for spills or noise disturbance.

The Projective/Fantasy Zone

A sand area or an outdoor table that can be used with sand or water can accommodate projective/fantasy play with small objects. An adjacent area could contain small wooden or plastic cartons or containers that children can use in their sand or water play. A sandbox or sand area that lets them sit, kneel, or stand best suits the combination of sand and water play that young children enjoy.

The Focal/Social Zone

A place for children to sit and talk with friends or with their teachers is often overlooked in play yards. A well-shaded garden table placed in a central location adjacent to or bordering the other zones could fulfil this focal/social function. Here, the teacher can support children's activities by discussing with them the insects, rocks, leaves, or grains of sand they have found during their play. This zone can also provide children with a comfortable site from which to observe, without any obligation to participate in the more active play.

The Social/Dramatic Zone

The playground's social/dramatic zone can take many forms. The basic consideration in furnishing such a zone is the enhancement of the children's symbolic play possibilities as they engage in parallel, associative, or cooperative activities. The setting could be a ground-level playhouse furnished with tables and benches and further supplemented with pots, pans, pails, shovels, spoons, and dress-up clothes. Sand should also be available, so that the potential for combining sand-cake cooking with dress-up play can add complexity to the nature of the play and stimulate the use of more diversified language. With the addition of large hollow blocks and interlocking boards, the focus of play in this area can change from residential to commercial, allowing it to serve as a garage, a storefront, or anything else the children imagine. Making it possible to park wheeled toys close to this area could further extend play possibilities.

The Physical Zone

While the zones proposed in the previous sections do not give a high priority to gross motor skill development, children develop both their fine motor and gross motor competence as they move around the overall play space. A site that provides topographical changes—for example, mounds, small hills, or clusters of rocks and boulders—can provide a variety of motor challenges. These challenges can be increased by the addition of paved paths and wheeled toys, including wagons, wheelbarrows, tricycles, and scooters. In addition to all this, children need a zone with stationary equipment on which they can balance, swing, sway, climb, and slide together—a *physical zone*. This zone should be at some distance from most of the quieter activity zones. However, it could be close to the social/dramatic zone, since the play equipment could enhance the complexity of role-playing activities. The equipment in the physical zone should be scaled to enable the child to grow from the challenges it provides. It should offer children risk-taking experiences—opportunities to accept or reject challenges to their skills and courage. The challenges should complement the overall development of young children without providing unnecessary hazards.

The Natural-Element Zone

Throughout the outdoor play space, it is desirable to provide natural materials that enable children to become familiar with the textures, colours, and scents of nature. Sand, water, grass, and a variety of non-toxic plants and trees can fulfill this function. However, nothing pleases children so much as watching vegetation grow in their own garden plot, where flowers and vegetables can be cultivated and cared for as part of the curriculum. Vegetables, as well as bulbs and hardy annuals, grow easily and show rapid results. Garden plots that can be reached easily and that have some means of preventing the children from walking on the vegetation by mistake are recommended. There might also be a natural area where digging is possible, where children can use shovels, spades, and rakes to explore earth and perhaps dig a tunnel to a land of their dreams. As mentioned earlier, slopes, mounds, and other landforms can be used to provide gross motor experiences (for example, rolling or sledding, depending on the season). Areas with tall grass and wild flowers will introduce a variety of insects and birds to the yard. Such natural-element areas complement the playground equipment furnishing the outdoor classroom.

If the outdoor play environment is to provide safe and challenging opportunities for learning, it is not enough to give attention to design and organization of the site and to selection of the furniture and equipment. For the outdoor learning environment to be effective, it must also be well maintained. Combined with good design and proper furnishings, careful and regular maintenance will make it as good a place for children and adults to enjoy interacting and learning together as is the indoor environment.

CONCLUSION

The attention given to designing and organizing the space for play will permit teachers to focus their attention on providing quality experiences for young children both indoors and outdoors. The design-zone framework presented in this chapter should help teachers of young children to arrange the space so that it invites positive interaction and stimulating play experiences for the children. Creating zones allows the teacher to group compatible play areas by analyzing the kinds of activities that occur in the zones and determining whether such activities are compatible with the stated objectives. The design-zone framework has been used effectively in a variety of settings—child-care centres, nursery schools, and kindergartens—and it should help in the arrangement of materials in most early childhood environments. Organizing both the indoor and outdoor space according to this framework should complement the curriculum recommendations presented in the other chapters of this book and assist teachers and young children in achieving high-quality experiences together.

REFERENCES

Campbell, S. (1984). *Daycare: Facilities and equipment*. Ottawa: Health and Welfare Canada.

Canadian Council on Children and Youth (1980). *Play space guidelines*. Ottawa: CCCY.

Esbensen, S. (1980, March/April). Legislation and guidelines for children's play spaces in the residential environment. *Ekistics* 281, 123–125.

Esbensen, S. (1981). Where can the children play? *Challenge, 12*(2), 13–20.

Esbensen, S. (1982a). An international and comparative study of children's play space requirements in residential environments. In N. Nir-Janiv, B. Spodek, & D. Steg (Eds.), *Early childhood education: An international perspective* (pp. 333–343). New York: Plenum.

Esbensen, S. (1982b). Where can children play? *High/Score Resource* 2(1), 1, 6–7.

Esbensen, S. (1987). *The early childhood playground: An outdoor classroom*. Ypsilanti, MI: High/Scope Press.

Fraser, B.J., & Fisher, D.L. (1983). Use of actual and preferred classroom environment scales in person-environment fit research. *Journal of Educational Psychology, 75*(2), 303–313.

Getzels, J.W. (1974). Images of the classroom and visions of the learners. *School Review, 82,* 527–540.

Hendricks, B. (1986). *A safe place to play: Guidelines for safe public playgrounds*. Vancouver: The Playground Network.

Kritchevsky, S., Prescott, E., & Walling, L. (1977). *Planning environments for young children: Physical space*. Washington, DC: National Association for the Education of Young Children.

Lovell, P., & Harms, T. (1985, March). "How can playgrounds be improved? A rating scale." *Young Children, 40*(3) 26–33.

Moore, R.C. (1985). *Childhood's domain*. Kent, U.K.: Croom Helm.

National Playing Fields Association (1985). *Children's outdoor playground equipment: National Playing Fields Association, Recommendations*. London: NPFA.

Parten, M. (1932). Social play among preschool children. *Journal of Abnormal and Social Psychology, 28,* 136–147.

Rosenfield, P., Lambert, N.M., & Black, A. (1985). Desk arrangements effects on pupil classroom behavior. *Journal of Educational Psychology, 77*(1), 101–108.

Schweinhart, L.J., Weikart, D.P., & Larner, M.B. (1986). *Consequences of three preschool curriculum models through age 15.* Ypsilanti, MI: High/Scope Press.

15

Infants and Toddlers

Sue Martin

THE NEED

More Canadian women are re-entering the work force after only brief absences for pregnancy, birth, and the first few weeks of their babies' lives. Where both parents need or want to work, families seek but cannot always find suitable child-care arrangements (Cook et al., 1986). Despite being aware of their own requirements, and more knowledge-able than ever before about the needs of their offspring, parents often have to make compromises and accept less than perfect arrangements. They may find themselves without the child-care arrangements necessary to enable them to work. This issue may cause the parents considerable stress both on and off the job. Accepting a situation that is less than ideal for them or their young child cannot be good for parents or infants.

Care does exist for infants and toddlers in Canada, but there are not enough spaces to meet the demand. In 1988, only 38,464 (16.5 percent of the total) child-care centre spaces available were intended for children under age three. Although this represents an increase of more than 10,000 spaces in a one-year period, 1987-88 growth was not yet keeping pace with need (Status of Day Care in Canada, 1988).

A shift in Canadian attitudes is leading to a new recognition that child care exists not primarily for the socially disadvantaged, but for all those families who desire it. This shift is especially dramatic with regard to the care of infants and toddlers—traditionally considered the exclusive responsibility of mothers.

New spaces for infants and toddlers are being made available in both the private and public sectors, in profit and non-profit organizations. Child-care facilities in public-school buildings are increasing rapidly. Provision is being made for pre-school programs, after-school programs, and infant and toddler programs. These child-care programs are administered separately. They are so desperately needed by parents that many have waiting lists.

Employers in Canada are beginning to see the wisdom of providing workplace child-care as a way of attracting and keeping workers; the younger the child they can provide for, the more likely they are to retain their staff.

Fast expansion of services brings with it a greatly increased need for training, and a concern about the quality of infant and toddler care. In some provinces community colleges have begun to respond to these training needs, either by establishing new basic courses or by upgrading or expanding existing programs. Some regard infant care as a new specialty that requires postdiploma expertise.

TOWARD QUALITY OF CARE

Infants and toddlers cared for in settings other than their own homes are not known to be either any better off or worse off than those who remain at home with a parent. There is as yet insufficient research to make a statement in support of one or the other type of setting. Although clarification of the needs of babies and young children, and how we can best provide for them, is increasing, research and observational information does not yet answer all our questions.

The standardization of training, particularly the adoption of common skills and competencies, is necessary to raise the standards of infant and toddler care. Equivalency is another issue that must be addressed if the child-care professional is to develop and win increased recognition.

Graduates of early childhood education diploma programs may be given the task of looking after babies without sufficient training. They may be well motivated and enjoy the work, but not be sufficiently knowledgeable. Those who hire child-care workers often look for "earth mother" qualities in staff who will look after babies, and do not recognize that specific skills are required. Fortunately, there is an increasing awareness of the need for training, as demonstrated by requests for in-service or postdiploma courses from the caregivers themselves as well as from directors of child-care centres.

We are beginning to acknowledge the nature of care required for infants and toddlers. It is expensive to provide an ideal environment and low child/staff ratios. We must also make a commitment to staff training: high-quality care for infants and toddlers can be provided only when staff are trained to acknowledge and respond to the needs of very young children.

NEEDS OF INFANTS AND TODDLERS

Physical needs are the most obvious. Infants let us know about their most immediate needs for food and comfort. They live in the "here and now," and protest loudly when their needs are not responded to instantly. The mother may not be the person to provide for all the infant's needs, but if we examine the components of positive maternal care we can draw out relevant features, learn from them, and in some cases reproduce them. Physical contact is the key to understanding both the mother's role and the infant's need.

Breast-fed infants are at an obvious advantage. Shortly after birth they begin to receive nutrient-rich colostrum, followed by an easily digested milk designed especially for them. They also enjoy increased immunity due to the antibodies contained in breast milk. But possibly the most important aspect of breast-feeding is the intimate physical and social contact involved. Establishing breast-feeding soon after birth is important for filling infants' nutritional needs as well as their need for physical contact. Whether or not mothers continue to breast-feed may, in part, be related to the care arrangements they have planned. An early transition to formula-feeding may seem expedient. But separation from mother need not always mean that the infant must suffer loss of her breast. Child care in or near the workplace may make continued breast-feeding possible. It is also possible for the mother to express breast milk for feedings later.

Bottle-feeding, although a second choice, should not be considered an unacceptable alternative. It can be a very positive experience. Modern bottle design can reduce the problem of babies ingesting air. Disposable bottles or careful sterilization procedures reduce bacterial infections. Formula can provide an alternative that is close enough to mother's milk. Most important, time, contact, and cuddles can be provided by nurturers, whatever their relationship to the infant.

The importance of meeting the infant's physical needs cannot be overestimated. Infant and toddler development will be adversely affected in every area if the baby's needs for physical comfort, food, sleep, space, movement, and fresh air are not catered to. We must recognize that the infant needs an immediate response. Quick responses lead to a contented infant who is likely to be more easily calmed (Ainsworth, 1977). Caregivers must individualize the daily schedule, therefore, in order to be responsive. The caregiver can most easily do this by tuning in to the individual child's personal rhythms rather than imposing a routine.

This is the critical period for the development of trust in the infant (Erikson, 1963). Adults need not worry that they will spoil children by running to them every time they whimper. We must understand that a prompt reaction to crying not only brings peace more quickly, but also produces a generally more contented baby who has learned to trust the caregiver. Although babies may not cry less often if they are responded to quickly, they are likely to cry less vehemently and to calm more quickly. Crying is a signal of distress; infants produce a range of sounds indicating varied causes of discomfort. Crying is part of infancy and should not be thought of as indicating poor care, but continued crying is a sign that the baby's distress is not being relieved. Physical reasons for crying may be the ones we can most easily react to, because they are the most obvious, but other reasons may be just as significant. Fear, shock, or loneliness may be triggers of equal importance.

Infants who lack physical contact and are not responded to will typically fail to thrive. The amount and quality of contact that infants receive contribute to their health and general well-being. The way we handle infants tells them how we feel about them. Babies become tuned in to their primary caregivers to such an extent that it may be impossible for caregivers to hide their feelings from their charges.

Attachment to the parent or primary caregiver is commonly described as *bonding*. The *affectional bond* (Bowlby, 1969) can be seen in both the child's and the adult's behaviour. Klaus and Kennell's research (1976) seemed to show that the first hours after birth were a critical period for the formation of this attachment. More recently, Lamb and Hwang (1982) have suggested that although attachment is important, the early theorists were misguided about its formation. Infants *can* form the necessary attachment through a relationship with someone other than their mother—or, for that matter, their father: in fact, attachments can be formed with several people, including those not present immediately after birth. Thus, infant care can be entrusted to an institutionalized care setting, as long as each infant has a primary caregiver in order to reinforce attachment. The personalized contact this allows avoids the problems caused by lack of continuity in caregiving.

It is particularly important to appreciate the difficulties associated with separation. If we predict possible outcomes, we can minimize the effects of parting from parents or caregivers. It is helpful to expect that the infant, quite normally, passes through a sequence of attachment phases (Ainsworth et al., 1978). Caregivers and parents must handle the situation appropriately for each child (Batter & Davidson, 1979). Protest, despair, and even the detachment of the child can result from the experience of separation. These are positive indicators of developmental progress, but must be understood and treated very sensitively if we are to avoid damage to the child.

Infants also need time and space to play. They move in an uncontrolled way at first, but gradually their movements become deliberate and skilled. The surroundings in which they can explore and experiment are important. We understand this from our own observations; Piaget's observations (1952) clarify our knowledge and add detail to it. In the process of acting on the environment, the child builds up an *internalized* notion of the world. The first two years of life are termed the *sensory-motor stage*. During this period, children learn about the world from sensory interaction with the environment (that is, everything in their experience). Children develop the concepts of self and of others and gradually build up information—*cognitive schemata*—from their sensory experiences.

The infant needs to explore and does not have to be shown how to play. Everything in the environment will be experimented with in play—the natural learning mechanism of the child. Everyday materials will stimulate play; the very young child needs not a curriculum, but opportunity for experience.

As children grow, change their perspective, and increase their ability to move around, they extend their experience and their skills. They need a full range of play materials, particularly sand, water, and other basic and messy play substances in combination with many ordinary domestic items. The infant is rooted in the real world and not yet involved in fantasy or symbolic play; this will occur later. At this stage, children need play in and experience with reality; they can only make sense of new happenings and objects in relation to previously understood experience.

New physical skills, and an appreciation of the difference between self and others lead to the possibility of free choice. During the second and third year of life, as young children learn to walk and acquire some control of their bodies, they struggle with the issue of independence. Erikson calls this stage the stage of *autonomy versus shame and doubt* and suggests that it is a time when children need to experience success, self-control, and self-worth. These experiences can be hard to provide if we do not acknowledge children's inner conflicts. We must guide children, knowing their egocentricity, and help them balance their needs to create, to destroy, and to manipulate.

We need to recognize the individuality of babies and young children, and thereby see that different temperaments require different handling. Buss and Plomin (1984) and Chess and Thomas (1984) offer ways to describe the temperamental differences between babies. Their research work can help us formulate strategies for dealing with the individuality of babies. Personalities are shaped by experience, but are evident very early in life. Some children are placid, others are more irritable. Individual temperaments are evident in the behaviour and reactions of each child. Differences that are clear in the infant may increase in the toddler;

the disposition of the individual determines the specific needs of each young child.

INTERRELATEDNESS OF DEVELOPMENT

When we study even the youngest infant, the newborn, we must accept the unique nature of this individual and recognize that this is a dynamic and developing small person. Appreciating that all the aspects of this young person's development are interrelated is the key to making sense of what we observe.

It is obviously useful to consider one aspect of development at a time. For example, we study visual perception because we need to know the rules babies look by to understand what they see. To know how they perceive their environment enables us to respond by making appropriate eye contact, and providing appropriate visual stimulation. We must avoid, however, considering this aspect (or any other) without relating it to other areas of development.

We need to study and observe young children in each area of their development without losing our perspective on the whole child. The impact of one area of development on another is significant even where we do not have research to confirm it. This is particularly true in the case of very young children because they lack conscious thought and action. Physical development is apparently the key to understanding every other aspect of infant development. Thriving growth depends on emotional well-being but emotional well-being depends largely on having physical needs met. The way babies respond to their environment is affected by their physical skills and emotional state; consequently, their intellectual activity is in part determined by these other areas of development. Infants are simply responsive; they are unaware of the interrelatedness of the components of their development.

Infants do not categorize their experience into separate compartments. They not think to themselves, in response to some stimulation, "This is cognitive information." Division of children's development, therefore, into "physical," "cognitive," and so forth, without recognizing the relationship of one to the other, signifies a lack of understanding of children.

THE NEEDS OF PARENTS AND FAMILIES

Parents need to be involved with their children; the younger the child, the more this is true. They need involvement on several levels; they need to feel that they have taken part in a real decision-making process about the care of their children. If they assume total responsibility, they need to experience it as a choice. If they share the children's care, that too should feel like a choice.

When choosing a caregiver, parents need to know something of the person, the philosophy, and the program; they need to meet a number of caregivers to make comparisons; and they need to discuss issues important to them—feeding, sleeping, discipline, and the needs of this particular family. When caregivers are chosen in this way, a relationship of trust is much more likely. In a group setting, parents need to know who will be the primary caregiver and who will play supporting roles. Parents need good relationships with the supervisor of the centre, and with all the staff their child has contact with, but their relationship with the primary caregiver is the most important.

Trust and mechanisms for successful communication are essential to this relationship. Parents need to know that they are considered partners in the care of the child. Verbal communication between adults is essential in this context, but good record-keeping about daily routines, activities, and the infant's skills and development must be kept, and must be accessible to parents. Confidentiality is crucial to avoiding any feeling that the child no longer "belongs" to the parent. Parents' anxiety over handing over their small children can go far beyond anxiety about the quality of care. Not "being there" for the child might make them feel less loved and needed. Parents need to have ongoing, private interactions with caregivers to share information for its own sake, but also to retain their parental role.

Continuing contact with the infant or toddler is essential for parents, particularly if they spend less time with their child than the caregiver. Infants' relationships with adults other than their parents are important but are still secondary. However successful other attachments may be there is nothing more important than the relationship between parent and child. The caregiver's role is transitory; the parents', one hopes, is not. The caregiver must act as the source for the child's security and maintain the child's trust for a larger proportion of the day than does the parent. The fact that the relationship will end is no reason for it to be shallow. The child's security depends on high-quality relationships. The self-confidence security produces makes it easier to accept partings. The quantity, quality, and kind of care must never diminish the importance of the parents' role.

Caregivers can take care to encourage parents' involvement with their infants or toddlers. Parents need to feel that although they may not be present all day, or involved with every aspect of care, they can still be appropriately involved in their child's experiences. Periods of time spent in the child-care centre or caregiver's home can be important for all.

Parents need to know that caregivers acknowledge their situation, socially, culturally, and even financially. Although respecting the parents' rights can be difficult—particularly when the caregiver has fundamentally different child-rearing attitudes or practices—it is essential to do so. Information given to caregivers by parents must be accepted without judgement. Parents know that their child is an individual and needs to be treated as such; part of this individuality is the child's background. Cultural and personality differences may lead some parents to explain more about themselves. All parents need to know what is going on. Being informed about their child will make them feel much more able to cope. Parents are much more likely to feel like clients if we are reticent.

A PHILOSOPHY FOR INFANT AND TODDLER CARE

We need a common philosophy for the care of infants and toddlers and the place of this care in the context of other forms of child care and education. This will enable us to provide appropriately for children. We also need a philosophy so that we can improve professional direction and credibility.

Some of our beliefs about young children may be based on instinct; some are absorbed from the care we received in our own childhood or from our own parenting; some are learned from theory or research; and some are tried and tested in practice. Checking the validity of our beliefs may be difficult, but must be done as thoroughly as possible. Acceptance of handed down beliefs can lead us to some inappropriate conclusions. If we look to theorists we may find conflicting views. Research may not be sufficient, appropriate, or applicable. So what do we do? We accept that we may have to alter or refine first principles, but we must begin by adopting some, at least provisionally.

A philosophy of care for infants and toddlers should embrace the following:

- the individual infant or toddler in the context of his or her own family and culture;
- individual areas of infants' and toddlers' development;
- the interrelatedness of each area of development;
- the basic needs and rights of all individuals;
- the privacy, respect, and dignity that each individual infant and toddler deserves;
- the need of the infant and young child for warm relationships that can grow into attachments;
- the caregiver's responsibility to provide for all the child's physical needs—health, nutrition, general well-being, and safety;
- the need to be aware of the each child's individuality and personal rhythms, and to tune into them appropriately;

- the provision of a warm, caring, safe, and stimulating environment where the infant can grow in self-concept, self-esteem, and knowledge of the world; and
- time, space, and opportunity to play.

These are very broad areas that most professionals would be willing to support based on current theory, research, and knowledge about the growth and development of infants and toddlers.

Consistency and continuity of care are necessary at any stage of the child's development to support the child's emotional balance and sense of security. While caregivers need to be flexible and'spontaneous in response to the child, they also need to develop some elements of sameness in the kind and quality of their responses.

The day must be organized in response to the rhythms of the infants in our care. A large part of that day is taken up by our routine care of them, our seeing to their bodily needs. If we can recognize that these times are essential to children's experience of the world, we can allow them to be opportunities for contact and communication. Gerber (1987) offers us an excellent model of infant care; the role of the person she terms the "educarer" is to respond to infants via their physical needs and provide a wealth of opportunity for interaction at times of routine care. Infants and toddlers experience routine care—bathing, diapering, feeding, and so on—as part of their day; it needs to be a positive experience, not something to be done as quickly as possible.

The caregiver is responsible for appreciating all the needs of young children (Honig & Lally, 1981). The most imperative need of all children is for their caregivers to understand "where they are at" and to respond fully to each child, offering interactions of consistently high quality.

Conscious acknowledgement of needs leads to appropriate, but flexible, planning. Imposition of rigid schedules and highly structured programs is inappropriate for both infants and toddlers because it concentrates on the adults' immediate needs, not the children's. The child-centered approach is, in fact, easier for the caregiver because it works with, instead of against, the children's rhythms.

Group settings for infants and toddlers must not have group routines and group activities. Primary caregivers responding to the needs of individuals will find the day progresses much more smoothly when each child is catered to as and when required. Routines can be much more relaxed and fulfilling when every child can move at his or her own pace, rather than being "processed" simultaneously.

THE ENVIRONMENT

Heated arguments about individual in-home child-care versus group care in child-care centres has both sides certain that their type of care is best. The research is, as yet, inconclusive. Most available research deals with information collected from high-quality child-care centres. There is little research comparing care in different settings.

The quality of environment for the infant and toddler is second in importance only to the quality of caregiving. If we think of ourselves as responsible for this environment, then we are responsible for everything in that environment—including ourselves, the caregivers. This approach will bring greater responsiveness. A major indicator of quality in provision is found in the way the environment reflects child-centredness. The child, not the routine, needs to be the centre of the program. In group settings we must see a set of individuals rather than a group of children.

Every item in the infant's or toddler's environment needs to be considered for its safety. Each object has to be proved safe, rather than accepted until proven unsafe.

Hygienic practices are essential to maintain an appropriately clean environment. Differing levels of sanitation are required for feeding, diapering, and general disinfection.

Atmosphere is not something that just happens; it must be planned. Although the caregiver's role is significant in setting the tone of relationships, we should not forget that the physical environment contributes largely to the child's experience of the world (Harms, 1980). Colour, lighting, visual stimulation, texture of surfaces, sounds, music, and smells may sound more important for an interior decorator's mandate than for ours, but if we think of each separately, we can see how each affects both our own perceptions and behaviour and the young child's.

We need sufficient space that is organized for safety, efficiency, and optimal use. Staff must be able to move without collision; space planning must take account of traffic patterns as well as use patterns. Some areas may have more than one purpose; other areas may be designed specifically for sleep, or for a particular activity. Adaptability may not be desirable when organizing space for the use of very young children; contrasts between high-stimulation areas and quiet areas are important to the infant's experience. The toddler's mobility affects space arrangement; as children grow in physical skill, boundaries need to be safe and effective.

Are we supposing that the infant's environment must be separate from that of older children? Common practice in Canada would lead us to suppose that it is "correct," in group care, to separate the age groups. This may be easier, safer, and cleaner for the management of infants, but it is not necessarily developmentally appropriate practice. Interaction between children of different ages is certainly normal and advantageous in the home environment. Group-care settings need to address this issue, even if the benefits of "family grouping" are not strictly measurable.

INFANT AND TODDLER CAREGIVERS

Caregivers must like young children and must be prepared to give time, effort, and energy to infants and toddlers. They must be communicative, responsive, stable, and consistent. Most particularly, they must be able to put others before themselves. What kind of martyr can do all this? Individuals who can acknowledge and take care of their own strengths and limitations.

Traditionally, the child-care profession has been blighted by the notion that the "practical girl" is the person most suitable for the task. The notion of practicality implies a limitation, not an aptitude. The required breadth of information, theoretical understanding, and ability to apply and adapt knowledge in changing situations has been grossly underestimated. Nevertheless, level of academic attainment is not a sure sign of effectiveness; a combination of skills is needed. The assumption that women will perform this task has obvious restrictions. It makes little sense when we appreciate the need for caring to be offered by both men and women. A female-only scenario, without male influence or role models, is unacceptable.

Competence for the task of caregiving lies in personal attributes and motivation, in experience on the job, and in education and training.

Broad areas of competence in caregiving can be identified as follows:

- facilitating infant and toddler development in each interrelated aspect
- responding to the needs of individual infants and toddlers
- observing, assessing, and keeping records on the children
- identifying deviations from the normal pattern of development and responding appropriately.
- giving care and nurturing in a communicative relationship with the children
- planning routines in accordance with the individual rhythms and patterns of behaviour of these particular infants and toddlers
- organizing and maintaining an environment that is stimulating, safe, and secure for the children
- providing space, opportunity, and materials for the play and exploration of young children
- supplying a healthy environment and taking care to minimize infection and disease
- recognizing and handling common childhood ailments, and administering first aid

- establishing and maintaining effective communication with parents
- communicating and cooperating with co-workers
- supporting professional standards of dress, personal hygiene, behaviour, and confidentiality
- working with professionals in other disciplines, and making appropriate referrals

CONCLUSION

Caring for very young children requires a blend of disciplines. A truly professional approach to infant and toddler care involves acknowledging the breadth of skill demanded by the job and ensuring that caregivers are not called upon only to be good people. We must provide them with the necessary learning, support, and skills for this important task.

REFERENCES.

Ainsworth, M. (1977) Social development in the first year of life: Maternal influences on infant-mother attachment. In J.M. Tanner (Ed.), *Developments in psychiatric research*. London: Hodder and Stoughton.

Ainsworth, M., Blehar, M., Waters, E., & Wall, S. (1978). *Patterns of attachment*. Hillsdale, NJ: Erlbaum.

Batter, B.S., & Davidson, C.V. (1979). Wariness of strangers: Reality or artifact? *Journal of Child Psychology and Psychiatry, 20*, 93–109.

Bowlby, J. (1969). *Attachment and loss: Vol. 1. Attachment*. New York: Basic Books.

Buss, A.H., & Plomin, R. (1984). *Temperament: Early developing personality traits*. Hillsdale, NJ: Erlbaum.

Chess, S., & Thomas, A. (1984). *Origins and evolution of behavior disorders: Infancy to early adult life*. New York: Brunner/Mazel.

Cook, K., London, J., Rose-Lizee, R., & Edwards, R, (1986). *Report of the federal task force on child care*. Ottawa: Ministry of Supply and Services.

Erikson, E. (1963) *Childhood and society* (2nd ed.). New York: Wiley.

Gerber, M. (Ed.) (1987). *A manual for parents and professionals*. Los Angeles, CA: Resources for Infant Educarers.

Harms, T., & Clifford, R.M. (1980). *Early childhood environment rating scale*. New York: Teachers College Press.

Honig, A.S., & Lally, J.R. (1981). *Infant caregiving: A design for training* (2nd ed.). Syracuse, NY: Syracuse University Press.

Klaus, H.M., & Kennell, J.H. (1976). *Maternal infant bonding*. St. Louis: Mosby.

Lamb, M.E., & Hwang, D. (1982). Maternal attachment and mother-neonate bonding: A critical review. In M.E. Lamb & A.L. Brown (Eds.),

Advances in developmental psychology (Vol. 2). Hillsdale, NJ: Erlbaum.

Piaget, J. (1952). *The Origins of intelligence in children*. New York: International Universities Press.

Special Parliamentary Committee on Child Care. (1987). *Sharing the Responsibility* (Shirley Martin, Chair). Ottawa: The Committee.

Status of Day Care in Canada. (1988). *A review of the major findings of the National Day Care Study*. Ottawa: Health and Welfare Canada.

16

Peace and Human Rights Education in Early Childhood

Catalina Ferrer and Joan Gamble

The Rationale for Peace Education
History and Philosophy of the Peace Education Movement
A Canadian Program for Early Childhood
Objectives for a Peace Education Curriculum
Conclusion
References

This chapter will present a general overview of a program for peace and human rights education in early childhood that has been prepared at the request of the New Brunswick Minister of Education (Ferrer, Gamble, & Didier, in press).

The chapter will be divided into two main parts. First, we will explain the rationale behind the peace and human rights education movement and why this education should begin in early childhood. This will be followed by a brief history of the movement and an explanation of the characteristics of the approach. Then we will present some of the most important aspects of the program we have prepared, explaining in detail each of the program's four principal underlying objectives and outlining some of the program's implications for designing activities, selecting materials, and planning the educational setting. The methodology applies more to five- and six-year-olds than to three-and four-year-olds. The program is developmental in nature and must therefore be adapted to the age of the children involved.

THE RATIONALE FOR PEACE EDUCATION

As the human race enters the twenty-first century, we face challenges to our very survival and to the survival of the planet as we know it. Canadians, like the people of all other nations, live daily with the possibility of a nuclear holocaust. The news media bring into Canadian households an awareness of the injustices associated with poverty, violence, racism, and sexism. The natural environment faces imminent destruction due to the excesses of industrialization.

Because of the urgency of these problems, ever-increasing numbers of people and organizations are turning to education for possible solutions. While recognizing that the issues are complex and that solutions lie, to a great extent, in the arena of international economics and politics, many see education as playing an important role in contributing to the construction of a new social order that recognizes the human rights of all people and respects the ecology of nature. As Canadians we have a role to play in this process.

The former world president of OMEP (Organisation mondiale pour l'éducation préscolaire, or World Organization for Early Childhood Education), Madeleine Goutard (1985), has stated that "as education for international comprehension and peace develops, evidence shows that this education should begin as early as possible" (p. 4). She continues, "Little by little we have become aware that the most profound action should be undertaken as early as possible, at the age when the fundamental attitudes are learned and personality is forming" (p. 7, author's translation).

Because of the age of the children, however, the approach and the content of peace education in early childhood require considerable thought. Some of the concerns about educating for peace in early childhood arise from a fear of manipulation, of lack of respect for children's free expression, and of creating stress in children by exposing them to social problems.

These concerns, though not unfounded, arise more from a desire to protect children, to maintain the myth of childhood innocence, and to keep children apart from society than from a deep analysis of the social reality in which children live. The fact is that all children, in Canada and elsewhere, are exposed in some way to violence, sexism, and racism in their homes, their communities, and through the media. A large number of Canadian children live in poverty, and many are objects of physical and sexual abuse, violence, and abandonment. They live in a world that is highly militarized and in which they are often objects of consumerism, perhaps most blatantly in the sale of war toys.

What a peace education approach proposes, then, is to take into account children's daily reality, to help them understand those issues that they are able to grasp, and to help them develop the attitudes and behaviours required to construct a society free of violence and exploitation.

In this endeavour, the real dangers of manipulation and indoctrination must not be ignored. Because of the idealistic nature of this approach, it runs the risk of inspiring over-zealous actions and dogmatic attitudes. Early childhood educators must be willing to criticize their own actions and attitudes in order to avoid these pitfalls. They must also be very sensitive to children's reactions in order to avoid over-burdening a child's conscience. As in other child-centered approaches, children's free expression remains the focus of the curriculum.

HISTORY AND PHILOSOPHY OF THE PEACE EDUCATION MOVEMENT

The concept of peace education originally grew out of the New Education Movement, which arose in Europe around the turn of the century. This psychologically oriented movement attacked traditional education on many fronts: its detachment from the daily life of children, its authoritarianism, its verbalism, its individualism, and the value it placed on obedience. Some of the authors connected with this movement are Ovide Decroly, John Dewey, Celestin Freinet, Friedrich Froebel, Maria Montessori, and Jean Piaget.

Although there is considerable divergence of opinion among these authors, they are all concerned with humanizing education. The child's well-being is their prime focus. They advocate active teaching methods that allow children to develop as autonomous, responsible individuals, capable of cooperation and respect. These methods are based on the active interaction between children and their environment. Curriculum content is chosen according to the experiences, interests, and needs of the children in the group and according to the sociocultural situation in which they live. Rather than merely teaching specific activities or imparting a specific course content, this approach transforms education by promoting egalitarian relationships between teachers and children and creating a climate of respect for each individual.

After World War II, a world movement developed to promote peace and respect for human rights. The United Nations assumed a leadership role of historic importance in this regard: in 1945, it created the United Nations Educational, Scientific, and Cultural Organization (UNESCO); in 1948, it proclaimed the first Universal Declaration of Human Rights; and in 1959, it adopted the Declaration of the Rights of the Child.

In Canada, educating for peace and human rights is entering the mainstream of the education community. For example, the Canadian Teachers Federation has adopted a comprehensive policy supporting peace education (Macintosh, 1987). Study guides on peace and human rights education have been produced by several institutions, including the Department of the Secretary of State of Canada in 1984, the Canadian Human Rights Foundation in 1986, and the Centrale de l'enseignement du Québec (1986). Peace education is being integrated into the classroom curriculum in schools across the country (Kalmakoff, 1986; Macintosh, 1987; Walkley, 1988).

The approach to peace and human rights education advanced by Erich Fromm (1981) and Amadou Mahtar M'Bow (1982) adopts a positive conception of peace as a state of justice and respect for the rights of all. This approach questions, among other things, social relationships based on domination, the extolling of the virtues of war, the mindless exploitation of the natural environment, individualism, conformity, and uncritical obedience to authority. It puts education at the service of the construction of a peaceful world. It proposes a double undertaking: the transformation of the individual and of the social structures in order to put into practice universal respect for human rights. It is an approach based on

- interaction, interdependence, and pluralism
- respect for cultural diversity
- cooperation, mutual respect, and critical thinking
- character formation and attitude-building
- using children's present situations and involving them in concrete action
- directing aggression toward constructive action
- a long-term process, not a short-term endeavour
- a way of looking at the human condition, not a new religion
- dynamic dialogue between people and nations
- a systematic effort to build comprehension among people.

Educating for peace involves not only educating children to become builders of peace, but also educating teachers and parents so that they all grow in personal awareness and in awareness of others and the world (Freire, 1970).

A CANADIAN PROGRAM FOR EARLY CHILDHOOD

We are currently experimenting with the concrete application of our ideas in various early childhood settings in New Brunswick, including the laboratory kindergarten at the Faculté des sciences de l'éducation at the Université de Moncton. Over the next year or two, using the feedback and ideas of the teachers involved in these experiments, we plan to produce teaching guides that will help clarify how to implement peace and human rights education in early childhood settings in Canada.

In addition to the educational principles cited above, there is a fundamental principle underlying the program we have developed: the right for people to live personally fulfilling lives. This principle involves values on two levels: on an individual level, the values of freedom, autonomy, and responsibility; and on a social level, those of justice, the appreciation of social diversity, and solidarity. These values are applicable to a peace education curriculum at any age level.

As in other humanistic, child-centred approaches, play remains the focus of this curriculum. In order to better ensure that children's play allows them to develop the attitudes and values underlying the program, special attention is given to selecting materials and organizing the physical environment. For instance, it is important to provide anatomically correct dolls of different cultural and racial groups, beautiful and plain; dress-up clothes that represent women and men in various types of blue-collar, pink-collar (beautician, retail salesperson), and white-collar work; and materials that invite cooperation and enrich children's cultural awareness—works of art, music, and musical instruments. Pictures and books are selected to actively counteract stereotypes and to ensure that children are exposed to cultural diversity: for example, photographs and books depicting differently abled people actively involved in community life; women construction workers; working-class life; children from various parts of the world; and differently abled children engaged in everyday activities such as going to school, playing, and eating.

Although play has an important place in this approach, children also engage in work or activities that have a social purpose (Freinet, 1969). These activities are planned by adults to allow children to take responsibility for themselves and for others, and to expose them to social realities and to problems facing the natural environment. For example,

- children assume responsibility for tidying the room, watering plants, and caring for animals
- teachers help children determine the rules of conduct for the group and modify the rules as required
- teachers help children solve problems faced by the group—for example, noise level or infringement by some children on others' play
- teachers encourage children to assist others in the group who are having difficulties and help them better understand one another's feelings
- teachers might lead a discussion about a local industry that is causing damage to the environment and explore possible solutions.

OBJECTIVES FOR A PEACE EDUCATION CURRICULUM

The program's values are expressed in four principal objectives, each identified with a specific aspect of peace and human rights education. We will provide an explanation of each objective, as well as some suggestions of related activities.

Developing self-acceptance, self-awareness, self-respect, and a sense of inner harmony

In our peace education program, spontaneous play and freedom of choice are emphasized to allow children to develop their autonomy, imagination, and creativity. Through actively manipulating open-ended materials in a stimulating environment, children encounter problems and discover solutions. Their play allows them to express their inner world and to develop a sense of harmony between their inner world and outer reality.

In early childhood, children are often very spontaneous in their emotional expression. In a peace education classroom, children are encouraged to express, identify, and accept their emotions, including their feelings of aggression. Early childhood educators help them find ways to express negative emotions without infringing on the rights of others in the group. A teacher might suggest, for example, using body movement, or paint, or clay to express an emotion of the moment. This could be followed up by looking at how emotions are expressed through the arts—perhaps looking at an illustrated book on the theater or examining how sculptors convey different emotions.

Masks from various cultural and theatrical traditions can also be used to help children understand emotional expression. Hand-held masks can be made by photocopying pictures from books, colouring them, gluing them onto cardboard, and adding a holding stick. These can then be used as props in the dramatic-play area. (Traditional masks for Canadian Indian tribes provide interesting possibilities along these lines.)

Another aspect of this objective, which is very important to a peace education approach, is the emphasis placed on specific activities that help children focus their attention inwards. Many of these activities are inspired by yoga; they often involve relaxation, breathing, and gentle stretching, as well as massage.

The quality of the educational setting also has a great impact on the children's and the teacher's sense of well-being. In order to "soften" the environment, preference is given to pastel colours; colour are harmonized; plants abound; and attention is given to music, keeping it baroque and lyrical. Cushions, rugs, and fur; soft, natural lighting; and wood (as opposed to, say, plastic) are used as much as possible.

The focus of this objective is on building a sense of inner peace, which is achieved through increasing self-awareness, gaining an understanding of emotions, finding creative ways to express them, consciously focusing inwards, and learning to relax and listen internally.

Developing the ability to interact with others in mutual respect, cooperation, and empathy

Through spontaneous, informal interactions and planned activities, teachers encourage children to recognize and value the similarities and differences among the children in the group—in appearances, attitudes, ideas, and values. One of the benefits of group experiences in the early years is that children are exposed to different ways of doing things; this exposure can increase their understanding of human diversity. When following this approach, an early childhood educator organizes specific activities aimed at expanding children's awareness. For example, each child may make a book entitled "My Family," which describes the members of his or her family and the family's daily activities and routines. Through these books, the teacher can explore, with the children, the different types of families represented in the group, filling in where there are gaps: two-parent families, divorced families, extended families, children living with grandparents, families from cultures not represented in the group, families headed by homosexuals. These books can also provide source material for illustrating various types of cultural expression. (For other ideas along these lines, see Derman-Sparks, 1989.)

It is important that, while making children aware of differences, we also identify common elements among the various groups. For example, we might explore with children how different cultural groups express affection, as well as the different ways of expressing affection within the same cultural group.

Conflict resolution is also very important in a peace education curriculum. Rather than avoiding conflicts, teachers use them to help build tolerance and understanding. One way to increase children's self-awareness and their understanding of the importance of dialogue in conflict resolution involves a directed activity in which the teacher discusses with children why they get into fights and what frustrates them. Teachers can also express their own feelings about things that cause them stress and frustration.

Teachers must realize that although children may understand the importance of dialogue in conflict resolution, they will not necessarily be able to apply these ideas to their personal conflicts in any systematic way.

Helping children realize this fact can increase their awareness of the difficulty of achieving peace—whether it be inner peace, peaceful conflict resolution, or peace on a larger social scale. It is nevertheless important that teachers continue to help children develop the skills required for peaceful conflict resolution.

In the area of power relationships between children, both domination and submission are seen as problematic because they impede egalitarian relationships. Teachers work closely with submissive children to help them stand up for their rights and express their feelings, while at the same time helping dominant children develop their leadership abilities and their sensitivity to and respect for the needs of others. This is one way to help children develop feelings of empathy for each other.

Conflicts that occur in free play offer ideal opportunities for children to develop the skills required to cooperate—for example, negotiating, bargaining, and learning to listen to another point of view (Goffin, 1987).

Although cooperative games are used in peace education, competition is not completely eliminated. Teachers emphasize the pleasure of participation in group games and actively downplay the importance of winning, often taking cues from the children themselves—encouraging, for instance, children who spontaneously modify the rules of a game to eliminate the competitive aspect.

To further encourage cooperation among the children, teachers might propose group projects in which children work together for a common goal. For example, the children might produce a mural for a local senior citizens' residence. Teachers can help children decide together on the theme, the materials, the procedures, and how to transport the final product.

Another aspect of this objective is the role of the group in determining the rules required for the smooth functioning of group life. When problems arise, the group can be appealed to for help in finding solutions. For instance, if the play of some children is infringing on that of others, a teacher can discuss with the group the nature of the difficulty with a view to collectively identifying and implementing solutions.

Through this objective, teachers seek to increase children's appreciation of human diversity and their recognition of what people have in common, and to increase their ability to resolve conflicts in mutually respectful ways, to empathize with one another, to cooperate, and to affirm their rights and assume their responsibilities as group members.

Developing an awareness of social realities, an appreciation of cultural diversity, and feelings of solidarity

In this objective, the two sides of human expression are considered: on the one hand, the creative genius of humans and their ability to love, and on the other, people's inhumanity to one another.

Children are, for example, introduced to the world of music and to the great artistic and theatrical traditions of various cultures. Exposure to artists such as Chagall, van Gogh, and Jackson Beardy, who are of particular appeal to children and who have an important message to communicate about the human condition, enriches the program. Teachers can guide children to explore the theatrical traditions of various cultures in order to broaden their appreciation of human diversity and their understanding of creative ways to communicate ideas and express emotions. Children are introduced to the musical expression of their own culture and of others—Chinese, African, Arab, Greek, Amerindian.

This program also seeks to make children aware of social issues. The goal here is to empower children with the feeling that they can contribute, at their own level, to finding solutions. The program builds on children's sense of justice and encourages them to think critically and to speak up in the face of injustice directed at themselves or others. With three- and four-year-olds, the issues dealt with would be directly related to their daily experiences in the early childhood setting. However, as Derman-Sparks (1989) states, "Five-year olds can begin to understand people's struggles for justice and a better quality of life" (p. 64). At this age it is appropriate to look at social issues that affect the immediate community of the children in the program and eventually at other issues of injustice in the larger community.

Great care must be taken, however, to avoid overwhelming children with social problems. Early childhood educators must think critically about which issues are appropriate for three-, four-, and five-year-olds and which issues are beyond their intellectual and emotional comprehension. Teachers must be willing to risk controversy by confronting troublesome issues rather than covering them up. It is also important that they become personally committed to the cause of justice.

In choosing content, early childhood educators are encouraged to relate issues to children's personal experiences and knowledge and to use their spontaneous questions as departure points.

Role models are used to make children aware of how one person's commitment can influence a movement for social justice. (For examples of activities along these lines, see Clement, 1988.)

Exploring the issue of violence is another important aspect of this program. Children have intimate knowledge of violence through their daily experience: the violence of their own feelings and actions; the violence they often suffer at the hands of their caregivers and friends; the violence they are exposed to through the media. Although violence cannot be eliminated from the environment or from children's interactions with each other, teachers can help children to better understand this troubling aspect of human expression. They can discuss with children the violence in their daily lives and help them discover its origins, distinguishing between violence that has its roots in the environment (that is, violence related to such social conditions as over-crowding, poverty, lack of choice and challenges, and the commercialization of violence in the media) and violence attributable to the human condition (that is, violence stemming from more individual sources, such as personality conflicts and moods). Teachers can help children find ways of improving the environment in order to reduce violence, as well as ways of dealing with violence. To do this effectively, it is important that early childhood educators look honestly at how they deal with their own aggressive and violent feelings—how they cope with stress, how they deal with personality conflicts, how they express anger, and so on.

In order to broaden children's understanding of their social world—since they are often exposed to and affected by sexism and racism and often have limited knowledge of and contact with differently abled people—teachers make conscious efforts to expose them to non-sexist, non-racist, and differently abled models. Books, display materials, and dramatic-play props are selected to break down stereotypes—by depicting and/or describing, for example, a black woman doctor, a male dancer, a differently abled computer operator. Mere exposure is not enough, however, to change the attitudes that underlie stereotyping. Teachers also actively intervene in spontaneous situations and planned activities to help children develop positive attitudes toward members of the opposite sex, people with a different skin colour from their own, and people with different levels of physical and mental ability.

The theme file is a technique that can be used to increase children's social awareness—that is, their awareness both of human creativity and of social problems. The teacher can help children put together files on different themes. The children, their parents, and the teacher seek information and pictures to put in the files. The following list of possible themes for these files is inspired, to a great extent, by the ideas of Viviane Fava (1988), director of a UNESCO-associated kindergarten in Nanterre, near Paris:

- discovering artists
- discovering scientists
- dolls—through the ages in different cultures; in art; male and female; of various skin colours; beautiful and plain; children's drawings of
- houses around the world
- war toys (helps children and parents develop their critical awareness of the war toy industry and its exploitation of the child as consumer)
- friendship—its expression in different cultures
- masks—use in theatre and in various cultures
- the world of jazz (can serve as a departure point for introducing children to slavery and its impact on black culture, as well as for exploring the richness of black culture—for example, listening to jazz, becoming familiar with some jazz musicians and the instruments they use and so on)
- hands—of artists; of the elderly; of babies; of different colours; of

labourers; of dancers; in sculpture; in painting; hands destroying, hands creating

Through this objective, children are led to broaden their understanding of social reality, to appreciate various types of cultural expression, and to recognize and denounce situations involving injustice.

Developing an appreciation of the material and natural environment and a respect for the ecology of nature

Children's tendency to wonder at nature is encouraged in this approach. Time is taken to observe simple, everyday "wonders"—the newly formed ice in a puddle, a spider patiently spinning its web. Children are also encouraged to respect the natural environment—to become aware, for example, of the harmful effects of taking branches from trees or of removing insects from their natural habitats.

Pollution and problems of ecological imbalance are explored, using children's daily and personal experiences as points of departure. Teachers help children learn which of their own actions cause pollution, and discover pollution sources in their community and what they, as children, can do about these problems. One example of an activity that helps develop awareness of the natural environment and the threats posed by pollution entails constructing a theme file about water. This file might include information about and images of water in nature, in various forms; water's use to humanity; clean water; polluted water; water and trees; and drought. The teacher can also help children become aware of how they can reduce their wasteful use of water.

Natural objects have an important place in the classroom: having them available provides children with hands-on experiences (for example, exploring an abandoned wasp nest, or observing worms or spiders in a terrarium). Within this approach, teachers and children spend a great deal of time outdoors—in the woods, by streams, on the beach—and teachers use these experiences to heighten children's appreciation of their natural environment and to inspire them to engage in ecologically sound practices. A teacher can have children do a spring cleanup of their play yard and in the process reinforce their sense of personal responsibility to be "non-polluters" and to criticize the behaviour of litterers. Local industries can be scrutinized for their environmental practices; if they are found wanting, the teacher can explore with the children what they can do as a group to try to change the situation.

Through this objective, therefore, teachers seek to encourage children's sense of wonder; to increase their awareness of the problems of ecological imbalance; and to help them take positive actions, at their level, to combat pollution.

CONCLUSION

This program of peace and human rights education seeks to empower children, so that, based on feelings of personal well-being, they become concerned with building a world in which all people have the opportunity to fulfill themselves and to live in harmony with each other and with the natural environment. (Teachers must work with parents and children to build a greater awareness of situations of injustice and ecological imbalance and to engage in positive action to contribute to finding solutions to these issues.) This program cannot be "taught", it must be lived. To accomplish the objectives, teachers must be willing to engage with children and parents in a process of mutual growth.

The question of what issues to address and how to address them remain largely unanswered. The experiments which are presently being undertaken in the laboratory kindergarten at the Université de Moncton and in other early childhood centers in New Brunswick will begin to provide some answers. Other efforts of individuals and organizations across North America and in various places throughout the world are contributing to our understanding of this area.

The peace education movement is a response to the challenges humanity faces as the end of the century approaches. The efforts can begin in early childhood and continue throughout the child's education, reaching beyond the formal educational and care settings to include the larger community. Through peace education children are inspired with a new world vision based on the recognition of the right of all people to live in justice in a healthy environment.

REFERENCES

Canadian Human Rights Foundation. (1986). *Guide for teaching human rights.* Montreal: CHRF.

Centrale de l'enseignement du Québec (1986). Cahier pédagogique. *Éduquer à la paix c'est contribuer à bâtir la paix.* Québec.

Clement, S.G. (1988). Dr. Martin Luther King, Jr., curriculum: Playing the dream. *Young Children, 43*(2)11.

Department of the Secretary of State of Canada. (1984). *Canadian Charter of Rights and Freedoms: A guide for students.* Ottawa: Secretary of State.

Derman-Sparks, L. (1989). *The anti-bias curriculum: Tools for empower-*

ing young children. Washington DC: National Association for the Education of Young Children.

Fava, V. (1988, October). [Interview.]

Ferrer, C. Gamble, J., & Didier, B. (in press). *Programme d'éducation préscolaire*. Fredericton: Ministère de l'Education.

Freinet, C. (1969). *Pour l'école du peuple*. Paris: François Maspero.

Freire, P. (1970). *Pedagogy of the oppressed*. New York: Seabury.

Fromm, E. (1981). *On disobedience*. New York: Seabury.

Goffin, S.G. (1987). Cooperative behaviors: They need our support. *Young Children, 43*(2), 75–81.

Goutard, M. (1985). *Grains de paix: Contribution de l'éducation préscolaire à la compréhension internationale et à l'éducation pour la paix*. Paris: UNESCO.

Kalmakoff, S. (1986). *Peace education in a public school system: Report of a curriculum implementation project*. Paper presented at the annual conference of the Canadian Peace and Rights Educators Association, Winnipeg.

Macintosh, R. (Ed.). (1987). *The Canadian peace educators' directory*. Drayton Valley, AB: Pembina Institute for Appropriate Development.

M'Bow, A.M. (1982). *Las raices del futuro*. Paris: UNESCO.

Walkley, A. (1988). *Curriculum for education for peace: Developing interpersonal communication skills in children*. Paper presented at the annual conference of the Canadian Peace and Rights Educators Association, Windsor.

PART 4

CANADIAN PROGRAMS AND SERVICES

The content of Part Four focuses on the dynamics of programs and services for young children. In chapter 17, Jean Stevenson introduces the parent-cooperative model and its current adaptation, the parent resource centre. Chapter 18, by Margie Mayfield, extends the emphasis on children's parents, illuminating the role parents can and should play in any early childhood program. Patricia Canning and Mary Lyon shift the focus to one particular child population that is served by Canadian programs and services children with special needs. The two final chapters offer the reader a perspective on the future of programs and services by introducing two current research thrusts. The Victoria and Vancouver projects described by Hillel Goelman and Alan Pence in Chapter 20 will undoubtedly be the forerunners of other research of this type in Canada, and will, as well, push our knowledge about the impact of child-care programs and services to a new point. In chapter 21, the Quebec team of Madeleine Baillargeon, Raquel Betsalel-Presser, Donna Romano-White, and Ellen Jacobs also help draw the reader's attention to what the future might hold with their work on the issue of child-care-to-school transitions.

17

The Cooperative Preschool Model in Canada

Jean H. Stevenson

Within the broad spectrum of Canadian child-care services and educational programs for young children, parent cooperatives have emerged as strong, viable alternatives to municipal or commercial operations. This chapter offers a retrospective view of the earliest manifestations of the movement in North America and a study of the ensuing years as its influence spread in Canada. This is followed by a description of the origin and development of a philosophy and style of operation indicative of non-profit parent-participation programs. The chapter explores the expanded role of parent co-ops, along with their impact on the early childhood community, and concludes with a speculative look at the future of this remarkable institution.

INCIDENCE OF PARENT COOPERATIVES

In cities, towns, and rural communities all over North America there are early childhood programs known as "parent cooperatives". Their existence today, in many forms and in widely varied premises, is proof that this grassroots movement, through some 70 years of progress, continues to offer valuable experiences and needed services to parents and to their young children. This is possible through the efforts of the parents themselves, with the help of experienced and committed people who believe in cooperation as a democratic and fulfilling way of achieving their goals.

It is impossible to determine the exact number of parent co-ops currently functioning in North America. Although some statistics may be derived from the membership records of regional co-op councils, many groups that qualify as co-ops by the nature of their operation choose to remain independent.

A 1988 poll of eleven councils in Canada (two in British Columbia, one in Quebec, and the remaining eight in Ontario) provided a reasonable estimate of 500 member groups serving about 20,000 families. This does not include co-op preschools known to exist in other provinces or in areas with no coordinating council.

ORIGINS

Canadian parent co-ops are the proud inheritors of a style of children's program based on parent participation and shared learning. The co-op movement received its earliest encouragement from the work done by Katherine Whiteside Taylor in the 1920s in Cambridge, Massachusetts, and in Berkeley, California. The Children's Community in Berkeley, begun in 1927, is the oldest known cooperative nursery still in operation, although the honour of establishing the earliest known co-op goes to a group of 12 faculty wives at the University of Chicago in 1916.

Many American educators and parents contributed to the rapid spread of parent cooperatives in the United States. Large concentrations of parent-participation nursery schools appeared in Maryland, New York, New Jersey, California, Michigan, Washington, northern Virginia, and Oregon. Grouped under regional councils, they set an example that led to the initiation of similar preschools in almost every state of the union, including Alaska and Hawaii.

Although the movement's spread across the border into Canada has not been clearly chronicled, pockets of co-op preschool activity appear to have existed in Canada in the 1930s and 1940s. Toronto's Manor Road Nursery School, for example, is believed to be the oldest cooperative nursery in Ontario, and possibly in Canada, having been established in 1935. Founded by the Junior League at the Church of the Transfiguration, it was transferred to a committee of parents in 1937 and continues to operate in the same location to this day (Turvey, 1987).

Vaughan Road Nursery School, also in Toronto, was established in 1950, with Daisy Dotsch, a most enthusiastic teacher, in charge. Daisy and the Vaughan Nursery became leaders in the development of the co-op preschool philosophy in Ontario. As the numbers of co-ops grew, a coordinated approach to solving operational problems led to the establishment of the Parent Co-operative Preschool Corporation of Toronto and District. Like many of its sister councils, it functioned informally for some 10 years before becoming incorporated in 1974.

During the 1960s and 1970s, other regional councils appeared in Ottawa, Hamilton, London, Niagara, Shoreline (between Toronto and

Hamilton), and Kitchener. For short periods of time, councils also functioned in Brantford, Sarnia, Kingston, and Sudbury. The determination of these councils to work together culminated in the formation of the Committee of Councils of Parent Participation Preschools of Ontario in 1971. This group has provided support through a newsletter and biannual meetings. In 1989 the Ontario Committee took leadership in establishing a training course for co-op teachers and parent board members.

The earliest documentation in western Canada, a booklet entitled *Cooperative Play Groups for Preschool Children* (McGill, 1947), provides information on the establishment of the first cooperative playgroup when, in 1944, Gertrude McGill founded the Children's Garden Library in Victoria, British Columbia. She was convinced by Katherine Whiteside Taylor, whom she met in Seattle, Washington, to include mothers in the supervision and play experiences of their children. It was the diligent work of Gertrude McGill that inspired the first parent co-ops on Vancouver Island. In 1949 the Vancouver Island Play Group Association, precursor to the Vancouver Island Cooperative Preschool Association, was formed.

The early 1940s was also a period of development for playgroups in the city of Vancouver, where nine groups helped form the first association of Cooperative Playgroups of Vancouver in May 1947. Early records of this group credit a Mrs. Whittaker of Holden Playgroup with taking the initiative to draw the groups together into a working unit. This was the forerunner of the Council of Parent Participating Groups in British Columbia, which was inaugurated in 1960 (Roosdahl, 1986). It serves mainland British Columbia and the Queen Charlotte Islands, and is separate from the Vancouver Island Preschool Association, which serves Vancouver Island and the Gulf Islands.

Another spin-off of the co-op preschool activity on the West Coast appeared in Saskatchewan in 1945, when the first cooperative playgroup in that province was established at Community Apartments in Saskatoon. Here, 88 veterans' families, living in a housing development in a former army/air-force station, initiated a cooperative playschool. A booklet, *Parents Cooperative Play Schools*, that chronicles the activities of this group was prepared by the Adult Education Division of the Saskatchewan Department of Education (Saskatchewan, 1946). It refers to Taylor and her work in Seattle, and quotes her as saying, "Playschools are schools of democratic living. They promote among children and adults, mutual consideration, respect, and a genuine will to understand the needs and rights of all". (p. 3)

To develop their program, this parents' cooperative persuaded Maeli Kals, a Vancouver psychologist, to advise and guide them in their first months of operation. Supervisors as such were rarely to be found in Saskatchewan at that time, so the play sessions proceeded with alternating parent leaders, faithful participation of all the parents, and on-going study sessions to keep the supervision consistent and educationally sound. It was believed that professional leadership was essential during the early stages. These preschool pioneers hoped that, by the time a large number of communities in Saskatchewan wanted cooperative play-schools, there would be well-trained supervisors to meet the need. Surprisingly, however, no widespread development of parent cooperative preschools occurred in Saskatchewan in the wake of this valiant start, although a few are known to exist now in larger centres such as Regina and Saskatoon. In recent years the greatly accelerated demand for child-care services has produced a variety of non-profit centres in the midwest. Two or three under co-op auspices have broken new ground with the introduction of 24-hour, or "extended-day", child care.

Alberta's kindergartens, which operated for many years as recreation programs outside the school system, were largely parent-participating, though they seldom used the "cooperative" name. A few nursery schools for younger children functioned here and there under the co-op banner, but without a unifying organization, their whereabouts have not been consistently recorded.

Historically, the East Coast of Canada has been a hive of activity for cooperatives of many kinds—other than those for preschool children and their parents. However, parent cooperative preschools emerged slowly there, in small pockets of activity in Nova Scotia, New Brunswick, and Newfoundland. It is likely that they were established by migrating indivi-duals with co-op experience or with contacts elsewhere. Through their continuation they have demonstrated again the remarkable strength of the co-op philosophy at the grassroots level.

In the same way that across-the-border fertilization took place on the West Coast in the 1940s, there was considerable communication between Quebec and the New England states concerning child care and family-life education, which was embodied by two publications. One was Taylor's book *Parent Cooperative Nursery Schools* (1954/1971). The other, *Parent Cooperative Preschools of America*, was a newsletter, which later became *The Parent Cooperative*. The latter was initiated by Taylor and was devoted to the organization and support of groups based on the philoso-phy of parent participation. Concurrently, Quebec and Ontario teachers of young children were sharing ideas and establishing links between parent co-op groups in both provinces through personal exchanges, conferences, and visits.

In Quebec in the late 1940s there were known to be eleven parent co-ops: five in Montreal proper, three in the West Island, and three in off-island locations. Through the concentrated efforts of parents in the West Island region and the yearly development of new groups, the Lakeshore Council of Cooperative Preschools (LCCP) was established in 1956 (LCCP,

1965). Now known as the Quebec Council of Parent Participation Preschools, this group has given strong leadership in the advancement of parent-owned, parent-operated preschools (Muir, 1987). In a province with two languages, it was appropriate that a number of French-language preschools developed alongside their English neighbours. Quebec Council's *Communiqué* became a bilingual publication. This council also succeeded in establishing, in 1968, a unique centre that provides early childhood services and parent education. It serves as a model for community integration.

Given the communication links between U.S. and Canadian groups, it is not surprising that, when the formation of an umbrella organization of parent co-ops was under discussion, Canadians were active participants. Four who attended the inaugural meeting of Parent Cooperative Preschools International (PCPI) at Columbia University's Teachers College in 1960 were Daisy Dotsch and Elsie Stapleford of Toronto, Kay Calder Crowe of Montreal, and Jean Stevenson of Pointe Claire, Quebec.

From the ranks of Canadian co-op councils, quality leadership has been supplied to the PCPI. A number of Canadians have served as president or have held responsible positions on the board. From time to time, the international conference has been held in Canadian centres, including Montreal, Hamilton, Toronto, London, Vancouver, and Victoria.

Clearly much of the impetus for the emergence of parent cooperatives in Canada stemmed from the enthusiasm and activity of the American parent co-op movement. Taylor's international travels as a Fulbright Scholar brought her in contact with areas of growing interest in playgroups in New Zealand, Hong Kong, India, and Great Britain. In 1948 the New Zealand Playcentre Federation was established. As of 1988 it could claim 640 centres as members.

British playgroups flourished after the earliest groups were started around 1960. A visit from Beverly Morris of New Zealand in 1961 further spurred these playgroup pioneers, so that the Preschool Playgroups Association was born. Thousands of playgroups have found homes in England, Scotland, Ireland, and Wales, where they take an active role in early childhood care and education. Once considered a middle-class phenomenon, British playgroups moved their programs into many economically disadvantaged areas, extending services more broadly to children and encouraging parents to understand and provide for their children's needs.

Canadian parent cooperatives have been the fortunate beneficiaries of these international efforts. In the ensuing years, communication through both publications and international exchange visits has nurtured the sharing and given inspiration to those who continue in parent cooperative programs today.

THE PHILOSOPHY OF PARENT COOPERATIVES.

The development of the human personality is a theme that has permeated the parent cooperative movement from the earliest expression of the philosophy of cooperative preschools.

In the first issue of *Parent Cooperative Preschools of America*, Taylor's editorial included the following statements:

> Children in the early formative years are learning to live, play and grow in ways developing respect for others' rights yet releasing to individual activity. . . . In the socialization of children, cooperatives help lay the groundwork for a more socially mature future world. By developing parents and teachers dedicated to larger social values, and by giving practice in the democratic ways needful for their realization, cooperatives provide more adults capable of contributing to the world's present desperate need for social vision in the face of hysterical competition for instruments of power. (1958, p. 1)

It is the parent/teacher partnership that is the foundation of the cooperative preschool's operation. All policies and procedures emanate from a commitment to define goals, formulate plans, and carry out responsibilities together, on behalf of the children in the group.

As they set about planning and organizing a cooperative play experience for their children, only a few of the adults involved may be aware of this broader, deeper philosophy, because the focus of their efforts is the children. It is this focus on the children that engenders the activities and relationships found in parent cooperatives, which in turn foster adult personality development. In working together, in establishing an incorporated business, and in planning and carrying out a children's program, parents and teachers begin to sense the influence on their own attitudes and practices.

"From joint planning comes the perspective that the best development of one's own children is inextricably linked with that of all others" (Taylor, 1970). Taylor viewed the parent cooperative as a kind of "intentional community," which, despite the relatively short period of time a family may be involved, can provide a sense of kinship that is much needed amongst the isolating pressures of daily life.

The use of the word "parent" in "parent cooperatives" properly describes the concept of family involvement inherent in the co-op philosophy. At first, parent co-ops tended to maintain contact with families chiefly through the mother, who usually was not employed and therefore had time to devote to participation or to study groups. Very soon such jobs as creating equipment or addressing financial problems brought more fathers into active participation on committees. More of today's parents show a heightened interest in sharing child-care duties, especially when both parents are employed outside the home. As a result, some fathers have made time to visit or even to assist in their children's preschool or child-care programs. They may also be found attending special Saturday nursery sessions, conducting field trips to their worksites, giving time and effort to fund-raising projects, and taking part in the business sessions of their nursery boards. In co-ops, the importance of the paternal role in the family has been recognized, and participation in the child's care and education encouraged.

The principles of cooperation had been formulated and published as early as 1884 under the Rochdale Society of Equitable Pioneers in England. However, we have found no proven statement suggesting that the earliest parent-participating groups drew directly upon this source as a guide for operation. Child care and education were later concerns of formally described cooperatives. In their own unsophisticated way, these early groups embraced the tenets of personal involvement, democratic decision-making, and the sharing of resources and responsibilities. Gradually, as experience refined their policies and procedures, non-profit parent-participating groups found themselves identifying with the particular style of action labeled "cooperative."

An interesting connection between cooperative housing and cooperative nursery schools is recorded in a publication of the Play Schools Association. *Community Living in Co-operative Housing* (Fox, 1958) describes a two-year pilot project to assist parent groups in providing programs for their children within co-op housing units in the city of New York. Cooperative nursery schools developed, with the guidance of the Play Schools Association, a play-implementation agency that was active during that time.

The current upsurge in cooperative housing in Canada has brought with it several on-site cooperative nursery-school and child-care operations. An early example began in Mississauga, Ontario, around 1974. The Cooperative Union of Canada has shown some interest in cooperative preschools, with particular regard to their incorporation. The U.S. Cooperative Union has participated with the PCPI in projects pertaining to administration and public relations.

Providing the best possible service for the lowest possible cost is an accepted cooperative principle. "Making do"—for example, using surplus resources from lumberyards and paper companies and creating home-made equipment—is a typical economy. In some areas groups combine for bulk purchasing of common supplies at lower prices.

Using volunteer parent assistants in the classroom saves some of the outlay for staff salaries. It also opens the door to a variety of learning opportunities. Ongoing observation of different children, as well as of the teacher's techniques of child guidance, are coupled with actual practice, as parents work directly with the children in the classroom. All of this is done under the supervision of a qualified leader or teacher, whose task it is to provide a high-quality children's program while guiding the semi-trained assistants.

From these activities have emerged the practices of parent education, parent orientation, and the production of parent-participation handbooks. Parent Cooperative Preschools International has compiled an annotated bibliography of 60 resource materials that are representative of the many published by cooperative groups and councils. Available at minimum cost, these materials assist other groups in starting or improving their operation.

Once the co-op assumes the role of owner/operator, it must conduct the operation in a businesslike manner. In replacing the intermediary, co-ops have assumed incorporation, asserting their goals through policies and procedures stated in by-laws. Insurance, audits, fund-raising, and decision-making at executive, general, and annual meetings have all become part and parcel of running a co-op. Of necessity, teachers and parents (particularly board members) have had to acquire skills to handle each of these tasks. Sometimes these skills are developed through experience, but more often through planned workshop sessions with co-learners and with the advice of experts.

The initial efforts in the area of leadership development came from two Canadian women who had been long-time supporters of the Hamilton and District Council of Cooperative Preschools. These two women recognized the advantages of specialized training for parents and teachers who attempt to guide groups through the co-op preschool experience, and they introduced the first PCPI Leadership Development Workshop. Another basic principle of cooperatives is provision for the education of co-op members. Parent co-ops fulfil this to a high degree, using local and regional conferences to expand the horizons of both their members and the community regarding the children and their families. They also promote cooperation among cooperatives by forming councils in which individual groups work together to strengthen the efforts of each. As a result parent co-ops continue to flourish.

Cooperatives are self-determined groups, in which the members are the owners of the service. Through democratic procedures the members determine their objectives and how they will achieve them. For the members of a parent co-op, this represents an element of control that is unusual in the field of education, where state-run schools are the norm. Sometimes co-ops have provided a service where nothing comparable exists, as for example, a nursery school, a child-care centre, a kindergarten, or a school-age child-care program. Some offer a variation of or an enriched alternative to the standard programs of the community. Non-participating groups generally lack the personal talents and resources of parents, which can enhance the curriculum. Field trips with a learning focus, integration of children with special needs, parent education through observation and discussion are ways in which parent co-ops respond to the needs of the community and the wishes of their members.

In all cases, the realization that they have power over decisions relating to their children encourages parents to participate in the process. This in turn strengthens the group, bringing it ever closer to its goal. That prime goal is the planning and presentation of the children's program.

Most parents seek for their children a group experience that will stimulate and nurture them as they grow and develop every area of their physical and mental capabilities. They also want them to be happy, to enjoy their early out-of-home experiences in the care of adults other than their own parents or family members.

To become the best judges of the value of these experiences, co-op parents accept the responsibility to understand and use principles—such as the paramount importance of play—as the framework on which most of the children's activities are based. Respect for the individuality of each child, the value of choice in giving a child opportunities to exercise skills in decision-making, and the role of language and other modes of communication in expanding social skills are often issues that expand parental knowledge and teaching skills. Opportunities are offered to talk about them, to see the principles demonstrated by teachers, and to take a personal role by putting them into action in the classroom or in their everyday lives at home. Better still, it is a comfort to parents that their efforts take place in the accepting, supportive, non-threatening company of other parents and teachers who share similar aims. In the process, they learn to view their children more objectively and to build their own adult self-confidence as the foremost influence in their child's care and education.

The credo of Parent Cooperative Preschools International, which has become the benchmark for all its members, was originally composed by Beth Stephenson and published in 1960 in *The Parent Cooperative*. With minor changes, it was adopted by PCPI in 1975. In it, Stephenson distils clearly the values of the cooperative nursery for children, parents, teachers, and the community. It begins, "We believe that the parent cooperative is an especially good environment for the young child because it is created and maintained by people who trust one another." It concludes, "Joy in achievement to which all have contributed. Cooperation is the heartbeat of the parent cooperative nursery. Cooperation is love in action."

Such exalting words invest parent cooperative ideals with a highly spiritual quality, yet these ideals continue to be translated effectively in the decisions and actions of the everyday operation of parent-participating co-ops.

THE COOPERATIVE IN ACTION

As much as possible, each family is encouraged to take part in the classroom program from time to time. Some parents participate more specifically in the administration, on the board of directors or on designated committees. The duties involved demand additional time to review goals, to address problems, and to formulate action, as well as the energy to carry out the necessary tasks that follow. Advertising, registration, housing, transportation, hiring teachers, purchasing equipment and supplies, licensing and the implementation of health regulations, and program development become the on-going responsibilities of the board. Most successful co-ops carry out these tasks, having consulted fully with the teaching staff, often inviting them to attend board or committee meetings. Sometimes, as in the case of fathers and working mothers, a board or committee job may be their main form of participation.

Traditionally, participation of parents in the children's classroom has been a basic requirement of membership in a cooperative nursery, but the social and economic evolution of the family has necessitated some adaptation in recent years. The purposes of this participation still include the provision of sufficient staff at an affordable cost, the promotion of parent learning, and the encouragement of parents to take an active role in their children's care and education. It requires parents to accept the responsibility of assisting in the classroom on an assigned rotation basis once or twice a month, depending on the number of children they have enrolled and the number of teaching staff employed.

In the classroom the qualified, hired teacher is the leader. This individual is responsible for organizing and guiding the children's program and for arranging the classroom-participation activities of the parents. These could include assisting the teacher in supervising the children in the daily routines of washing, dressing, eating, or taking rest periods, as well as in program activities. According to personal interests or talents, parents could be assigned to help with art, music, story-reading, water play, science, cooking, physical activity, or trips. Orientation sessions with the teacher often precede such participation; during these, parents could be given opportunities to try out the media, and to learn about the value of play experiences in the child's development and about how best to present them.

If being present in the classroom is a problem—as in the case of a parent who is ill, pregnant, working, or a student—other forms of participation are accepted. In practice, these include a variety of jobs, such as performing secretarial tasks, cleaning the nursery, or doing laundry. Yet other cooperative groups have approved the provision of a duty-parent substitute on a volunteer or paid basis. Mothers and fathers commonly assist in the classroom, but grandparents, neighbours, and others have been accepted by arrangement with the participation committee.

There are some major benefits to the child in having a parent in the classroom or as a visitor to the program from time to time (as in the case of co-op child-care parents). These derive from the security it gives the child in this first step away from home and into a group setting. Such security allows the child to accept the classroom as a safe environment in which to try new things, and to trust other adults as caregivers and guides, and it provides an opportunity to see adults cooperating to provide the program, thus demonstrating respect for each other's contribution.

For their part, parents and substitute parents can observe good skills for child guidance, and then put them into practice. Not only do their talents enhance the program, but also they gain a sense of accomplishment and personal satisfaction from participation. They begin, too, to appreciate the art of the teacher, who must orchestrate the plans and the participants that compose each preschool day.

Seeing parents in action, teachers become more aware of how they can best use the natural skills of their assistants or best help them to develop new approaches. The extra hands of parent assistants can also free the teacher to devote more individual time to children, to observe growth, and to foster learning.

There is no doubt that the teacher in the parent co-op holds a key position in assuring that the members of the group, parents and children, achieve their potential. The co-op style of operation demands of its teacher superior skills in administration and personnel management, as well as expertise in program planning, in child development, and in undertaking the parenting role. Acceptance of parents as assistants and employers, whatever their level of capability, requires a teacher whose own strong self-confidence still permits the sensitivity and the flexibility so essential to this unique position.

With so many details to be taken care of in the day-to-day operation of a parent-participating program, success depends on general agreement on the principles of a quality curriculum, on good communication, and on a well-delineated division of duties. Many groups accomplish this with carefully planned handbooks. Discussion sessions clarify rules and procedures while encouraging the expression of expectations from all parties.

It is not an easy process. As many groups have found, there are times of frustration and misunderstanding, which can threaten the stability of the operation. Experience has taught that a first defence is to accept that there will be times of conflict and to recognize these as opportunities for growth. Planning for this inevitability involves setting up prescribed ways to deal with difficulties. What if I don't like what's happening in the classroom? How do I get action on a problem relating to the performance of a committee member? Co-ops try to use proven methods for alleviating such concerns. Establishing a written policy and designating a liaison parent to facilitate communication can reduce the incidence or intensity of conflict. Now that both parent board members and teachers have recognized the importance of being skilled in interpersonal relationships, more and more of them are taking advantage of the type of leadership-development course offered through Parent Cooperative Preschools International and local co-op councils.

Financing a quality children's program on a modest budget is a perennial challenge to parents in a co-op. Participating in fund-raising projects has a high priority on the activity agenda of most groups. Bright, creative ideas (T-shirts, buttons, fun-fairs, puppet shows, raffles, trike-a-thons—their ingenuity is endless!) regularly attract dollars from co-op members and their communities. At the same time as the groups' team spirit grows, the community becomes more aware of the co-op's contribution to local families.

Participation in a parent co-op has many faces, depending on the needs and resources of the group. Beyond the classroom or the board table, car-pooling children to school, sharing child-care, weekend boarding of classroom pets, and the saving of all manner of beautiful junk for creative centre, are but a few of the ways in which these parents help their children and their teachers.

THE INFLUENCE OF THE
PARENT-COOPERATIVE MODEL

Parent co-ops have developed many resources to facilitate the operation of their particular programs. At the same time, their publications, workshops, and conferences often have been made available to the public. Across the country, information on family life and parenting, as well as on the fundamentals of preschool curriculum, have become part of the basic agenda under conference themes such as "Great Beginnings," "A Family Happening," "Making Tomorrow," "The Magic of Childhood," "The Changing Family," and "Growing Together." Attendance in the hundreds verifies the appeal of these workshops and conferences to the community beyond the co-op nursery doors.

In their concentration on parent learning as fundamental to participation and in their extension of opportunities and resources to the community at large, parent co-ops have been in the forefront of the parent-education movement. Co-op councils have become the repositories of a large volume of materials on operating a parent co-op program, on child development, on preschool curricula, and on promoting parent education. Some co-op councils have organized these collections as loan libraries and outlets for children's books and records. Some, under government grants, have established parent resource centres, and a few have undertaken the operation of a toy library.

The current remarkable growth of parent/child resource centres, in many communities and under a variety of auspices, can be attributed, in part, to the application of parenting-skills development and the non-profit approach used in parent co-ops. Drop-in–style programs suited to the in-home mother or family child-care provider tend to emphasize the learning value of play, the parents' role in child-rearing, and the accept-ance and support of the community.

Since 1982 the Toronto Board of Education has shown admirable initiative and progress in promoting Parenting Centres in more than 21 public schools (Gordon, 1988). Parents and caregivers of preschoolers are welcomed with their little ones to facilities and programs where the children play while the adults observe and discuss the children with each other and with a Parent Worker. As well, books and toys may be borrowed for home use. Mary Gordon, the Parenting Advisor for these projects, has a background of co-op experience. These groups, with the support and endorsement of the Board of Education, are reaching families with a wider variety of cultural and economic backgrounds than may have been part of cooperative preschools to date. Parent co-ops, which pioneered some of these concepts, are now encouraged by their use in an ever-widening variety of ways.

The concept of parent participation itself is being accorded greater acceptance in the early childhood field. In no small way, this can be attributed to the successes of the parent co-op movement. A major breakthrough came in the 1960s, when co-op child care arrived on the scene, fostered mainly by determined student groups on university campuses. To the old concept of a co-op with a middle-class, half-day, parent-in-the-classroom profile, a new face was added in the form of non-profit, parent-run, full-day centres. As child care needs rapidly outgrew the available spaces, the "we can do it ourselves" idea gave birth to what are now hundreds of non-profit child-care groups with parent involve-ment, even parent control. They may be found in co-op housing, in employer-related facilities, in churches, and in elementary and high schools. Some operate in their own single-use premises.

The continuing challenge to each group lies in finding ways to initiate and sustain parent involvement on the board of directors, as well as in activities that relate directly to the children's program. Parents who work outside the home have little time and energy that they can devote to the support of their child-care services. However, parent representation on the board, parent meetings, family social functions, and the encour-agement of visits or participation in the children's program have all been used successfully to sustain involvement. In addition to standard pre-school child care, services for infants and toddlers or for young school-age children have been added as needed. Acting as agencies, a few parent-run centres have provided supervision of private-home child care.

In response to government emphasis on the integration of handicapped persons into the everyday community, a number of cooperative councils in Ontario have undertaken to promote and facilitate the integration of preschool children with special needs into cooperative nurseries in their own communities. Government funding for the coordination of such services, with resource teachers assigned to work with individual children, with their families, and with the integrated group, has stimulated the development of preschool integration services in co-ops under their own councils in London, Hamilton, and Toronto.

From time to time, parent co-ops have played influential advocacy roles by voicing their concerns to school boards or government committees. The introduction of junior kindergartens, seen by some as a threat to the existence of cooperative nurseries, became an opportunity for parent co-ops to lobby for appropriate class size, adequate facilities, and teacher qualifications. In some areas where kindergartens for five-year-olds did not exist in the public system, parent cooperatives often ran their own programs for this age group until the introduction of kindergartens under school-board auspices.

With an ever-increasing number of "graduate" co-op parents arriving with their children in the kindergartens of the country's school systems, the ideal of participation as a benefit—or even, as some feel, a right—has been put to the test, with varying results. Parent involvement appears to be becoming more accepted, depending on the attitudes of school boards, principals, and teachers. The use of volunteers and parent aides in elementary classrooms is popular in some areas. In other areas, alternative parent-participating schools have emerged. In Victoria, British Columbia, when an inner-city school became vacant, a visionary group of parents and community members organized and achieved school-board approval to develop a parent cooperative school. This school, begun in 1974, continues today in downtown Victoria as Park Street School. Another example is the APPLE (Alternative Parent Participating London Elementary) School in London, Ontario. This group, with parent participation from junior kindergarten to grade four, sanctioned by the London Public School Board, is a special part of Brick Street Elementary School. An informative study of the project's inception in 1985 and its first year of operation was made by two researchers from the Faculty of Education of the University of Western Ontario (1986). In the conclusion of their report, Patricia Allison and Mary Lou Bedrosian-Vernon state, "When all of the information is processed and all of the images completed we are left with very positive feelings about APPLE. . . . APPLE has achieved something really different and really special" (pp. 104, 105).

While developing their own strong administrative skills and procedures, parent co-ops have indirectly influenced other early childhood programs. Fulfilling the requirements for incorporation, and functioning as employers or tenants or property-owners or fund-raisers all demand business and management expertise. To focus on the essentials and the legal implications of such activities, workshops and handbooks were created by co-ops and shared with the public. Insurance schemes have been examined and reduced group rates have been arranged through councils for their member schools.

Achieving this advanced standard of operation has helped co-ops to open the doors to government funding for a variety of children's services. Where formerly much had to be accomplished by the parent co-ops through the good will and energy of committed members, grants can now help to reduce the risk of volunteer burnout and give greater assurance of continuity.

Throughout the developmental period of parent cooperatives, their members have been sensitive to the need to encourage higher standards for all teachers of young children. In 1954, in British Columbia, they took part in a provincial government drive to establish a minimum of ten courses of training for all preschool teachers. At this time also, in Ontario, extension programs at Toronto and McMaster universities included a number of courses relating to parent-participation programs. In the 1960s and 1970s, Quebec's only cooperative preschool council helped to stimulate night courses for preschool teachers through McGill and Sir George Williams universities. Then, in 1973, a trail-blazing summer extension course specifically for co-op teachers was given at Seneca College in Toronto.

Over the years it became exceedingly apparent that the teacher's role in a co-op style, parent-participating program is unique. The parents are the teacher's employers, and yet may be classroom assistants as well. Assuredly, parents have a decision-making role in the operation of the group. Achieving the delicate balance of who leads when, and why, is an on-going challenge. At the heart of it is the working relationship between the teacher and parents. A breakdown of this vital relationship is generally the cause of failure in a program (Allison & Bedrosian-Vernon, App. C., p. 4).

This potential has serious implications for the training and selection of personnel to work as teachers in such settings. How does a teacher gain the confidence and enthusiasm, as well as the commitment needed, to work with and for parents? By and large, new graduates from early childhood training courses have not been ready for a full-fledged co-op program. Perhaps their own professional development has not yet reached that stage of confidence that allows them to be less protective of their leadership role.

Not surprisingly, a parent who has experienced participation in a parent co-op often goes on to take early childhood education training, emerging as a very capable teacher. More and more training programs are including a practicum in a parent co-op as a worthwhile experience. There is growing support for the idea that the greatest benefits could be derived through courses and experiences aimed at promoting positive interpersonal relationships based on a deeper sense of awareness of self and others.

The need for additional information and study to best prepare a teacher to share in co-op parent participation has been recognized and addressed with orientation and seminar sessions, usually provided by co-op councils. These courses, offered to preservice or in-service teachers, attempt to enhance learning about the history and philosophy of the cooperative movement and promote skills in leadership, problem-solving and group development. Additional experiences in observing and participating in a cooperative program are also facilitated. Parent co-ops in British Columbia have long supported preservice orientation for teachers new to their co-ops. During 1988 and 1989 a training module was under development, sponsored by the Committee of Councils of Parent Participating Preschools of Ontario and subsidized by the Ontario Ministry of Community and Social Services. Placing great faith in the value of shared learning, the designers of the module stress a mixed enrolment of teachers and parent board members in order to assure that the discussions reflect the two key viewpoints.

THE FUTURE OF THE COOPERATIVE PRESCHOOL MOVEMENT

What of the future? Formal schooling systems are extending their interest in the younger child, and tax-supported education is becoming more broadly available for four-year-olds as well as five-year-olds. In Ontario in 1988 the government made provision of child-care services in all new elementary schools mandatory. A large number of child-care centres are already located in schools where diminished enrolment has made space available. If these can be interpreted as indications of a probable future meshing of education and care services, what then will become of the parent-participating cooperative? Will it, should it, survive?

The response of cooperative groups already facing a reduced access to preschool children has been interesting. For some the move has been toward introducing programs aimed at two-year-old toddlers and the three-year-old preschoolers whose parents value the opportunity for small-group play, one or two mornings a week, while they themselves share in the economic, social, and educational benefits of participation.

For some others, the choice has been to maintain their own co-op for junior- and senior-kindergarten-age children as a preferred alternative to publicly operated programs, where their ideas of curriculum and their participation may be less welcome. This could be one kind of private or independent school of the future.

As long as child care remains under the jurisdiction of a social services ministry, and given a preference for funding of non-profit corporations, parent cooperative child care will continue to have the potential to increase in numbers and in influence. The lack of affordable, accessible child-care spaces across Canada could be sufficient reason for determined parents and communities to consider cooperative child care as a viable alternative. Ontario's policy paper *Child Care Directions* (1988) promotes parent participation on parent boards and actively supports projects which strengthen them.

The very best situation would be one in which the school system and its personnel would gradually move towards a more open and receptive attitude, so that parents have a recognized voice in school affairs and a stronger influence on their child's education. Greenberg (1989) raises many urgent reasons why parent participation in elementary schools has not achieved general support in the United States, in spite of lip-service acknowledgement that parent involvement can improve a child's self-esteem and indirectly affect academic success. To some degree it can be assumed that the roadblocks—racism, classism, and gender bias—cited by Greenberg (pp. 66, 70, 71) apply to Canadian schools as well. Too often, the subtle resistance shown by some of our empowered institutions and educators to acknowledging parents' rights and capabilities and to sharing equally the role of educating children has negated or prevented the true involvement of parents. Nevertheless, it is reassuring to find some exceptional examples of successful efforts in this direction in schools where parent advisory committees exist, and in others where parent volunteers contribute to the day-to-day classroom activities. In Metro Toronto, some trustees and principals are showing much stronger commitment to parent participation, encouraging parent information sessions (for example, Scarborough's Family Math program), and introducing "parent rooms" for informal drop-in visits. These commendable efforts bear witness to the growing recognition of the benefits to be gained when home and school work and learn together.

In a current Canadian study, Glenn Dixon and his associates at the University of British Columbia are exploring the concept of a "non-deficit" approach to parent/teacher relations. It stresses the credibility of parents as their own child's most dependable resource and the application of this idea in a collaborative relationship between parents and professionals. The ANCHOR Project (Answering the Needs of Children through Observation and Response) has promoted groups in the lower mainland of British Columbia, in Nova Scotia, and in other geographic locations across Canada (Fraser, Kasting, & Dixon, 1988). The observation-and-discussion format implemented to facilitate parent/teacher collaboration is similar to study-and-sharing sessions practised by exemplary parent co-ops since early in the history of the movement. Canadian research such as ANCHOR is welcome, and could lend much-needed authenticity to some of the precepts long esteemed in the parent cooperative philosophy.

CONCLUSION

As far back as 1963, James Hymes, Jr., in addressing the Montgomery (Maryland) Council of Cooperative Preschools, proposed that the job of parent co-ops would be done when the essence of the movement had permeated the formal system of education. "Public education," said Hymes, "could markedly be improved by the adoption of the same concepts at work in the co-op." This aim is not unrealistic. The journey toward its achievement will continue to be a challenge, yet one that will be met in the spirit of the parent cooperative movement.

REFERENCES

Allison, P., & Bedrosian Vernon, M. L. (1986). The first year experiences of the APPLE (Alternate Parent Participating London Elementary) program. London, ON: University of Western Ontario, Faculty of Education.

Fraser, S., Kasting, A., & Dixon, G. (1988). Breaking down barriers to collaboration between parents and educators: A "non-deficit" approach. *Canadian Children, 13*(1), 41–48.

Gordon, M. (1988). Toronto Board of Education Parenting Centres. *Canadian Children, 13*(1).

Greenberg, P. (1989). Parents as partners in young children's development and education: A new American fad? Why does it matter? *Young Children, 44*(4).

Hymes, J. Jr. (1963). *The Parent Cooperative,* 6(3).

Hymes, J., Jr. (1978). Living history interviews: Book 1. Beginnings. Carmel, CA: Hacienda.

Ontario. Ministry of Community and Social Services. (1988). *Child Care Directions, 1*(3).

Siska, H.S. (1978). Canadian co-ops: From the West . . . : A look at the beginning, *PCPI Journal, 8*(3), p. 7.

Stephenson, B. (1951). Untitled poem, *Parent Cooperative Preschools of America 2*(1), p. 3.

Stephenson, B. (1955). Mothers in a cooperative nursery school. Washington, DC: National Association for the Education of Young Children.

Stevenson, J.H. (1971). Parent Cooperative Preschools International: A brief summary of the growth and development of the organization, April 1966–April 1971. Montreal, PCPI Archives.

Stevenson, J.H. (1978). Canadian co-ops: To the East . . . : Tell us about the olden days, *PCPI Journal*, *8*(3), p. 11.

Taylor, K.W. (1958). Editorial. *Parent Cooperative Preschools of America*, *1*(1), 1.

Taylor, K.W. (1967). *Fiftieth anniversary: History of the parent cooperative movement*, 1916–1966. Parent Cooperative Preschools International Archives.

Taylor, K.W. (1970). *PCPI Journal* 1(1), p. 3.

Taylor, K.W. (1971). *Parents and Children Learn Together* (rev. ed.). New York: Teachers College Press. (Original work published as *Parent Cooperative Nursery Schools* 1954, revised and retitled 1967).

18

Parent Involvement in Early Childhood Programs

Margie I. Mayfield

What Is Parent Involvement?
Rationale for Parent Involvement
What Research Says About Parent Involvement
Types of Parent Involvement
Issues in Program Development and Implementation
Conclusion
References

In the past two decades, there has been a growing trend to increased parent participation in early childhood programs in North America (Berger 1981; Lapides, 1980) and internationally (Nir-Janiv, Spodek, & Steg, 1982). Parent involvement in the education of children is not new; indeed, "its history goes back many centuries" (Berger, 1981, p. 4). In the relatively recent past in Canadian history, many children were educated solely in the home by the family.

Early childhood educators have been recommending parent involvement in their children's early development and education for hundreds of years. The twenty-eighth yearbook of the National Society for the Study of Education included this comment:

> Interest in the young child and his parent has spread so rapidly within the past ten years as to appear to be a new development, but the movement is not altogether modern. A search through the annals of ancient history reveals the occasional philosopher, preacher, and educational reformer contemplating the significance of parent-child relationships and planning for improved education of infants and young children. (1929, p.7)

Although this statement was published in 1929, it is really in recent years that parent involvement has received significant and increasing attention from educators, professionals, and policy-makers.

A recent review of Canadian early childhood programs identified three trends in this area:

(a) the notion that early childhood education must consider family and parent as well as child needs; (b) the idea that parents are really partners in, not clients of, early childhood programs and services; and (c) the acceptance of the school as a partner in developing programs and services for preschool-age children and their families. (Biemiller, Regan, & Lero, 1987, p. 45)

This chapter will discuss (a) what is meant by the term parent involvement; (b) why parent involvement is part of early childhood programs; (c) the types of parent involvement found in Canadian early childhood programs; and (d) some of the issues and concerns in planning and implementing parent involvement in early childhood programs.

WHAT IS PARENT INVOLVEMENT?

Parent involvement is a comprehensive term that can mean different things to different people. To some people, it means parents receiving newsletters or attending school meetings, while to others it means parents being very actively involved in the program, including the decision-making. Parent involvement can be all of this, as well as many other types of involvement, as we shall see later in this chapter.

Parent involvement includes parents, children, and the program. Morrison (1988) defined parent involvement as "a process of helping parents use their abilities to benefit themselves, their children, and the early childhood program" (p. 322). This definition emphasizes the triadic nature of parent involvement. It is not "for parents only"; It is a *process* that implies an ongoing interactive relationship and mutual development among parents, children, and the program, rather than a single activity.

RATIONALE FOR PARENT INVOLVEMENT

The importance of involving parents in the early education of their children has been described by child developmentalists, psychologists, program evaluators, policy-makers, national commissions (for example, Martin, 1987), national surveys (for example, Mialaret, 1976), international foundations (for example, van Leer, 1984), and early childhood professional organizations (for example, Association for Childhood Education International [ACEI], 1983). The two recent Canadian federal reports on child care (Cook, 1986; Martin, 1987) both commented on the importance of involving parents in their young children's early education, as well as the need for additional parent education opportunities.

Reasons for involving parents in early childhood programs include the following:

1. *The changing nature of the Canadian family.* With the increase in

labour-force participation by women with young children, the growing number of mothers who are single heads of households, and fewer extended families, there is an increasing need for more early childhood programs, especially those which also provide support, information, and assistance to parents.

2. *The continuity of home and school.* This recognizes that "childrearing and education are overlapping enterprises" (Peters, Neisworth, & Yawkey, 1985, p. 189) and that parent involvement in an early childhood program can foster continuity for the child, parent, and teacher between home and school. When parents are aware of what is happening in the program, and teachers are aware of the home situation, each can build on and reinforce the resources of the other.

3. *The importance of the early years.* With the growing recognition of the importance of the early years has come the desire by parents, policymakers, and program planners for more programs "for the first 5 years of life during which education traditionally has been the responsibility of parents" (Lapides, 1980, p. 241). Because parents wish to be involved, and because of the crucial role of parents during this time in their children's lives, many early childhood programs include parent involvement.

4. *A multidisciplinary focus for family/child programs.* In recent years, there has been a broadening of the goals of early childhood education programs, from an emphasis on children's cognitive and social development to a wider perspective, including health, nutrition, and a variety of family concerns. This multidisciplinary approach can be seen as helping to provide some of the resources that may no longer be available within, or easily accessible to, today's family. In addition, "there seems to be a growing interest in using some form of educational or developmental pre-school programming... to act on the general cycle of socio-economic deprivation within marginal communities through nutrition, health and parental education activities focussed through children" (Shaeffer & Bernard, 1983, p. 1). In the past 20 years, early childhood programs have also been used as a means to redress inequalities and social problems. Some of these programs resulted in significant changes in the lives of many young children and their families (Lazar & Darlington, 1982).

5. *The era of advocacy.* The growth of parent concern about and involvement in education may be one reason for the legacy of an "era of advocacy" (Berger, 1981), in which parents have become more active in targeting specific needs and lobbying for rights, services, and programs. In Canada, examples of this advocacy can be seen in demands for more funding and programs for special-needs children, Native Indian and immigrant families, abused children, and teen-aged mothers (Martin, 1987).

6. *The positive effects of parent involvement.* Many research studies (see below) over the past 20 years have reported wide-ranging positive effects for children, parents, and other family members. Many *types* of parent involvement have proved to be effective.

WHAT RESEARCH SAYS ABOUT PARENT INVOLVEMENT

Numerous reviews of the literature and research on parent involvement have reported that parents' involvement in education programs for their young children can have long-term positive effects on children, parents, and other family members (Berrueta-Clement et al., 1984)

Many positive effects have been reported:

1. The parents became more aware of their role in teaching their children, became more confident in their parenting skills, and became more concerned with educational and life goals for their children (Slaughter, 1983).
2. The parents and children developed more positive attitudes towards education (Berger, 1981).
3. The children were retained in grade or assigned to special classes less frequently than control-group children (Berrueta-Clement et al., 1984).
4. The parents became more responsive to and with their children, used more complex language, and became less authoritarian and more confident (Love et al., 1976).
5. Positive effects on siblings and other family members were also noted (Karnes & Teska, 1980).

In addition, parent involvement in early childhood education has also been perceived positively by teachers, administrators and parents (for example, Mayfield et al., 1981).

Even though these positive outcomes have been found for many early childhood programs with parent involvement, it is important to keep in mind that such outcomes are not guaranteed to any program that merely includes parent involvement. Good parent involvement requires much thought and effort to best meet the needs and goals of the children, the parents, and the program. In order to do this, a variety of types of parent involvement have been included in Canadian early childhood programs.

TYPES OF PARENT INVOLVEMENT

Parents can participate at a variety of levels and in a variety of ways in early childhood programs. Some programs try to provide more than one type of involvement to better accommodate each individual parent's needs, interests, and abilities. The following typology describes the different types of parent involvement using six levels (Gordon et al., 1979).

The first level, *parents as audience*, "means that parents will either be an audience getting the message and listening to the word or will be involved as bystanders and observers visiting the school, or the day care center, or nursery" (Gordon, p. 27). This represents minimal parent involvement. Other examples of this level are open houses, group meetings, children's performances, and the provision of newsletters for parents. For many parents who work and care for a young family, this level may be their preferred, and most realistic, level of involvement in their child's early childhood program.

The second level, *parents as adult learners*, describes many parent-education programs, where parents learn about topics such as child development and child-management techniques. Parent education can be (a) structured, "commercial" programs such as Parent Effectiveness Training (Gordon, 1975) and Systematic Training for Effective Parenting (Dinkmeyer & McKay, 1975); (b) films, television, and radio programs on child development, as recommended by the recent federal report (Martin, 1987); or (c) courses for parents on child development, offered through local community colleges, church groups or community organizations such as the YW/YMCA or the British Columbia Council for the Family. One innovative program of this type is the Preschool in Prison Project offered in provincial and federal correctional institutions in Alberta, which provides parenting courses for inmates and parent/child interaction programs during weekly family visits (OMEP [Organisation mondiale pour l'Éducation préscolaire, or World Organization for Early Childhood Education] Canada, 1987). A program for immigrant families, Ontario Welcome House, provides care for infants, toddlers, and preschoolers while their mothers attend language and citizenship classes (Mock, 1986).

Another level of parent involvement involves *parents acting as teachers of their own child at home*. Probably the most frequent example of this is a parent who reads to his or her young child (a very important early reading activity). Infant development or intervention programs, such as those in Ontario and British Columbia, train parents to work with their at-risk or special-needs child in their own home, Resources for parent involvement at this level include toy libraries, whose objective is to provide toys and games that foster play and parent/child interaction (Mayfield, 1988). Toy libraries may be associated with special-needs programs (for example, the Alvin Buckwold Centre in Saskatoon, and the CNIB in Vancouver), public libraries (for example, in Edmonton, Regina, Windsor, and in North York, Ontario), parent/child centres (for example, those sponsored by the Toronto Board of Education and the Winnipeg School District), and community organizations (for example, the Kiwanis in Oshawa and the YW/YMCA in Pickering, Ontario).

Parents as volunteers can take part in such activities as "reading stories, collecting resource materials, helping with special days, working with the library, making games and instructional devices, publishing a cooperative newsletter, or serving as a resource visitor, foster grandparent, or listener" (Ramsey & Bayless, 1980, p. 261). Parents can be volunteers both in the classroom (for example, playing games with the children) or in the home (for example, making or repairing materials).

Many programs, such as kindergyms, mom-and-tot swim classes, playgroups, drop-in centres, and parent/child centres can operate only if parents are available to help with activities and supervision. Parent-cooperative nursery schools are typically staffed by one early childhood educator and two or three parent volunteers (on a rotating basis). In addition to providing extra help for programs, the parents benefit by observing their children, the program, the modelling of professionals, and other parents. Some parent volunteers in early childhood programs may then choose to pursue additional training to become program leaders, supervisors, paid aides, or teachers (Pugh & De'Ath, 1984).

Yet another level of parent involvement described in Gordon's study is *parents as paraprofessionals or paid workers*. In some early childhood programs, parents are trained specifically as paraprofessionals. In many kindergarten classes, a parent works as a trained teacher aide, assisting the teacher, organizing materials, and working with individuals or small groups of children, among other tasks. The use of paraprofessionals from the community is also found in some home-based programs—for example, the Native Infant Program, in which women from the local reserves were trained as infant-development workers and then hired for a home-based program for Native infants and their families on Vancouver Island (Mayfield & Davies, 1984).

The last of Gordon's levels involves *parents as decision-makers*. Parents involved in parent-cooperative nursery schools throughout the world not only function as volunteers but may also serve on the board that runs the program. Parent/child centres also typically have parents on their governing boards (Gordon, 1987) and some parent/child centres have been established due to the initiatives of parents (Regan, Mayfield, & Stange, 1988).

ISSUES IN PROGRAM DEVELOPMENT AND IMPLEMENTATION

Although early childhood programs that include parent involvement tend to share a common focus on young children and their parents, these programs can vary widely in objectives, scope, sponsorship, delivery models, size, and level of parent involvement. There are five key development and implementation issues to consider when planning parent-participation early childhood programs:

1. Assessment of parental and program needs;
2. Determination of the level of parent involvement;
3. Diversity of parent-involvement delivery models and strategies;
4. Program development concerns and cautions; and
5. Evaluation of parent-involvement programs.

Assessment of Needs

Needs assessment has been defined as a process that helps to identify and examine both values and information. This information is essential for planning effective early childhood programs for children and their families: "Programmes for children must be based on a knowledge of their environment and a recognition of the most important problems" (Cano, 1979, pp. 149–150).

The many variables that have an impact on the lives of families with young children need to be examined and considered in planning for parent involvement in early childhood programs, if these programs are to be optimally effective. For example, one might want to find out if the potential parent participants work full-time or if they have younger children or other family members at home needing care. One might also want to know what language(s) is/are spoken in the home, what the parents' concerns are, what type of information they would like, at what level of involvement each parent would feel comfortable, what services for young children and their families are already available in the community, and other such details. This information could be gathered by talking to parents individually or in groups or by a written questionnaire.

A needs assessment should not only assess current conditions and needs but also provide information on what the parents' goals are for their children and for a potential parent-involvement program. It is unrealistic and arrogant of professionals to assume that they know for certain what is needed, desired, and best for these families. In one American study, when the goals for children in a Head Start program were ranked by the parents and then compared to those of early childhood professionals, there was agreement on only one goal—the least important one (Lewis, 1980). Studies from the West Indies (Olsen & Olsen, 1979) and from Canada

(Mayfield et al., 1981) have also reported differing perceptions of program goals by parents and professionals.

A thorough needs assessment can do' much to reduce the potential for future problems by providing accurate information on the children, the families, and the community situation. Planners of early childhood programs should "respect the very different needs of families and... respond to them in such a way that schemes and services are not only available but also accessible, appropriate and above all acceptable" (Pugh & De'Ath, 1984, p. 203). The best of programs is a waste if it is not accessible, appropriate, and acceptable to the participants. The needs assessment is so important in the process of establishing effective parent involvement in early childhood programs that it should receive as much attention and care as other stages in program development and implementation.

Determination of the Level of Parent Involvement

Once the needs, attitudes, interests, and goals of the parents, the children, and the program have been identified, one must decide which level(s) of parent involvement would be appropriate for this group of parents in the context of this early childhood program at this particular time. For example, if parents are working full-time, participating as volunteers in the classroom on a regular basis is probably not possible. However, they might be interested in receiving information, working with their child at home, or serving on the program's board. Other parents may be willing to help out for an occasional field trip or special celebration, but cannot or do not wish to participate frequently. Still others may wish to work directly with the children in the classroom on a regular basis.

Many early childhood educators have found that what works best in their programs is to provide for more than one level of parent involvement. Some educators new to parent involvement may decide to begin slowly with one level (for example, newsletters to parents), and then expand parent involvement gradually (for example, add parents as resources or volunteers in the classroom). Often several levels of parent involvement are necessary to meet a variety of needs, wishes, and interests.

The Head Start program in the United States made parent involvement on policy and advisory boards mandatory as a condition of federal funding (Zigler & Valentine, 1979). One difficulty with requiring parent involvement was noted by van der Eyken (1982): "Not only do many parents not seem to want to exercise control, but some are surprised, disconcerted and discomfited by being asked to become involved in a manner they perceive is not 'their' function" (p 71). This is an example of the need to provide a satisfactory match between what may be perceived by program staff as an ideal level of parent involvement in an early childhood program and what is realistic in terms of parental interests, background, and preferences. What works with one group of parents or in one program may not work for another group or program.

Diversity of Parent-Involvement Delivery Models and Strategies

After the needs, goals, and level of parent involvement have been identified, the delivery models and specific strategies can be examined. There is a wide diversity of options for meeting the needs of young children and their families.

For example, if parents wish to work with their own child, several choices are available. First, they could participate in the centre, or in the school, or in their home, or in all of them. The program staff could send home periodic newsletters containing suggested activities to do and books to read with their child, or a home visitor could work with the parent and child to demonstrate activities and strategies appropriate for young children.

Throughout the world, innovative delivery models such as mobile classrooms housed in vans or buses, information hotlines, radio and television programs, video courses, correspondence schools for pre-school and primary children in isolated areas, and evening or weekend activities have been used to meet the needs of parents with young children.

Some Program Concerns and Cautions

One concern in developing parent involvement in early childhood programs is ascertaining how much flexibility and adaptability exists for the implementation of the program. For example, some Canadian early childhood programs in Native Indian communities may have to be flexible in what language is used, since some families may still speak the Native language, while others may speak only English or French (Mayfield, 1986). Another factor in certain communities is the varied literacy levels of the participants.

To meet the needs of young children and their families, an early childhood program must be culturally relevant and appropriate. This involves respecting and understanding the cultural and ethnic diversity of the participants and their community, including the child-rearing practices.

Some groups in Canada and elsewhere have kept their languages and cultures, and for these groups "cultural differences in fact constitute a vital resource, a social strength rather than an educational disadvantage, for families and young children" (van Leer, 1984, p. 7). Some Canadian early childhood programs have included Native Indian elders in the initiation and development of the programs, thereby rendering the programs more culturally relevant and acceptable to the families and the community. The continuing involvement of the community elders, and the recognition of their special expertise and knowledge, facilitates community acceptance of, interest in, and participation in these programs. In many cases, it would not be possible to successfully operate such programs without this type of support from the local community.

The current economic situation has exacerbated the perennially difficult task of obtaining adequate, continuous funding for programs for young children and their families. Too often, program staff must spend a great deal of their time trying to secure funding, instead of working with the children and families. Unfortunately, the level of funding frequently determines the type and scope of the program that can be developed, rather than the type and scope of the program determining the level of funding.

One caveat that should be included in discussing parent involvement is that although there is evidence that the effects of early intervention programs for children are strengthened by the involvement of the child's parents, not enough is yet known about *how* parent involvement works to warrant sweeping conclusions about its effectiveness and potential (Castro & Lewis, 1984). Two major questions remain to be answered: Which factors promote or reduce parent-involvement effectiveness in a variety of settings? Which factors are most important and crucial in providing the best possible match of children and parents with early childhood programs?

A second caveat when discussing parent involvement is that caution and realism are necessary. Although parents are the people most knowledgeable about their own children and their circumstances, and although they genuinely wish to help their children, it is important not to over-romanticize or over-idealize the family and its participation. In a few cases, "the family," as a traditional unit, may have "so lost cohesion that it is now suffering a crisis" (van Leer, 1984, p. 14). In such cases, the causes of the crisis must be addressed and dealt with if the parents are to be able to participate effectively in the early childhood program.

Evaluation of Parent-Involvement Programs

Evaluation of parent involvement in early childhood programs can provide program validation, feedback for program personnel, and information on changing family or community situations that could have an impact on the program or could suggest program modification. An early childhood program has a greater chance for success if "through the use of constructive evaluation techniques ... the leadership team can acquire feedback on the usefulness of various projects and activities. Future programs can be designed around some of the suggestions given by participants during this evaluation process" (Swick, 1984, p. 133).

There are obviously many ways to evaluate a parent-involvement program. Whether to use individual telephone interviews, review of program attendance records, written questionnaires, group interviews, checklists, or some other method depends on the nature of the questions one wants answered and on who is likely to have the answers.

There are also hundreds of questions one might ask in evaluating parent involvement in an early childhood program. Some of the following general questions may be helpful in developing an evaluation:

- What are the goals and objectives for parent involvement in this program? (At the end of an evaluation, one should be able to ascertain to what degree these goals and objectives were accomplished.)
- Have the parents seen any changes in themselves or their children since participating in the program? Do they do anything differently as a result of being involved in the program?
- Do the parents and program staff have any suggestions for improving the program?
- Do staff members see any changes in themselves, the parents, or the children that may be a result of the parents' involvement in the program?
- Is there a need for more or fewer types of parent involvement? Which types are used most frequently, and by whom are they used?
- Are the parents aware of the types of parent-involvement activities that are available? If not, how could communication between home and school be improved? Which activities are most liked, most useful, and so on?
- Are there any special needs of parents or children (for example, needs related to divorce or health) that should be addressed?
- Do staff members discuss parent-involvement activities with one another? Do they have access to resources to help in planning and implementing parent involvement (for example, professional organizations, conferences, workshops, or opportunities to observe other programs)?
- Is the parents' involvement in the program recognized (for example, with thank-you notes, recognition days, or certificates)?
- What steps must be taken to provide a better program in the future?

CONCLUSION

Hildebrand (1981) stated, "Nowhere in the long educational continuum is the parent–teacher relationship more important than in the child's early years" (p. 443). One way to make this relationship a rewarding and beneficial one for children, parents, and early childhood educators is to involve parents in their children's early childhood programs.

REFERENCES

Association for Childhood Education International. (1983). *On families and the re-valuing of childhood: A position paper.* Washington, DC: ACEI.

Berger, E.H. (1981). *Parents as partners in education: The school and home working together.* St. Louis: C.V. Mosby.

Berrueta-Clement, J.R., Schweinhart, L.J., Barrett, W.S., Epstein, A.S., & Weikart, D.P. (1984). *Changed lives: The effects of the Perry Preschool Program on youths through age 19.* Ypsilanti, MI: High/Scope Educational Research Foundation.

Biemiller, A., Regan, E., & Lero, D. (1987). Early childhood programs in Canada. In L.G. Katz (Ed.), *Current topics in early childhood education* (Vol. 7). Norwood, NJ: Ablex.

Cano, M.T. (1979). From the child to community participation: Lessons from two Peruvian experiences. *Assignment Children, 47/48,* 143–164.

Castro, G., & Lewis, A.C. (1984). Parent involvement in infant and preschool programs. *Journal of the Division for Early Childhood, 9*(1), 49–56.

Cook, K., London, J., Rose-Lizee, R., & Edwards, R. (1986). *Report of the federal task force on child care.* Ottawa: Ministry of Supply and Services.

Dinkmeyer, D., & McKay, G.D. (1975). *S.T.E.P.: Systematic Training for Effective Parenting.* Circle Pines, MN: American Guidance Service.

Gordon, I.J. (1968). *Parent involvement in compensatory education.* Champaign, IL: University of Illinois Press.

Gordon, I.J., Olmstead, P.P., Rubin, R.I., & True, J.H. (1979). How has Follow Through promoted parent involvement? *Young Children, 34*(5), 49–53.

Gordon, M. (1987). Toronto Board of Education parenting centres. *Journal of the Association for Young Canadian Children, 12* (2), 41–46.

Gordon, T. (1975). *P.E.T.: Parent effectiveness training.* New York: Wyden.

Hildebrand, V. (1981). *Introduction to early childhood education.* New York: Macmillan.

Karnes, M.B., & Teska, J.A. (1980). Toward successful parent involvement in programs for handicapped children. In J.J. Gallagher (Ed.), *New directions for exceptional children: Parents and families of handicapped children*. San Francisco: Jossey-Bass.

Lapides, J. (1980). Working with parents of preschoolers. In M.J. Fine (Ed.), *Handbook on parent education*. New York: Academic Press.

Lazar, I., & Darlington, R.B. (1982). Lasting effects of early education: A report from the Consortium for Longitudinal Studies. *Monographs of the Society for Research in Child Development, 42*(2-3, Serial No. 195).

Lewis, M.S. (1980). Parents' goals and preschool education. In N. Nir-Janiv, B. Spodek, & D. Steg (Eds.), *Early childhood education: International perspectives* (pp. 209-214). New York: Plenum.

Love, J.M., Nanta, M.J., Coelen, C.G., Hewlett, K., & Ruopp, R.R. (1976). *National Home Start evaluation*. Cambridge, MA: ABT Associates.

Mayfield, M.I. (1986). Policy and planning implications of home-based infant stimulation programs for Native Indians in North America. *Early Child Development and Care, 24*, 181-195.

Mayfield, M.I. (1988). Toy libraries in Canada: A research study. *Canadian Children, 13*(2), 1-18.

Mayfield, M.I., & Davies, G. (1984). An early intervention program for Native Indian infants and their families. *Canadian Journal of Public Health, 75*, 450-453.

Mayfield, M.I., Dey, J.D., Gleadow, N.E., Liedtke, W., & Probst, A. (1981). *Kindergarten needs assessment*. Victoria, BC: Ministry of Education.

Mialaret, G. (1976). *World survey of pre-school education*. Paris: UNESCO.

Mock, K.R. (1986). Child care needs of cultural minorities. Report prepared for the House of Commons Special Committee on Child Care.

Morrison, G.S. (1988). *Education and development of infants, toddlers, and preschoolers*. Glenview, IL: Scott, Foresman.

National Society for the Study of Education. (1929). *Preschool and parental education*. Bloomington, IL: Public School Publishing.

Nir-Janiv, N., Spodek, B., & Steg, D. (Eds.) (1982). *Early childhood education: International perspectives*. New York: Plenum.

Olsen, J., & Olsen, M.A. (1979). Early childhood education in the Caribbean. *Prospects, 9*(4), 477-85.

O.M.E.P. Canada, (1987). *Preschool in Prison Project* (Kit). Edmonton, AB: The Preschool in Prison Project.

Peters, D.L., Neisworth, J.T., & Yawkey, T.D. (1985). *Early childhood education: from theory to practice*. Monterey, CA: Brooks/Cole.

Pugh, G., & De'Ath, E. (1984). *The needs of parents: Practice and policy in parent education*. London: Macmillan.

Ramsey, M.E., & Bayless, K.M. (1980). *Kindergarten programs and practices*. St. Louis: Mosby.

Regan, E.M., Mayfield, M.I., & Stange, B.L. (1988). Canadian alternatives in early childhood programs. *International Journal of Early Childhood, 20*(1), 3–11.

Shaeffer, S., & Bernard, A.K. (1983, May). *Early childhood education activities—International Development Research Centre.* Paper presented at the meeting of the Consultative Group on Early Childhood Care and Development, New York, NY.

Slaughter, D.T. (1983). Early intervention and its effects on maternal and child development. *Monographs of the Society for Research in Child Development, 48*(4, Serial No. 202).

Special Parliamentary Committee on Child Care. (1987). *Sharing the Responsibility* (Shirley Martin, Chair). Ottawa: The Committee.

Swick, K.J. (1984). *Inviting parents into the young child's world.* Champaign, IL: Stipes.

van der Eyken, W. (1982). *The education of three-to-eight-years-olds in Europe in the eighties.* Windsor, UK: NFER-Nelson.

van Leer Foundation. (1984). *Multi-cultural societies: Early childhood education and care.* The Hague: Bernard van Leer Foundation.

Zigler, E.F., & Valentine, J. (Eds.). (1979). *Project Head Start: A legacy of the War on Poverty.* New York: Free Press.

19

Young Children with Special Needs

Patricia M. Canning and Mary E. Lyon

This chapter will describe the nature and prevalence of special needs in young children and discuss current trends in programs for these children in Canada. Principles of good practice for early childhood educators working with special-needs children will be considered. We will focus on how these principles apply to all good early childhood programs whether or not they include special-needs children.

THE NATURE OF SPECIAL NEEDS

Young children are considered to have special needs for a wide variety of reasons. According to Thurman and Widerstrom (1985), we describe a child as having special needs whenever that child needs help and information beyond what is normally required to assure the best developmental outcome. Relevant factors may include physical, mental, or sensory impairment; family situation; or social background. A child may have special needs because of a specific physical disability (for example, cerebral palsy) that limits motor ability and development. A child may have intellectual limitations because of a specific genetic disorder (for example, Down's Syndrome). Children who have limited hearing or vision will also need special help.

In addition to children whose special needs arise from clearly established disabilities, other children are said to have special needs because they are seen as "at risk" of experiencing developmental problems (that is, they have a greater than average chance of having such problems). Children are considered *biologically at risk* if they have experienced certain events early in life—for example, prematurity, low birth weight, or asphyxia at birth. Children are considered *environmentally at risk* if their living conditions are not conducive to optimum developmental outcomes. For example, children living in poverty constitute a disproportionately large percentage of children who repeat a grade, are placed in special-education programs, or drop out before completing school (Brooks-Gunn & Furstenberg, 1986); many children of adolescent mothers display lower cognitive functioning that appears in preschool, continues into elementary school (Broman, 1981; Maracek, 1979), and on into high school (Brooks-Gunn & Furstenberg, 1986); children of minority and immigrant groups may also have special needs. Still other children, for unknown reasons, may display delays in the development of age-appropriate skills—for example, language, cognitive, and motor skills—that indicate the possibility of more serious problems later. Clearly, there are many circumstances that may result in children having special needs.

There is increasing evidence that the population of children at risk of experiencing developmental problems is growing. This increase is seen both in the numbers of biologically at risk children, and in the numbers of those environmentally at risk. Recent and rapid advances in medical science have resulted in smaller and sicker babies surviving (Guralnick & Bennett, 1985). In general, these babies have less favourable outcomes than full-term healthy babies. The number of children living in poverty is also growing rapidly. More children live in single-parent families, often below the poverty line. The growing numbers of immigrants from countries where neither of Canada's two official languages is spoken bring us another group of special-needs children (Winzer, Rogow, & David, 1987). Early childhood educators and other providers of services to children and families must be aware of all the factors that may contribute to children's special needs.

There is wide acceptance of the idea that optimum developmental outcome depends on the earliest possible identification of any special needs and early provision of appropriate help. Research into the effectiveness of special programs is problematic (Simeonsson, Cooper, & Scheiner, 1982), but there is a growing body of evidence indicating that well-designed programs can both promote development and prevent future problems (Guralnick & Bennett, 1985).

Comprehensive educational programs for young children with special needs are a phenomenon of the past three decades. Similarly, courses preparing early childhood educators to work with these children are relatively new. We still have many unanswered questions concerning both children's programs and preparing educators. However, the knowledge we have acquired over the last 25 years does allow us to identify the essential components of programs that encourage development in all children, including those with special needs.

THE PREVALENCE OF SPECIAL NEEDS

It is difficult to compile a clear and accurate picture of the prevalence of special needs in young children due to problems in defining, locating, and identifying this population (Lesson & Rose, 1980; Lindsay, 1984). Only a relatively small percentage of young children with special needs receive a clear diagnosis of disability. The vast majority of children with special needs are those who are either biologically or environmentally "at risk." It is often difficult to identify young children with significant problems, or those at risk for developing them, even though it is important to do so as early as possible. Early detection gives us an opportunity to prevent the risk factors from adversely affecting development, or to minimize their effects as much as possible by providing appropriate programs and services.

Reported figures on the prevalence and incidence of special-needs children invariably refer to school-age children. Traditionally in North America, we have accepted a figure of 12 percent as accurate (Karagianis & Nesbit, 1980). When children whose special needs are mild and transitory but still educationally significant are included, the percentages are higher—ranging from 15 percent (Canada, Council of Ministers of Education, 1983) to 20 percent (Department of Education and Science, U.K., 1978).

While we have information about the number of school-age children with special needs from school records, we have no such source of information for children five years of age and younger. Canning and Lyon (1988, in press) report initial data on the number of children five years of age and younger with special needs in Nova Scotia. Their sources of information were public-health nurses, child-care providers in licensed centres, and teachers of children in "grade primary" (that is, kindergarten) throughout the province. Each group was asked to provide information on the special-needs children in their care during the previous 12 months. Data were collected on the number of children already identified as having special needs, the number suspected of having special needs, and the number in each category of special need. In all, information about approximately 29,000 preschool-aged children was obtained.

The reported percentages of children diagnosed as having special needs varied across the three groups, ranging from 7 percent (preschool directors), to 13 percent (public-health nurses) to 24 percent (grade primary teachers). All three groups reported an additional 10 to 13 percent of children whom they suspected had special needs as yet undiagnosed. The differences in the figures reported by the three groups may be due to a number of factors, but one factor is clear—not all children are enrolled in preschool programs (only about one-sixth of the total sample attended such programs). At the grade-primary stage, however, all children in Nova Scotia attend school. It is also clear that a number of milder or more subtle special needs are not apparent until we see their effect on the child's ability to meet the new demands that come with school entrance.

The categories of special need most commonly identified or suspected in children attending any type of preschool program were emotional/behavioural problems (2 percent identified and an additional 6 percent suspected); language problems (2 percent and 0 percent, respectively); and hearing impairment (1 percent and 4 percent). Public-health nurses reported environmental disadvantages (3 percent) and language problems (2 percent) as the most prevalent categories. By the time children were in grade primary, the most common categories of special need were speech and language problems (8 percent identified and 2.5 percent suspected); hearing impairment (3.7 percent and 4 percent); and "significant immaturity" (5 percent suspected). The most prevalent special needs among all three groups were those related to language and speech, and the factors leading to such difficulties (for example, environmental factors, social and emotional development, and hearing problems). Figures from all three groups, particularly the grade-primary teachers, show up to 20 percent of children as having difficulties in one or more of these areas. A much smaller percentage of children (3–5 percent) have a special need due to a clearly identified condition such as mental retardation, a physical handicap, or severe sensory impairment.

Clearly some special-needs children are identified during the pre-school years, but many are not identified until they enter elementary school. All the groups surveyed indicated that early identification of special needs should be a priority. Medical personnel, educators, and parents share the responsibility for monitoring children's development and identifying problems as early as possible. Thus one of the major responsibilities of early childhood educators involves monitoring each child's development and ensuring that children who need help are identified before they get to school.

LEGISLATIVE ISSUES

In several countries over the past 20 years, legislative documents dealing with special-needs children have supported the development of programs for preschool children. These documents include the Education Act (1981) in the United Kingdom, as well as the Education for All Handicapped Children [EAHC] Act (1975), and the Education for the Handicapped Act Amendments [EHAA] Act (1986) in the United States. The

U.S. laws provide mandates and federal funds for the development of services for preschool children who have, or are at risk of developing, handicapping conditions. The legislation also mandates family involvement in the total program, and a multidisciplinary approach coordinating professionals, programs and skills. Active participation by the family members who deal with the child is seen as essential to providing a high-quality service for young children.

In Canada there is as yet no similar legislation. However, major policy documents have recommended the extension of services to all preschool special-needs children and their families, for example, the CELDIC Commission (Commission on Emotional and Learning Disorders in Children) (Lazure, 1979). Except for services to children with visual or hearing impairment, there are currently no legal mandates to provide services to preschool special-needs children and their families in Canada. Programs serving this population are nevertheless increasing and seem to be influenced by legislation and resulting services in the United States.

Education in Canada is under provincial control; so far, only Ontario has comprehensive provincial legislation on the education of school-age handicapped children (Bill 82). Throughout Canada, programs and services for preschool-aged children (with or without special needs) are neither mandatory nor universally provided. Programs that do exist fall, for the most part, under the auspices of the provincial department of social services or health, where they are considered to be child-care services and are covered by provincial legislation concerning those services. Such laws vary from province to province. Most provinces have some regulations specific to children with special needs. These regulations typically deal with one or more of the following areas: numbers; space; staff training; reporting requirements; and funding provisions for grants, staff salaries, or additional subsidy payments. All provinces now offer some financial support to home-based programs for young special-needs children from birth to age three and their families. Many have developed or are in the process of developing guidelines and standards for such programs (Brynelson & Cummings, 1987).

WORKING WITH SPECIAL-NEEDS CHILDREN

Most children with special needs, including the largest group (that is, those at risk of developing problems due to either biological or social factors), attend—if they attend any program at all—regular early childhood programs rather than programs especially designed for them. Data from Nova Scotia (Canning & Lyon, 1988) indicate that at least 50 percent of preschool programs included one or more children with special needs. Thus, all those intending to work with young children should be trained to work with special-needs children. Fewer programs exist that deal only with special-needs children, and the current trend is toward mainstreaming and integrating special-needs children with "normal" children at the preschool, as well as at the school-age, level. For most such children—unless their special needs are very severe—this appears to be the most appropriate practice (Guralnick, 1981).

Whatever the caregiver's or teacher's context, and whatever the children's special needs, the most important preparation for working with special-needs children is a thorough understanding of normal child development. In any situation, it is most important to know the normal stages and sequences of development, and the conditions, contexts, strategies, and relationships that promote it.

Special education is sometimes expected to provide something unique or different from education for children who do not have special needs. However, the aim of all programs should be to create an environment in which any child can maximize the normal processes of development. The "special" in early childhood special education must refer to the children, not to our principles or approaches. Good programs for children with special needs are based on the same principles as those identified in other chapters of this volume.

PROGRAMMING PRINCIPLES

There are four key principles to consider in designing and delivering programs for special-needs children: individualization; the use of developmentally appropriate programs and practices; focusing on the family; and integration of services.

Individualization

It is necessary for everyone who works with young children to be familiar with the children's individual needs, whether or not they are considered to be "special." Professionals working with special-needs children must know the causes and characteristic manifestations of the children's specific disabilities or special situations: they must be familiar with what is known about the usual development in children with this particular type of special need, and they must be familiar with any specific strategies and techniques that have been found necessary or useful in dealing with children thus affected. For example, professionals must be aware of the most appropriate ways to move or place children with physical disabilities, and must encourage them to move on their own. With visually impaired children, educators must understand how vision aids work and how to structure the environment so that such children can be independently mobile. For some non-verbal children, teachers may need to learn a special mode of manual or visual communication. Children from socially disadvantaged backgrounds may need extra exposure to the language used in books and schools, as well as extra encouragement to use such language, if they are to cope well with the demands of school.

Teachers and caregivers need specific information about each individual child in their care. Children with the same category of special need, often described by a particular label (for example, "mentally retarded," "cerebral palsied," or "abused") tend to be more different than alike. Every child has distinctive abilities, strengths, weaknesses, temperament, likes, dislikes, ways of behaving and responding, favourite toys and activities, family background, and life experiences. How the individual child develops and learns will be a unique result of the complex patterning of all of these factors. Down's syndrome children may have some things in common—for example, certain physical characteristics, patterns of development, and common difficulties. However, they display a whole myriad of differences in health, sociability, physical strength, creativity, reading ability, and emotional maturity. Moreover, they come from a wide range of different family backgrounds, have experienced different kinds of family relationships, and different life situations. There is no "one best way" to teach all Down's syndrome children, any more than there is one best way to teach all children who wear size five shoes. Educators need specialized knowledge about the disability itself, the usual development of Down's syndrome children, and appropriate programs for them. But there is no substitute for careful and detailed observation of the individual child, continuous communication among all who deal with the child, and the provision of whatever will help that particular child at that particular time.

The principle that programs must reflect the individuality of each child's needs has been incorporated into recent legislation in the United Kingdom and the United States. In the United States, the EAHC Act requires that all children with special needs have an Individualized Education Plan (IEP) developed for them. Each IEP must contain an assessment of the child's present level of development, a statement of long-term goals for the child (goals for the next year in most cases), short-term objectives, a description of the strategies and means of achieving these objectives, and a way to evaluate the child's progress. The EHAA Act requires that an Individualized Family Service Plan (IFSP) be developed for preschool children. An IFSP must include the following: a statement of the child's present level of development; a statement of the family's strengths and needs related to enhancing a child's development; a statement of the major outcomes expected for the child and the family; criteria, procedures, and timelines for determining progress; the specific early-intervention services necessary to meet the unique needs of the child and the family (including the form, frequency, and intensity of services required); projected dates for the initiation of, and an estimate of the expected duration of the need for services; and procedures for easing the transition from home-based early intervention to the preschool program.

There is no corresponding legislation in Canada, but many programs and school boards now require that Individualized Education Plans be developed for school-age and even for preschool-age children, on the grounds that the U.S. laws enshrine good principles of practice. Similarly, many early-intervention programs, both centre-based and home-based, use Individualized Family Service Plans or their equivalent to ensure that programs are tailored not only for individual children, but also for their families.

Developmentally appropriate approaches and practices

Using IEPS, IFSPS, or similar types of individualization strategies represents only a first step in the process of meeting individual children's needs. Such plans are effective only if the goals they set and the strategies they propose are appropriate for each child's development. Goals, and plans to meet them, must reflect knowledge of developmentally appropriate practice for all children.

Research and theory in child development, from a wide range of perspectives, supports the view that development is not something that can be "done to" children, but is rather something they do themselves. It is a consequence of their actions on, and the responses and encouragement they receive from, their physical and social environments (for example, Piaget, 1952; Wells, 1981). The major contexts in which child development occurs are the everyday activities of young children— eating, dressing, shopping, watching TV, and playing (whether with parents and siblings, alone, or with friends). Programs for children with special needs, however, have often been conceptualized as programs that will provide something unique or different—the idea being that if a child is not normal, and has not developed certain abilities, we must take some abnormal or extraordinary approach.

In the past 20 to 30 years, many curricula and packaged programs have been developed for young children with special needs. These programs are often limited to assessments of children's current functioning, objectives, and suggested sequences of teaching activities. Examples include *The Portage Guide to Early Education* (Bluma et al., 1976); *The Brigance Diagnostic Inventory of Early Development* (Brigance, 1978); *The Portage Classroom Curriculum* (Brinckerhoff, 1987); *The HICOMP Curriculum* (Forsberg et al., 1983); DISTAR (Engelman & Osborn, 1976); *Small Wonder* (Karnes, 1979, 1981); and ECHO (Nash, 1981). These curricula and materials may be helpful in many instances. It is obviously useful to adopt a system for assessment and to find ideas for activities and materials rather than work out entirely new ones for each particular program. It is important, however, that such curricula are used in a way that supports optimal development.

Our aim should be to make the contexts and means of development as normal as possible for every child. This means doing more for special-needs children than we would for "normal" children. It means taking special measures to make the environment as normal as possible. For example, children with impaired hearing need the best possible amplification systems; we can monitor effective use of these; and we can, perhaps, explore communicating by a manual means such as sign language. However, the principles we use to communicate with such children, and to encourage them to communicate with us, should be the same as those we use with children whose hearing is unimpaired. For a mentally retarded child, we must develop activities that make features of the environment clearer and more differentiated than is necessary for a normally developing child. For a child with behaviour or attention problems, the environment and routines may need to be adapted to reduce distraction and to support consistent responses from caregivers. These are the types of necessary modifications that will help children learn in spite of their handicaps. However, within these adapted learning environments, we should support the same processes that promote development in all children.

The importance of play in the development of all children has been discussed fully in Chapter 2. Research has demonstrated that children who play well typically do well, both at the time and later. Recent studies have indicated, moreover, that this relationship holds equally true for many children with special needs, including those who are language-impaired (Udwin & Yule, 1983), mentally retarded (McConkey, 1985b), or socially disadvantaged (Smilansky, 1968). Play has not always been highly valued as an activity in early-intervention programs for special-needs children, but it is now clear that play is just as important for these children as for all others. Some children may not play spontaneously; they may need special encouragement and adapted materials. Once again, we must apply the principle that we should employ special means to make the learning environment as normal as possible.

Bricker (1986) describes a structured and planned approach to meeting children's goals and objectives in the context of play and the usual activities of a regular preschool program. She provides a number of principles for selecting and implementing individualized and developmentally appropriate activities within the regular preschool environment. These principles include choosing activities that incorporate a number of different learning objectives, are adaptable for varying ages and skill levels, minimize the need for adult assistance or direction, and can be initiated by the child (Bricker, 1986, p. 292).

Focusing on the family

Recent legislation and developments in other countries directly address a third general principle of early childhood programs for children with special needs: such programs must focus on the family, rather than exclusively on the child. Parents have the right and are entitled to the opportunity to play an integral role in every aspect of these programs, just as they do in the other programs discussed throughout this book. Not only should parents be given the chance to be involved in what is done with their children from an ethical and human rights perspective, but we must also recognize that families are the primary agents of children's development and their most influential context. Empirical research demonstrates that the effectiveness of a program for young children depends on the program's overall impact on the family (Bronfenbrenner, 1975; McConkey, 1985a; Trickett et al., 1982).

A great deal of the impetus for recent legislation in the United States has been provided by pressure from parents' organizations for the right to be involved in decisions about the placement of, and provision for, their handicapped children. In Ontario, Bill 82 incorporates parents' rights to participate in placement and education decisions regarding their handicapped children. In other Canadian provinces, parents have successfully fought in court for the right to make decisions about their own children.

Parents of preschool-age children have perhaps an even more obvious right to be involved in decisions about their children than do parents of school-age children. This idea is supported by findings on the impact of the parents' role from research into the effectiveness of programs for young children with particular special needs (Guralnick & Bennett, 1985).

We will describe three major aspects of the early childhood educator's role in connection with parents whose children have diagnosed special needs: (1) supporting parents as they come to terms with, and learn to deal with the stresses of, having a handicapped child; (2) giving parents access to professional information so that they can make their own decisions; and (3) helping parents understand their child's development and thus become more confident and competent as parents.

In order to support parents, we must recognize that families, like children, are distinguished by a myriad of differences—for example, in size and constellation, quality of relationships, education, socioeconomic status, and support networks. Individually and cumulatively, these factors affect the way parents cope with the handicapped child and with the short- and long-term stress this handicap has on family function-ing. Professionals must respect the individual feelings, reactions, and circumstances of parents and families just as they consider the differences of individual children. This involves, above all, being willing and able to listen to parents and to show respect for what they say.

The second important component of the educator's role is to help parents find relevant information, to act as a resource to answer or refer parents' questions, and to enable parents to locate and use other commu-nity resources. The professional acts as a resource to the parents to enable them to find out what they want and need to know at particular times. In order to do this effectively, early childhood educators must be knowl-edgeable about the role of other professionals, and aware of other services and resources.

Third, we must help parents understand and promote their children's development. This does not imply that parents should become formal instructors of their young children, or that teachers should expect them to follow lesson or activity plans. Parents are their children's first and best teachers: they are present during more of their children's early life than anyone else, and they have a special and close relationship to, and knowledge of, their children.

As McConkey (1985a) points out, it is somewhat presumptuous of us, as professionals, to assume that we know better what to do with a child than that child's parents—particularly if we do not first consider the parents' views. Parents are likely to know what works best with their own children. More importantly, telling parents (indeed, telling anyone) exactly what to do robs them of the feeling of competence they might get from figuring it out themselves. Directive behaviour toward parents is likely to increase their dependence on professionals rather than help them find their own way to function as autonomous families.

Parents must decide goals for themselves and their children. Profes-sionals, with theoretical and objective knowledge of stages of develop-ment, can help parents set appropriate and realistic objectives. Sugges-tions of activities can sometimes be helpful, together with discussions of how everyday routines and interactions with the child promote develop-ment. This discussion should not be seen as a one-way process. Parents can very often give teachers helpful advice and suggestions on how to best help their child. Both groups should be able to bring their own knowledge and perspective.

Integration of Services

The fourth general principle for comprehensive early childhood pro-grams is that programs be integrated into the whole range of services for children and families in the community. Legislation in the United States and in the United Kingdom, as discussed earlier, supports such a multidisciplinary approach to assessing the needs of and providing services to special-needs children and their families. Successful programs require cooperation from all professionals involved with young children. We must foster a working relationship among the disciplines providing services to children and families. Our training institutions must prepare students for this role.

The professionals involved in providing services to special needs children and their families come from a wide range of health, educational, and related disciplines. No one professional can be expected to provide all the expertise required by children with handicaps and their families. For example, a child with language and cognitive delays may be assessed by a psychologist, an audiologist, and a pediatric neurologist—all of these may suggest activities or additional services that may benefit the child. A child with cerebral palsy may see physical and occupational therapists in addition to all of the above professionals. Other children may need the services of a public-health nurse and a social worker, as well, while also attending a preschool program.

Many parents report being overwhelmed by the amount of information, advice, and directives they receive from various professionals. For example, an evaluation in a developmental clinic usually includes assessments by pediatricians, speech and language pathologists, occupational and physical therapists, and psychologists. Parents meet these professionals and receive information, instruction, or suggestions from each of them. It is unreasonable to assume that a short meeting will suffice for the parents to grasp all the implications of what is said.

In the United States, the EHAA Act explicitly addresses the need to coordinate professional services by requiring that each family be assigned a case manager. Similarly, in the United Kingdom one person is designated to coordinate information. An appropriate case manager must be found for a given situation to be responsible for implementing the program and for coordinating the agencies and professionals involved.

The early childhood educator is often the professional who sees the child most regularly and has the most consistent contact with parents. As such, she or he is often the person parents are most likely to approach. All early childhood educators must be prepared to serve as part of a multidisciplinary team by providing professional reports on the child's development and behaviour and by attending team meetings to help make appropriate program decisions regarding the child. They must also thoroughly understand the roles of all the other professionals and be able to collate and interpret information from each. All programs must establish and maintain good communication with the relevant agencies and professionals involved with individual children. In this way they can directly help the child and the family, and can also help the family deal with all relevant information.

CONCLUSION

While approximately 5 percent of young children are likely to be diagnosed as having severe handicaps, a much greater percentage (approximately another 15 to 20 percent), are likely to have some kind of special need that must be met in early childhood education programs. Because most of these children will be in regular settings, all early childhood educators must be aware of the nature of special needs in young children and be prepared to work toward meeting them.

The provision of appropriate programs for young children with special needs is based on principles that apply to all high-quality early education services. These principles include individualization, developmentally appropriate programming, a family focus, and a multidisciplinary, community-integrated approach.

Canada has no comprehensive legislation or service provision for this population, although programs providing services for young children with special needs have grown considerably during the past two decades. Many of the developments and trends seen in the field reflect the principles underlying legislation and services in other countries. As recent task forces on child care have confirmed, this is an area where a priority should be made to further extend services. It is likely that the provision of appropriate services to young children with special needs will continue to expand and be an area of increasing importance in early childhood education in the next decade.

REFERENCES

Bluma, S., Shearer, M., Frohmer, A., & Hilliard, J. (1976). *The Portage guide to early education*. Portage, WI: The Portage Project Co-operative Educational Service.

Bricker, D. (1986). *Early education of at-risk and handicapped infants, toddlers and preschool children*. Glenview, IL: Scott Foresman.

Brigance, A. (1978). *The Brigance diagnostic inventory of early development*. North Billerica, MA: Curriculum Associates.

Brinckerhoff, J. (1987). *The Portage Classroom Curriculum*. Portage: The Portage Project Co-operative Educational Service.

Broman, S.H. (1981). Long-term development of children born to teenagers. In K. Scott, T. Field, & E.G. Robertson (Eds.), *Teenage parents and their offspring* (pp. 195–224). New York: Grune and Stratton.

Bronfenbrenner, U. (1975). Is early intervention effective? In B. Fredlander, G. Sterritt, & G. Kirk (Eds.), *Exceptional infant: Vol. 3. Assessment and intervention.* New York: Brunner/Mazel.

Brooks-Gunn, J., & Furstenberg, F.F. (1986). The children of adolescent mothers: Physical, academic and psychological outcomes. *Developmental Review, 6,* 224-251.

Brynelson, D., & Cummings, H. (1987). Infant development programs: Early intervention in delayed development. In C. Denholm, R. Ferguson, & A. Pence (Eds.), *Professional child and youth care: The Canadian perspective* (pp. 133–154). Vancouver: University of British Columbia Press.

Canada, Council of Ministers of Education (1983). *Survey of special education in Canada, 1982–1983.* Winnipeg: Candid Research and Council of Ministers of Education, Canada.

Canning, P., & Lyon, M. (1988). A survey of young children with special needs. *Nova Scotia Medical Journal, 67(6),* 182–184.

Canning, P. & Lyon, M. (in press). Preschool-aged children with special needs: Implications for preschool and primary educators. *Canadian Journal of Education.*

Cook, K., London, J., Rose-Lizee, R., & Edwards, R. (1986). *Report of the federal task force on child care.* Ottawa: Ministry of Supply and Services.

Department of Education and Science, United Kingdom (1978). *Special Educational Needs* (The Warnock Report). London: Her Majesty's Stationery Office.

Engelman, S., & Osborn, J. (1976). DISTAR: *An instructional system.* Chicago: Science Research Associates.

Forsberg, S., Neisworth, J., & Lamb, K. (1983). *The HICOMP curriculum: Higher Competencies in Communication, Own care, Motor development and Problem solving.* Toronto: Bell and Howell.

Guralnick, M. (1981). The efficacy of integrating handicapped children in early education settings: Research implications. *Topics in Early Childhood Special Education, 1,* 57–71.

Guralnick, M., & Bennett, F. (Eds.). (1985). *The effectiveness of early intervention for at-risk and handicapped children.* New York: Academic.

Karagianis, L.D., & Nesbit, W.C. (1980). Educational landmarks accenting exceptional children: CELDIC Report, Public Law 94–142, Warnock Report. In G.M. Kysela (Ed.), *The Exceptional Child in Canadian Education: Seventh Yearbook* (pp. 75–83). Edmonton, AB: Canadian Society for Studies in Education.

Karnes, M. (1979). *Small Wonder I.* Circle Pines, MN: American Guidance Service.

Karnes, M. (1981). *Small Wonder II*. Circle Pines, MN: American Guidance Service.

Lazure, D. (Ed.). (1979). *The CELDIC report: One million children*. Toronto: Crainford.

Lesson, E.I., & Rose, T.L. (1980). State definitions of preschool handicapped populations. *Exceptional Children, 46,* 467–469.

Lindsay, G. (Ed.). (1984). *Screening for children with special needs*. London: Croom Helm.

Maracek, J. (1979). *Economic, social and psychological consequences of adolescent childbearing: An analysis of data from the Philadelphia Collaborative Perinatal Project. Final report to National Institutes for Child Health and Human Development*. Swarthmore, PA: Swarthmore College.

McConkey, R. (1985a). *Working with parents: A practical guide for teachers and therapists*. London: Croom Helm.

McConkey, R. (1985b). Play. In D. Lane & B. Stratford (Eds.), *Current approaches to Down's Syndrome*. New York: Praeger Scientific.

Nash, C. (1981). *ECHO: Early Childhood Identification Through Observation*. Don Mills, ON: Collier Macmillan.

Piaget, J. (1952). *The origins of intelligence in children*. New York. Norton.

Rubin, K.M., Fenn, G.G., & Vandenberg, B. (1983). Play. In E.W. Hetherington (Ed.), *Carmichael's manual of child psychology: Vol. 4, Socialization, personality and social development* (pp. 693–774). New York: Wiley.

Simeonsson, R., Cooper, D., & Scheiner, A. (1982). A review and analysis of the effectiveness of early intervention programs. *Pediatrics, 69*(5), 635–641.

Smilansky, S. (1968). *The effects of sociodramatic play on disadvantaged preschool children*. New York: Wiley.

Thurman, S.K., & Widerstrom, A.H. (1985). *Young children with special needs*. Boston: Allyn and Bacon.

Trickett, P.K., Apfel, N.H, Rosenbaum, L.K., & Zigler, E.F. (1982). A five-year follow-up of participants in the Yale Child Welfare Research Program. In E. Zigler & E. Gordon (Eds.), *Day Care: Scientific and Social Policy Issues* (pp. 183–199). Boston, Ashburn House.

Udwin, O., & Yule, W. (1983). Imaginative play in language disordered children. *British Journal of Disorders of Communication, 18,* 197–205.

Wells, G. (1981). *Learning through interaction: The study of language development*. Cambridge: Cambridge University Press.

Winzer, M., Rogow, S., & David, C. (Eds.). (1987). *Exceptional Children in Canada*. Toronto: Prentice-Hall.

20

The Victoria and Vancouver Research Projects*

Hillel Goelman and Alan R. Pence

The Generations of Child-Care Research
Fourth-Generation Ecologically Oriented Studies
The Victoria Project
The Vancouver Project
Future Directions
Conclusion
References

The Victoria Day Care Research Project (the Victoria DCRP, the Victoria Project) was the first major Canadian study to use an ecological design to address questions emerging from what has been termed the "fourth generation" of North American child-care research (Pence, 1983). The Victoria Project undertook data collection in 1983–84; research reports addressing various facets of the project were written primarily in the years 1984 through 1986 (Pence & Goelman, 1987). During the data analysis and report-writing period of the Victoria Project, it was determined that a follow-up study focusing on key questions and issues emerging from this project would be desirable. Subsequently, the Vancouver Day Care Research Project (the Vancouver DCRP, the Vancouver Project) received Social Sciences and Humanities Research Council (SSHRC) funding for a two-year period from April 1986 to April 1988. Research reports from the Vancouver Project were written during the fall and winter of 1988–89. Work on these should largely be concluded by late 1989.

This chapter will provide a brief overview and update of both the Victoria and Vancouver Projects, noting their common heritage in the fourth generation of child-care research and the continuing subjects of inquiry that link the two projects. Other North American studies that share a similar interest in the broader "ecology of child care" (Goelman &

*The research projects discussed in this chapter were supported by the Social Sciences and Humanities Research Council of Canada.

Pence, 1985) will be noted as part of a "family" of research studies seeking answers to the fundamental question posed by fourth-generation research: "What are the variables and interactions of variables that influence the development of children who experience various child-care arrangements?" While a detailed consideration of responses to this question is beyond our scope here, the generational framework leading up to this inquiry and a number of the studies involved in the undertaking will be noted.

THE GENERATIONS OF CHILD-CARE RESEARCH

Pence (1983) identified four post–World War II generations of North American child-care research. The first generation reflected the status of child-care services in a social environment that was strongly supportive of mothers staying at home with their children. Child-care was seen as a welfare "safety net" service for the few, not as a necessary service for the many. Social demographics supported such an attitude—less than 10 percent of mothers with young children were involved in the labour force outside the home. Research was enlisted to buttress the social belief with scientific facts.

Not surprisingly, few took note of or protested the fact that this research was based on studies of various forms of long-term and residential child care, rather than child care used on a day-to-day basis by the average family. The message, it was erroneously believed, was the same in either case: "Children need their mothers—child care by others is bad."

It was not until the late 1960s and early 1970s that social beliefs and demographics changed sufficiently to warrant a reinvestigation of the first generation's verdict. The second generation of research began in a number of university child-care and laboratory programs across North America (Fowler & Kahn, 1974; Saunders, 1972). Again the simple question was, "Is child-care good or bad?" The response from second-generation researchers was mostly "It's good."

Some expressed concern about the second generation's verdict, noting that university programs could not be seen as typical of the majority of child-care programs in North America. Thus a third generation of field-based research was inaugurated (Howes & Rubenstein, 1978; Prescott, 1973; Travers, 1979). To the same simple question—"Is child-care good or bad?"—these researchers provided a more ambivalent verdict than their predecessors: "It all depends."

The question "Depends on what?" became the impetus for fourth-generation child-care research in North America. Some research focuses on answering this question with regard to specific age groups (Belsky, 1986); other research, including the Victoria DCRP, examines the interaction of particular child, parent, and caregiver variables (Phillips, 1987).

One of the most useful frameworks for examining social and social systems' interactions and their possible effects on child development was Urie Bronfenbrenner's concept of *ecological research* (Bronfenbrenner, 1979; Pence, 1989). Bronfenbrenner's framework was system-based; the visual image he employed was that of the familiar Russian nested dolls, each one slightly smaller and fitting into the other. He identified four system levels:

- the *micro-system*: the child's immediate environment (for example, the caregiver, family, or school)
- the *meso-system*: two or more of the relevant micro-systems
- the *exo-system*: an environment that does not actually contain the child, but that can or does affect the child's micro-system (for example, a parent's work place or a child-care licensing body)
- the *macro-system*: the broader sociocultural system—the laws, beliefs, values, and so on that affect all the more restricted system levels.

Given the Victoria DCRP's interest in interactional and social systems, Bronfenbrenner's ecological framework was well suited to the researchers' purposes.

FOURTH-GENERATION ECOLOGICALLY ORIENTED STUDIES

Fourth-generation interactional research developed independently in various parts of North America. As these studies completed their data collection and began to appear in research presentations and publications in the middle 1980s, the awareness grew that a "family" of similarly oriented studies exists within this fourth generation.

A number of features characterize these studies. Most include children in different types of care and all include children in modal (as opposed to model) community-based child-care settings (the latter was also a characteristic of third-generation research). The studies all link developmental-outcome measures not to type of care *per se* (as was characteristic of many third-generation studies), but to such contextual features as quality of the caregiving environment and children's daily experiences in care. In addition, most of these studies consider the interaction of family sociodemographic, belief, and attitudinal features with caregiver attitudinal, training, and socioeconomic-status (SES) variables. Most display sensitivity to macro-level sociocultural factors; in addition, some incorporate such exo-system variables as licensing and regulatory characteristics. Also of note in considering the "family" of ecologically oriented studies is their diverse geographic locales, which include Bermuda, the United States, and Canada.

THE VICTORIA PROJECT

Bronfenbrenner's ecological-systems model was explicitly used in planning the methodology for the Victoria DCRP. Instruments were developed or incorporated to gather data from each of the micro- through macrosystem levels. Child-development measures focusing on language development were employed, and care was taken with the sampling procedure to include both licensed and unlicensed forms of care, and to include family child-care as well as centre-based care. The caregiving environments were evaluated using standardized rating scales (Harms & Clifford, 1980; Harms, Clifford, & Padan-Belkin, 1983), and child/adult interactions were observed using a system developed by Goelman (1984). In addition, structured interviews with both parents and caregivers were conducted.

The design of the Victoria DCRP allowed both for descriptive analyses of specific agents and systems within the ecology of child care, and for more complex, interactional analyses of factors affecting the children's development. For example, reports have focused on the characteristics of caregivers and parents across the three types of care (Pence & Goelman, 1987). A substudy of fathers was also carried out, and mother/father descriptive comparisons were developed (Pence & Early, 1988). In addition, reports were published on the interaction of variables associated with family structure and caregiver structure, and process variables (Goelman & Pence, 1987a). Finally, exo-system variables—for example, licensing and the interaction of licensing and quality—were considered (Goelman and Pence, 1987b).

Various results from the analyses of Victoria DCRP data were presented to the Special Parliamentary Committee on Child Care in the winter of 1987–88. Those findings included the following information:

Parents

- There are distinct preferences among families for either family or centre-based child care.
- There are distinct reasons for preferring specific types of child-care services.
- Parents report "good news and bad news" regarding the advantages and disadvantages of their current child-care arrangements.
- There are higher levels of friendship relationships between parents and family child-care providers.

- More parents using centre-based child care responded that they had "no negative concerns" regarding their current arrangements.
- There were high preferences for part-time employment by mothers using both centre-based and family child care.

Caregivers

- There was more scheduling flexibility in family child-care than in centre-based care.
- There was more flexibility in providing care for special-needs children in centre-based care.
- There were higher levels of formal caregiver training in centre-based care than in family child care.
- Most unlicensed family child-care providers would prefer to have other employment.
- There were higher turnover rates in unlicensed family child care than in licensed family child care.

Researchers' observation of children and child development

- Children in unlicensed family child care scored significantly lower on tests of language development than did children in licensed family child care.
- Children in lower-quality family child-care homes watched more television than did children in higher-quality family child-care homes or licensed child-care centres.
- Both the amount of caregiver training and level of maternal education affected the children's test scores.
- Children from low-resource family backgrounds (for example, single-parent families, or families where parents had low levels of income, occupational status, and education) were found to be disproportionately represented in low-quality family child-care homes.
- Low-quality family child-care homes were over-represented in the unlicensed family child-care sample.

These and other findings from the Victoria Project can be considered in two principal contexts: (1) as they contribute to an understanding of child care and the ecology of child care in Canada, and (2) as they contribute to the aforementioned "family" of similarly oriented studies in fourth-generation North American research.

The Victoria Project made a significant contribution to both these research agendas. The value and potential of the ecological approach led the investigators to seek follow-up funding for a Vancouver-based project focusing primarily on the families, children, and caregivers in a sample of family child-care homes.

THE VANCOUVER PROJECT

The Vancouver DCRP focused on the same meso-system triad of parent/child/caregiver that distinguished the Victoria Project. However, certain key modifications were made in the Vancouver Project: the study (1) focused primarily on family child-care arrangements and (2) sought richer detail on both the child's home environment and the caregiving environment. To accomplish the latter aim, several means were employed. First, Caldwell and Bradley's (1979) *Home Observation for Measurement of the Environment (HOME)* instrument was used, both in the child's own home and in the family child-care setting. Second, Moos's (1986) *Family Environment Scale* was administered to both parents and caregivers. And finally, the Harms, Clifford, and Padan-Belkin (1983) *Day Care Home Environment Rating Scale* (DCHERS) was again used in the caregiver's home (as was done in the Victoria DCRP).

For the Vancouver Project a decision was made to deepen our understanding of language use in the home and in the care setting, rather than to broaden the developmental focus to include a more specific cognitive measure. In order to provide a fuller understanding of the interaction of the effects of home and child-care settings on children's language development, the Vancouver Project collected detailed information on mother/child discourse patterns at home and caregiver/child discourse patterns in care. Observations were carried out in semi-structured play situations, at home and in care, with the dialogues being videotaped and later transcribed. The transcriptions were coded for a number of features that have been found to facilitate children's language development, including the frequency of use of psychological verbs, the cohesiveness of the child's discourse (that is, the ability of the child to stay on topic), and the difficulty of the questions (cognitive demands) asked by the child's conversational partners. Children were also tested using the *Peabody Picture Vocabulary Test* or PPVT (Dunn, 1979) and the *Expressive One-Word Picture Vocabulary Test* or EOWPVT (Gardner, 1979) to measure their receptive and expressive language abilities.

Data from the Vancouver DCRP were collected in the winter and early spring of 1986–87. Data analyses were undertaken in 1987–88, and the first data-based articles will be submitted for publication in 1989. Preliminary analyses indicate that findings from the Vancouver DCRP corroborate the Victoria DCRP findings in certain key areas. The preliminary data reveal strong relationships between the levels of cognitive stimulation in both the child's home and the family child-care home and the children's performance on the two measures of language development. Analyses of the discourse data also reveal that the frequency of such specific features as cohesiveness, psychological verbs, and cognitive demands, both at home and in family child-care, are closely associated with the children's level of language development. Further, the results on the *Family Environment Scale* (FES), our measure of social/emotional climate within the family structure, indicate high correlations between FES scores and levels of cognitive stimulation in both the child's home and the family child-care setting. These data also reveal strong associations between FES scores and the children's performance on both the PPVT and the EOWPVT.

FUTURE DIRECTIONS

The Victoria and Vancouver Day Care Research Projects have broken new ground in the ongoing effort to better understand child care in Canada and in North America. The work is an integral part of a "family" of child care research that emerged in various parts of North America in the 1980s. This body of research has focused largely on questions about the interactions among systems and system levels in the ecology of child care. Largely as a result of such fourth-generation studies, child-care specialists now have a heightened appreciation and understanding of the complex interplay among family, caregiving, and child variables.

In addition, the collaborative work of the Victoria and Vancouver Day Care Research Projects has been instrumental in the establishment of a communication and planning network of child-care researchers from across Canada. Members of that network were subsequently successful in securing funding for the *National Child Care Survey* (NCCS) (Lero, et al., 1988), a large-scale (*N*=25,000) survey of Canadian families, their child-care arrangements, and work-force participation characteristics. Now under way, the NCCS will meet a long-felt need for a reliable "base line" of information on Canadian child care. With such a base line established, other more focused local or regional studies will have an enhanced national context within which to interpret results and a stronger basis for understanding the generalizable findings of a given investigation.

There remain, however, many other significant needs that Canadian child-care research must address. One of the areas most urgently in need of attention is the collection of longitudinal data on the effects of various caregiving experiences on children in their early years. Only Bagley's Calgary-based study (1987) has systematically followed a sample of children from birth and incorporated a partial focus on their caregiving experiences. (Bagley's work is also valuable in the Canadian literature for its inclusion of mothers as one of the caregiving comparison groups.)

The next logical step in the Victoria and Vancouver Research Program would be a longitudinal follow-up of the two studies' sample groups. The Victoria children would, by the autumn of 1989, be an average of nine years old, and most would be in third grade. The Vancouver sample by that time would be largely in first grade. It is anticipated that a funding request for a longitudinal follow-up of the Victoria and Vancouver samples will be made in 1989.

CONCLUSION

The fourth generation of North American child-care research has been a productive era. It has seen child-care research move from simple societal questions and responses to more complex ecological research questions that facilitate more complex, interactionally oriented responses. Through such advances in the complexity of questions asked, the complexity of the phenomena in question will become better understood—and, in turn, through that more sophisticated understanding, appropriate social responses to the needs of children and families may be forthcoming.

REFERENCES

Bagley, C. (1987). *Day care and child development: Evidence from a longitudinal study.* Unpublished manuscript.

Belsky, J. (1986). Infant day care: A cause for concern? *Zero to Three, 6,* 1–6.

Bronfenbrenner, U. (1979). *The ecology of human development.* Cambridge, MA: Harvard University Press Press.

Caldwell, B., & Bradley, R. (1979). *Home observation of the environment.* Little Rock: University of Arkansas Press.

Dunn, L.M. (1979). *Peabody Picture Vocabulary Test, revised.* Circle Pines, MN: American Guidance Service.

Early, R., & Pence, A.R. (1988). *Fathers and mothers of children in the Victoria Day Care Research Project.* Unpublished manuscript.

Fowler, W., & Khan, N. (1974). *The development of a prototype infant and child day care centre in Metropolitan Toronto,* #1, year III Progress Report. Toronto: Ontario Institute for Studies in Education.

Gardner, M.F. (1979). *Expressive One-Word Vocabulary Test.* Novato, CA: American Therapy Publications.

Goelman, H. (1984). *Manual for observations in the Victoria DCRP.* Unpublished project manuscript.

Goelman, H., & Pence, A.R. (1985). Towards the ecology of day care in Canada: A research agenda for the 1980s. *Canadian Journal of Education, 10*(4), 323–344.

Goelman, H., & Pence, A.R. (1987a). Children in three types of day care: Daily experiences, quality of care, and developmental outcomes. *Early Child Development and Care, 36,* 52–66.

Goelman, H., & Pence, A.R. (1987b). The impact of day care, family and individual characteristics on children's language development. In D. Phillips (Ed.), *Quality in child care: What does research tell us?* (National Association for the Education of Young Children Monograph Series). Washington, DC: NAEYC.

Harms, T., & Clifford, R. (1980). *The Early Childhood Environment Rating Scale.* New York: Teachers College Press.

Harms, T., Clifford, R., & Padan-Belkin, E. (1983). *The Day Care Home Environment Rating Scale.* Chapel Hill, NC: Homebased Day Care Training Project.

Howes, C., & Rubenstein, J. (1978). *Toddler social development in two day care settings.* (ERIC Document Reproduction Service No. ED 160 250)

Lero, S., Pence, A., Goelman, H., & Brockman, L. (1988). *The National Child Care Survey.* Ottawa: Health and Welfare Canada.

Moos, R.H. (1986). *Family Environment Scale manual* (2nd ed.). Palo Alto, CA: Consulting Psychologists Press.

Peaslee, M.V. (1977) *Dissertation Abstracts International.* 37 (07), 4218.

Pence, A.R. (1983). Day care in the 80s: An overview of research and issues. *Canadian Children,* 8(1), 3–9.

Pence, A.R. (1989). In the shadow of mother-care: Contexts for an understanding of child day care in North America. *Canadian Psychologist.*

Pence, A.R., & Early, R. (1988). Fathers and child care: An exploratory study of fathers with children in day care. *Early Child Development and Care, 36,* 71–90.

Pence, A.R., & Goelman, H. (1987). Silent partners: Parents of children in three types of day care. *Early Childhood Research Quarterly.*

Phillips, D. (Ed.). (1987). *Quality in child care: What does research tell us?* Washington, DC: National Association for the Education of Young Children.

Prescott, E. (1973). *A comparison of three types of day care and nursery school home care.* (ERIC Document Reproduction Service No. ED 078 910

Saunders, M. (1972). *Some aspects of the effects of day care on infants' emotional and personality development.* Unpublished doctoral dissertation, University of North Carolina, Chapel Hill.

Travers, J., and Goodson, B.D. (1979). *Research results of the national day care study: final report.* Cambridge, MA: Abt Associates.

21

Child-Care Quality and Children's Transition to Kindergarten

Raquel Betsalel-Presser
Ellen Vineberg-Jacobs
Donna Romano-White
Madeleine Baillargeon

The increasing number of children attending child care prior to kindergarten has affected the kindergarten environment. Because the quality of available child-care services is not uniform, the kindergarten teacher is faced with a heterogeneous group of children who have had varied preschool experiences and exposures. New longitudinal studies are beginning to offer insight into the impact of child-care quality on the child's transition to kindergarten. Their findings suggest that child care, particularly high-quality care, may facilitate this transition.

Several problems make the study of child-care quality and transition to kindergarten difficult. In Quebec, as in other provinces, research is complicated by the diversity of child-care services offered and by the structural governmental provisions that favour parallel roles and responsibilities for the care and education of children. Most Quebec schools, for instance, offer a half-day kindergarten program for five-year-olds, which is sponsored and supervised by the Ministry of Education. Special half-day programs for four-year-olds and extended (full-day) kindergarten

*The authors wish to acknowledge support received from les fonds F.C.A.R. (M.E.Q.) and the Social Sciences and Humanities Research Council for several of the research studies summarized in this chapter.

programs for five-year-olds are available to some children identified as underprivileged. However, a Quebec Ministry of Social Services through its Office des services de garde à l'enfance (Child Care Services Bureau) licenses and supervises many different forms of full- and part-time care for children up to 12 years old. The child-care programs recognized by provincial legislation are day-care centres; family day-care agencies; school-based day care; nursery schools; and part-time care.

The artificial division between care and education may affect children's transition and adjustment to kindergarten—particularly when they have attended preschool programs, which vary widely in goals, methods, and philosophies. Those that offer high-quality, developmentally appropriate programs create a situation that requires kindergarten teachers to restructure their program plans in order to offer the experienced preschoolers new and different stimulating activities. This diversity can create classroom difficulties by obliging teachers to plan for those who have had high- or low-quality preschool experiences, as well as for those who have had none at all.

This chapter will address four issues: (1) the definition and measurement of child-care quality in group settings; (2) the relationship between child-care quality and child development; (3) the relationship between child-care quality and the child's transition to school; and (4) teachers' perceptions of the child-care child's transition to kindergarten.

DEFINING AND MEASURING CHILD-CARE QUALITY

For the past two decades, studies have persistently shown the crucial influence of early experiences (Belsky & Steinberg, 1979; Clarke-Stewart & Fein, 1983; McVicker Hunt, 1961). Child-care programs have thus been charged with an important mission—to achieve quality services. The aspects that determine the ecology of each child-care facility have been studied by researchers in both Canada and the United States, as Chapter 20 outlines.

Quality generally refers to those aspects of child-care environments that are associated with positive developmental outcomes in children. Any viable child-care system must answer the needs of children of different ages, sexes, and family backgrounds; the system must, therefore, be flexible. At the same time, however, there is considerable consensus in the literature with regard to the organizational characteristics thought to be related to high quality in group child-care environments. The National Day Care Study, carried out in 67 urban child-care centres in the United States in the late 1970s, examined the effects of structural characteristics such as caregiver training, group size, adult/child ratio, and resource availability on caregiver and child behaviour and on children's cognitive test performance (Ruopp et al., 1979). The study's findings support the relationship of such variables to developmental outcomes. Other research has indicated that staff stability is also an important variable related to development, particularly in infants and toddlers (Phillips & Howes, 1987).

Kontos and Stevens (1985) sought a definition of quality that went beyond reliance on structural features and reflected the multidimensional nature of any program. These researchers emphasized the idea that numerous variables define each child-care setting and exert a reciprocal influence on one another. They argued that a global measure of quality might best reflect child care's multidimensional nature, and suggested that the Harms and Clifford (1980) Early Childhood Environment Rating Scale (ECERS) was well suited for this purpose. Recent data collected as part of the National Child Care Staffing Study indicates that high global ECERS ratings are positively related to such structural dimensions as adult/child ratio in the child-care setting (Phillips, 1989).

CHILD-CARE QUALITY AND CHILD DEVELOPMENT

Early research into child care focused on comparing children in child-care centres and children reared at home. Peaslee's (1977) study, for example, indicated that home-reared children scored higher than their child-care peers when matched for age, sex, race, socioeconomic status (SES), and family structure. On the other hand, Winett et al. (1977) noticed no overall differences in language measures between children who attended child care and peers in their family. More recently in Canada, Baillargeon et al. (1989) found that child-care children scored higher than non-child-care children on receptive language, but similarly on expressive language.

On the whole, research has found that child-care children show no deleterious effects on language, intellectual, or social development. In fact, in some studies, child-care children have outperformed home-reared children. Differences in the quality of the child-care setting and in the children's SES may help explain the varied results. Research reviewers suggest that low-quality child care may have negative effects on young children, whereas excellent-quality child care may well have positive effects on development. Quality may be particularly important for children of low socioeconomic status.

More recent research has taken quality into account in trying to determine the effects of child care on child development. These studies have investigated language development, intellectual and social functioning and other dimensions. In general these studies offer support for the relationship of high-quality child care to positive developmental outcomes.

In a Bermuda study (McCartney et al., 1982), investigators found that children attending higher-quality centres had higher scores on measures of language development and were rated by their teachers as more social and considerate. McCartney (1984) found that high-quality centres were characterized by caregivers who used a low proportion of control statements; gave children information; and encouraged children to respond, initiate conversations, and converse. Schliecker, White, and Jacobs (1988) used the ECERS to rate the quality of child-care centres in Montreal. Attendance at excellent-quality child care was found to be related to higher vocabulary test scores.

Language is closely related to other fundamental aspects of human development—such as emotional, social, and cognitive development. It is tightly linked with thinking and learning. It plays a crucial role in expressing emotions and in controlling self and others. Verbal interactions are an important part of social relationships, since many social roles are related to and learned through language. Group situations such as child care invite such exchanges. Although verbal interactions with adults are necessary to language development, child-care studies indicate that children tend to interact more with peers than with adults. Child care introduces a growing number of children to a social milieu. Many children from immigrant families and linguistic minorities, for instance, have their first non-relative social contact while attending child care. As a result, other socialization agents, especially schools, must now recognize and share their socializing role with child care.

Child-care quality has also been related to social functioning in preschool children. White, Jacobs, and Schliecker (1988) found that attendance at excellent-quality child-care centres was related to peer play patterns that included more positive, verbal social interactions with peers; fewer negative interactions; and less teacher-directed parallel activity. The caregivers in the low-quality settings organized play situations so that cooperative or interactive play was difficult to achieve. In one setting, children were assigned seats and play items during each "free play" period.

There is little doubt that quality of any child-care experience may influence the competence of the child who comes to kindergarten. Positive developmental outcomes in intellectual, language, and social domains all seem to be related to higher-quality child care. Moreover, skills may be related to one another. For example, good language skills aid children in practising the social skills essential for successfully entering ongoing groups and for maintaining their subsequent inclusion in the group (Putallaz, 1983).

The myth of the child-care child as being characterized by excessive independence (Baillargeon & Betsalel-Presser, 1988), aggression (Schwarz, Strickland, & Krolick, 1974), and egocentrism and lack of consideration for others (Belsky & Steinberg, 1978) seems to be an overgeneralization. It is not child-care attendance *per se*, but the quality of the child-care environment, that seems to be related to the competence of the child who enters kindergarten. Home environments also differ, and the quality of home care may similarly affect children's competence.

CHILD-CARE QUALITY AND THE CHILD'S TRANSITION TO SCHOOL

Longitudinal research makes it possible to follow children in transition from a child-care experience through the early school years. Few longitudinal studies, however, have taken child-care quality into account. Baillargeon and Betsalel-Presser (1988) found that teachers reported that child-care children had difficulty respecting classroom rules, were aggressive, and had a tendency to form cliques. These teachers did qualify their views by indicating that the type of child care and the child's family background contributed to such behaviours. Nonetheless, a somewhat negative view of the child-care child emerges from these studies.

Longitudinal studies that have measured quality have found results supporting the view that attending high-quality child care may have positive effects on children. Vandell, Henderson, and Wilson (1988) studied the social behaviour of eight-year-old children who had previously attended child care that was rated as either high or low in quality. The high-quality centres had better-trained teachers, better materials, better adult/child ratios, lower enrolments, and smaller classes. The low-quality programs were characterized by larger enrolments, less teacher training, poorer adult/child ratios, and fewer materials. This study indicated that children from the high-quality child-care centres had more friendly interactions, were rated as more socially competent and happier, and were less frequently labeled shy by peers. Thus, high-quality preschool child care seems related to more positive social behaviours in eight-year-olds.

Another longitudinal study (Jacobs, Nathan, & Watkins, 1989) rated environmental quality and assessed the social competence of kindergarten children who had attended excellent- versus low-quality child care. The results indicated that high-quality child care was related to greater interest and participation in the kindergarten classroom.

Although more research is needed, several tentative conclusions seem warranted. First, quality is an important consideration in describing the preschool child-care experience. Second, the quality of the child-care experience affects development in kindergarten and the early elementary years. Finally, several of our ideas about child-care children may require revision. Based on teacher reports (Baillargeon & Betsalel-Presser, 1988), it had been expected that children who had not attended child care prior to kindergarten would display more interest and participation in activities than child-care children, who had "done it all before." This was not the case. Teachers rated children from high-quality centres as displaying more interest and participation in the classroom. Furthermore, based on research indicating that low-quality child care is more structured (White, Jacobs, & Schliecker, 1988) and that caregivers in such centres are more restrictive and controlling (McCartney, 1984), greater compliance was expected from children who attended these centres. The results did not confirm this expectation.

These findings might be related to the type of kindergarten classroom. (Jacobs, Nathan, & Watkins, 1989). These classrooms were similar to the high-quality child-care settings. There were special-interest areas, sand tables, blocks, reading areas, materials for dramatic play, and extensive art supplies. The majority of the teachers were warm and friendly and encouraged conversations with groups of children and individuals throughout the half-day period. Thus, children who had attended high-quality child-care centres entered an environment that was familiar, but offered sufficient challenge to maintain their interest. On the other hand, children from low-quality child-care centres, who had experienced many restrictions and a high degree of caregiver control, found themselves in an environment with different rules and expectations. This newfound freedom may have tempted them to "flex their muscles" and experiment with the rules.

The quality of child care may also be related to the parents'SES. That is, children from high-SES families tend to be in good- or excellent-quality child care, while children from low-SES families tend to be in minimal or inadequate care (Parent & White, 1989). This factor is often referred to as parental "selection" of child care. Fifteen of the seventeen child-care centres in three working-and middle-class areas of Montreal were rated by Parent and White (1989): of these, six were rated as minimal, nine as good, and none as excellent. Thus, parents' choice was restricted by the absence of excellent care. When there was only good or minimal care to "choose" between, the overwhelming majority of high-SES children were in good care. Low-SES families—who reported needing centres that were open for longer or more unusual hours, and for whom cost of care was an important factor—were more likely to have children in centres rated as minimal. In another study (Schliecker, White, & Jacobs, 1988) it was noted that mother-headed single-parent families often used low-quality child care. It would thus seem that family and child-care situations may interact to widen the developmental differences among children and contribute to variations in the child-care/school transition.

TEACHERS' PERCEPTIONS OF THE CHILD-CARE
CHILD'S TRANSITION TO KINDERGARTEN

In an attempt to obtain information regarding kindergarten teachers' perceptions of child-care children, a study was conducted with French-speaking kindergarten teachers from the Montreal and Quebec City areas. (Baillargeon and Betsalel-Presser, 1988; Betsalel-Presser, Jacques, & Lavoie, 1989; Betsalel-Presser, Lavoie, & Jacques, 1989). Teachers were asked to complete a questionnaire that addressed issues related to kindergarten adaptation and social competence for children attending or having attended a child-care program. The results suggest that teachers perceive such children as being able to adapt to the new environment, with some difficulty. On the one hand, teachers feel that these children show an interest in teacher-initiated activities, but on the other hand, they seem to prefer those activities related to creativity, such as dramatic play, arts and crafts, block building, pottery, and music. The least popular activities were the ones associated with formal learning. The results also indicate that teachers perceive differences in the children's concentration skills when faced with organized as opposed to free activities. This difference suggests that a child's attention span depends on the nature and the appeal of the activities and that a short attention span is not necessarily indicative of poor concentration skills in general. Although more than half the teachers supported the idea that the child-care child shifts quickly from one free activity to another, they were not ready to conclude that these children have difficulty fixing their attention, even though a majority of the teachers noted that they had to remind these children to finish their task more often when compared to non-child-care children.

When asked to express their opinion about the children's attitudes toward classroom instructions and discipline, a large majority of the teachers were quite negative. They indicated that child-care children lack discipline, do not automatically respect classroom rules, and challenge the teacher by creating their own set of rules. Teachers seemed to resent being forced to repeat and remind children frequently of rules. They considered their work to have become more difficult due to this kind of behaviour. However, a small percentage of teachers commented favourably on this issue, noting that child-care children tend to respect rules sooner than home-reared children do, since they have already been exposed to rules in previous child-care experiences. We may therefore question whether the discipline disturbances pointed out by teachers can be attributed principally to the child-care experience, or whether the ecology of the child's living context—for example, early-morning departure from home, exposure to more than one rearing environment, the change of nurturing agents, and the child's own family structure—might play a large part in such behaviours. For instance, a third of the teachers noticed that children who spent part of the day in another group setting arrived at school feeling tired. The majority associate such arrangements with "nervous," "tense," "hyperactive," and excited behaviours in children, while a few describe such children as smiling and self-confident.

From the perspective of individual development, teachers perceive child-care children as having a positive self-image expressed by a general state of well-being. This is reflected in such children's autonomous behaviour and in their ability to take initiative, make their own choices, and assume responsibilities. A large majority of the teachers noted that although child-care children maintain relative physical proximity to the teacher, they ask for help only after unsuccessful trials. Teachers seem to consider that these children have "numerous" interactions with peers that allow them to enhance their social competence. They are very involved in both affiliative and conflictual behaviours. They assume an important role in leadership and may also collaborate constructively in resolving social conflicts. But these rather positive comments are tempered by the teachers' disapproval of the level of aggression displayed by child-care children toward their peers.

In summary, this study indicates that although school teachers perceive some advantages for the child coming from child care, they also point out that such children create some degree of disturbance in the teacher's daily work. Since teachers are encountering more and more heterogeneous groups in most urban schools, we must look at ways of facilitating communication among child-care staff, school systems, and families in order to avoid stigmatizing children who have had early group experiences. Current knowledge about the importance of program quality underscores the need for a closer relationship between kindergarten and child-care services. A better understanding of their complementary roles may allow a smoother transition from one setting to the other.

CONCLUSION

Research on the interaction of family variables, child-care and school experiences, and the attitudes of kindergarten teachers has facilitated our understanding of the relationship between child-care quality and transition to kindergarten.

Positive transitions from child care to kindergarten depend on continuity among the various environments to which children are exposed. It is now possible to state that a high-quality child-care experience may facilitate positive transitions, while a poor-quality child-care experience may prepare the child to anticipate a similar experience in kindergarten and therefore set a negative attitude toward school learning.

High-quality programs offer developmentally appropriate environments in which staff, activities, materials, and the whole environment stimulate curiosity and interaction among children. Finally, the need to merge "care" with "education" requires systematic and regular communication among caregivers, educators, and parents. To achieve this goal, we must have offical recognition of the need to facilitate transition, as well as creative participation in the process. This can occur only if teachers, caregivers, and parents demonstrate a willingness to collaborate, and if those in positions of authority (for example, government officials and school and child-care administrators), support the need for both high-quality care and cooperation.

REFERENCES

Baillargeon, M., & Betsalel-Presser, R. (1988). Effets de la garderie sur le comportement social et l'adaptation de l'enfant: Perception des enseignantes de la maternelle. *Canadian Journal of Research in Early Childhood Education, 2*(2), 91–98.

Baillargeon, M., Gravel, M., Larouche, H., & Larouche, M. (1989, April). Day care: language and social development in kindergarten. Paper presented at the National Day Care Conference, Canadian Child Day Care Federation, Winnipeg, MB.

Belsky, J., & Steinberg, L.D. (1978). The effects of day care: A critical review. *Child Development, 49*, 929–949.

Belsky, J., & Steinberg, L.D. (1979). What does research teach us about daycare?: A follow-up report. *Children Today, 8*, 21–27.

Betsalel-Presser, R., Jacques, M., & Lavoie, C. (1989, April). How do kindergarten teachers view the day care child? Paper presented at the National Day Care Conference, Canadian Child Day Care Federation, Winnipeg, MB.

Betsalel-Presser, R., Lavoie, C., & Jacques, M. (in press). Les enfants de maternelle provenant des services de garde: Perceptions de leurs educatrices. *Revue des sciences de l'éducation 4*(3).

Clarke-Stewart, K.A., & Fein, G.G. (1983). Early childhood programs. In P.H. Mussen (Ed.), *Handbook of child psychology* (pp. 917–999). New York: Wiley.

Harms, T., & Clifford, R.M. (1980). *Early Childhood Environment Rating Scale*. New York: Teachers College Press.

Jacobs, E., Nathan, R., & Watkins, J. (1989). Day care environment and social competence: A longitudinal study. Paper presented at the Canadian Psychological Association Conference, Halifax, NS.

Kontos, S., & Stevens, R. (1985, January). High quality child care: Does your center measure up? *Young Children, 40*, 5–9.

McCartney, K., Scarr, S., Phillips, D., Grajek, J., & Schwarz, J.C. (1982). Environmental differences among day care centres and their effects on children's development. In E.F. Zigler & E.W. Gordon (Eds.), *Day care: Scientific and social policy issues.* Boston: Auburn House.

McCartney, K. (1984). Effect of quality of day care environment on children's language development. *Developmental Psychology 2*, 244– 260.

McVicker Hunt, J. (1961). *Intelligence and experience.* New York: Randal.

Parent, M., & White, D.R. (1989, June). Parental selection of day care: You take what you get. Paper presented at the Learned Societies, Canadian Society for Studies in Education, Quebec City, PQ.

Peaslee, M.V. (1977). The development of competency in two-year-old infants in day care and home reared environments. *Dissertation Abstracts International, 3*, 7, 4218–A.

Phillips, D.A., & Howes, C. (1987). Indicators of quality in child care: Review of research. In D.A. Phillips (Ed.), *Quality in child care: What does research tell us?* Washington, DC: National Association for the Education of Young Children.

Phillips, D. (1989). The contribution of caregiver characteristics, turnover, and caregiving competence to child care quality. Paper presented at the Society for Research in Child Development, Kansas City, KS.

Putallaz, M. (1983). Predicting children's sociometric status from their behavior. *Child Development, 54*, 1417–1426.

Ruopp, R., Travers, J., Glantz, F., & Coelen, C. (1979). *Children at the center: Final report of the National Day Care Study, Summary of findings and their implications.* Cambridge, MA: Abt Associates.

Schliecker, E., White, D.R., & Jacobs, E. (1988). *Predicting preschool language comprehension from* SES, *family structure, and day care quality* (Research bulletins, 7, No. 002). Montreal: Concordia University, Centre for Research in Human Development.

Schwartz, J., Strickland, R., & Krolick, G. (1974). Infant day care: Behavioral effects at preschool age. *Developmental Psychology, 10*, 502–506.

Vandell, D.L., Henderson, V.K., & Wilson, K.S. (1988). A longitudinal study of children with day care experiences of varying quality. *Child Development, 59*, 1286–1292.

White, D.R., Jacobs, E., & Schliecker, E. (1988). Relationship of day care environmental quality and children's social behaviour. *Canadian Psychology, 29*, Abstract no. 668.

Winett, R.A., Fuchs, W.L., Moffatt, S.A., & Nerviano, V.J. (1977). A cross-sectional study of children and their families in different child care environments: Some data and conclusions. *Journal of Community Psychology, 5*, 149–159.

Epilogue

Endings should be beginnings. The insights provided by this volume into the wealth of wisdom, initiative, and diversity in the field of early childhood education and care in Canada should inspire the reader to synthesize theory and practice—and then to translate that synthesis into positive action that builds on this bedrock of tradition.

To paraphrase an expression from folk wisdom, "The path leads to the future through the present." Although for some young children, the present means an inadequate level of either care or education, we can certainly be optimistic about the future when its architecture is in the hands of the type of committed individual the readers have met as authors in this book.

"Come let us live with our children."
Friedrich Froebel

The Contributors

Madeleine Baillargeon is a professor at the Faculté des Sciences de l'Éducation, Université Laval in Quebec City. She has authored publications for Office de Service de Garde à l'Enfance in Quebec and has done research on language and social development in preschool children.

Raquel Betsalel-Presser is a professor in the Faculté des Sciences de l'Éducation, Université de Montréal, and was recently appointed Vice-Dean of Human Resources. She has authored and co-authored articles, reports, monographs, and books and is currently Associate Editor of the *Canadian Journal of Research in Early Childhood Education*.

Patricia M. Canning currently directs a number of international development projects in child care from her base as associate professor in the Department of Child Study at Mount Saint Vincent University in Halifax. Her research and professional activities include child-care policy, young children with special needs, and the training of child-care professionals.

Deborah Chant is a faculty member of the School of Early Childhood Education at Ryerson Polytechnical Institute in Toronto, and is involved in the projects for teacher training in Jaipur, India, and in multicultural teacher education. Her teaching interests centre on the impact of family dynamics, particularly divorce and custody, on young children.

Barbara Corbett is the founder and principal of the Froebel Foundation School—a private school in Mississauga, Ontario, that she started in 1970 after her doctoral study. There she puts into practice Froebelian philosophy and pedagogy. Her most recent publication is *A Century of Kindergarten Education in Ontario* (The Froebel Foundation, 1989).

Patricia Dickinson is currently involved in a special project for the Halton (Ontario) Board of Education. Her career has included teaching in many settings in the early childhood field, contributing regular articles to the Federation of Women Teachers' Association of Ontario newsletter, and initiating an organization to integrate early childhood educators from the child-care and the education systems.

Isabel M. Doxey is a professor in the School of Early Childhood Education at Ryerson in Toronto. Her career has spanned teaching children and teachers; consulting nationally and internationally; serving on the boards and executive committees of numerous associations related to early childhood; and presenting many seminars, workshops, and conference addresses. She has researched teacher behaviour and is currently directing a project on school-based child care.

Steen B. Esbensen, a professor of early childhood education, has been engaged in research, teacher training, and advocacy on behalf of children for the past 20 years. He has authored numerous books, including *The Outdoor Classroom* (High/Scope Foundation, 19), articles and audio/visual presentations. He is currently on leave from the University of Quebec in Hull, while serving as Executive Director of the Social Science Federation of Canada.

Catalina Ferrer is an educational psychologist with a background in preschool education. She is a member of the Faculté des Sciences de L'Education at the Université de Moncton in New Brunswick. Her involvements centre on advocacy of and methodology for peace and human rights education both nationally and internationally through her presentations, research, and publications.

Joan Gamble currently holds a position as assistant professor in the Faculté des Sciences de l'Éducation at the Université de Moncton. She brings a background in home economics, child study, and sociology to her present project, which involves applying the methodology of peace and human rights education to the kindergarten and early primary grades.

Hillel Goelman is associate professor of Early Childhood and Language Education in the Faculty of Education at the University of British Columbia in Vancouver. His major research interests lie in the areas of children's language development and emergent literacy, and the effects of different preschool and child-care settings on these aspects of child development.

Anne Lindsay has extended her own teacher training and postgraduate study, after a recent move to the West, to undertake research with Indian children living in Canada. She is a member of the faculty of North Island College, Courtenay Campus, in Campbell River, British Columbia.

Mary E. Lyon has focused her research interests on the early detection of special needs and on the development of play in hearing- and language-impaired children after much experience working directly with special-needs children. She is currently chairperson of the Department of Child Study at Mount Saint Vincent University in Halifax, where she is an assistant professor.

Sue Martin qualified as a teacher at the Froebel Institute in England, with a nursery/infant specialization. She has been involved with the National Nursery Examination Board as teacher and examiner, contributed to journals, lectured, and served on the editorial board of *Nursery*

World. Currently she acts as a private consultant and faculty member at Toronto's Centennial College of Applied Arts and Technology.

Margie I. Mayfield has taught at the preschool, primary, and post-secondary levels in Canada, the United States, Saudi Arabia, and England. Since 1977, she has taught early childhood education at the University of Victoria. Her research interests include parent involvement in early childhood programs, employer-supported child care, children's early literacy development, and the home environment.

Karen R. Mock is a registered psychologist specializing in human development and race relations. A certified teacher, she has lectured at the University of Toronto, Ryerson Polytechnical Institute, and York University; has consulted on multicultural issues; and has served as president of the Ontario Multicultural Association. At present, she is national director of the B'nai Brith's League for Human Rights.

Ken Pierce is on the faculty at Holland College in Charlottetown, Prince Edward Island. With a background in psychology, he is the founding president of the Psychological Association of Prince Edward Island and a founding member of the Canadian Day Care Advocacy Association.

Alan R. Pence has been directly involved in child care as a child-care worker, trainer, director, and researcher since 1971. At present he is director of the School of Youth and Child Care at the University of Victoria; co-investigator (with Hillel Goelman) on the Victoria and Vancouver Day Care Research Projects; and co-director of the National Child Care Survey.

Ellen M. Regan is a professor at the Ontario Institute for Studies in Education (Toronto), where she is cross-appointed to the departments of Applied Psychology and Curriculum. Her research interests in teacher behaviour extend her own practical background as teacher and consultant.

Donna Romano-White has clinical and research interests in the effects of child-care and environmental differences on child development as well as on children's health. She is an associate professor of Psychology and Education at Concordia University, and a member of the Centre de Recherche en Développement Humain.

Ada Schermann was chairman of the Institute of Child Study, and principal of the Institute's Laboratory School, at the University of Toronto. She now teaches in the Educational Psychology Department of the Faculty of Education. As executive secretary for the Commission of Enquiry into the Education of the Young Child in Ontario, she co-authored the report *To Herald a Child* (1979).

Jean H. Stevenson, as a parent and teacher, has been a supporter of parent cooperatives for more than 35 years. A former president of Parent Cooperative Preschools International, she currently acts as an advisor to that organization. She has also served as assistant director of the Day Nurseries Branch of the Ontario Ministry of Community and Social Services and before her retirement was coordinator of the Early Childhood Education Program at Georgian College of Applied Arts and Technology in Barrie, Ontario.

Mary Taylor has collaborated for the past 15 years with Sister Valerie and other primary teachers in the search for greater understanding of children and their learning. Her career spans 35 years as a teacher, primary supervisor, principal, inspector, and education officer in Ontario.

Ellen Vineberg-Jacobs is an associate professor in the Department of Education at Concordia University, Montreal. She is director of the MA in Child Study program. Her research interests have covered different aspects of children's social development and preschool environments. She is the founder and editor of the *Canadian Journal of Research in Early Childhood Education.*

Otto Weininger is a professor of Educational Theory in the Department of Applied Psychology at the Ontario Institute for Studies in Education. A prolific author, he has published seven books and numerous articles. He was named Gold Medal Educator of the 1980s by Project Innovation, California, and has garnered other awards, both for teaching (from the Ontario Confederation of University Faculty Associations) and for his contributions to psychoanalysis (from the Ontario Psychological Association).

Index

social reform, 148–49
traditional, 145
traditional, failure of, 82–83
whole, 144

Dansky, J.L., 23, 24
Darlington, R.B., 242
Darwin, Charles, 68
David, C., 255
Davidson, C.V., 196
Davie, R., 77
Davies, G., 245
Davies, Robertson, 4
Day Care Home Environment Rating Scale
  (DCHERS), 274
De'Ath, E., 245, 247
Declaration of the Rights of the Child, 149,
  208
Decroly, Ovide, 208
De Laguna, G., 24
Demany, L., 23
De Mause, L., 47
Derman-Sparks, L., 212, 214
Dewey, John, 68, 173, 208
Dickens, Charles, 68
Dickinson, P., 160, 162, 163, 164, 165, 166
Didier, B., 206
Dinkmeyer, D., 244
DISTAR, 261
Dixon, Glenn, 237
Dotsch, Daisy, 222, 225
Dowling, M., 144
Down's syndrome, children with, 254
  programming for, 260
Dunn, L.M., 274
Duvall, Evelyn
  family life cycle theory, 48

Early childhood education
  acculturation v. progressive models, 166
  defined, x
  dichotomies within, 159–60
  implications of multiculturalism for, 110–
    11
  as tool for social reform, 146
Early Childhood Education for a Multicultural Society, 114
Early childhood educators
  categories, 158–60
  historical roots, 161–163
  impact on child's self-concept, 55–56, 58
  kindergarten, 164–65
  learning needs, 111
  as model for child, 58–59
  multicultural, 117–22
  nursery school, 163–64
    instruction-oriented v. enrichment-
      oriented, 164
  perception of child-care child's transition
    to kindergarten, 284–85

primary, 166–67
relationship with parents, 40, 41
roles, 56
role vis-à-vis special-needs child, parents
  of, 263–64
understanding family unit, 48–51
Early Childhood Environment Rating Scale
  (ECERS), 280, 281
Early Childhood Multicultural Services
  (Vancouver), 122
Early childhood programs
  changes, x
  history, 156–58
  integration, 264–65
  parent participation, 241–50
Early childhood setting, 178
  design, 180
  indoor environment, 180–84
  outdoor environment, 185–90
  traditional v. open classroom, 179
  See also Classroom, indoor/outdoor
ECHO, 261
Eckerman, C.O., 21
Eckler, J., 14
Education
  v. schooling, 41
Education Act (1981), 257
Education for All Handicapped Children
  Act (1975), 257, 260
Education for the Handicapped Act Amend-
  ments Act (1986), 257, 260, 265
Education of Man, The, 67
Edwards, E.P., ix, 146
Egan, K., 144, 147, 150
Eichler, M., 44
  definition of family, 45
Einstein, Albert, 71
Elkind, D., ix, 77, 146
Engelman, S., 261
English as Second Dialect (ESD), 15, 119
English as Second Language (ESL), 115, 119
Environmental readiness, 33
  See also Responsive environment
Equality Now!, 123
Erikson, Erik, 72, 96, 97, 196, 197
  stages of childhood, 75–76
Esbenson, S., 158, 178, 180, 188
Ethnocentrism, 113
Evertson, C.M., 22
Expressive One-Word Picture Vocabulary
  Test (EOWPVT), 274, 275

Faggott, B.I., 26
Fahlman, R., 114
Falicov, C., 49
Family, contemporary Canadian
  demographic model, 45
  legal model, 45
  monolithic/normative model, 45
  multidimensional model, 45